Q

Architect of Quality

The Autobiography of
Dr. Joseph M. Juran

Q

Architect of Quality

The Autobiography of Dr. Joseph M. Juran

Joseph M. Juran

McGraw-Hill

New York   Chicago   San Francisco   Lisbon   London
Madrid   Mexico City   Milan   New Delhi   San Juan
Seoul   Singapore   Sydney   Toronto

The *McGraw·Hill* Companies

1 2 3 4 5 6 7 8 9 0 DOC/DOC 0 9 8 7 6 5 4 3

ISBN 0-07-142610-8

Editorial and production services provided by CWL Publishing Enterprises, Inc., Madison, WI, www.cwlpub.com.

McGraw-Hill books are available at special quantity discounts to use as premiums and sales promotions, or for use in corporate training programs. For more information, please write to the Director of Special Sales, McGraw-Hill, 2 Penn Plaza, New York, NY 10128. Or contact your local bookstore.

 This book is printed on recycled, acid-free paper containing a minimum of 50% recycled de-inked fiber.

Dedication

To my beloved family

Contents

Preface

It is late. The year is 2003, and I am ninety-eight years old. I have devoted seventy of those years to the subject of managing for quality. "Quality" is an essential property of products (goods and services). High-quality products are those that meet customer needs, do not fail during use, and pose no threat to human well-being. "Managing for quality" consists of the decisions and actions needed to design and build high-quality products. This subject is of ancient origin but has recently moved to center stage. It is now high on managers' priority lists and has increasingly attracted public attention.

The public compares the quality of competing products. Consumers are irritated when the goods they have bought suddenly fail, or when they must endure outages of essential services such as energy, transport, and communication. They are fearful when hearing news of disasters such as Bhopal and Chernobyl, or of the traffic deaths that resulted in massive recalls of Firestone tires.

The products that produce those irritations and fears have nevertheless been welcomed; they are now an essential part of our industrial society. Those same products have enabled us to live longer, healthier lives than our forebears. They have liberated us from much of the toil and drudgery that was endured by past generations. We want to get rid of the irritations and fears, but not by going back to live in primitive villages. Instead we will get rid of them by doing a better job of managing for quality.

In primitive societies, managing for quality was carried out by primitive methods handed down from generation to generation. The growth of commerce and technology then intensified competition in quality, making the traditional methods obsolete and demanding a world revolution in managing for quality. That revolution accelerated during the twentieth century, and the leader has been Japan. Its astounding achievement in becoming the world quality leader has been the major reason for Japan's emergence as an economic super-power.

During my years in the field, I contributed extensively to that revolution by creating new aids to manage for quality—concepts, systems, and tools. These have been disseminated worldwide through my books, papers, lectures, training courses, and videocassettes. I have provided consulting services to hundreds of institutions in about forty countries. My writings have been translated into about twenty languages, and they remain influential in the field. Along the way I have received numerous honors, some quite prestigious. I am widely regarded as one of the chief architects of the world revolution in managing for quality.

Then, in 1996, I walked away from active participation in the field to give top priority to a huge backlog of neglected personal affairs and to begin a final major project—writing my memoirs. I have long wanted to discover what has been my journey through life—what my goals were, what forces confronted me, and how I responded.

I am an immigrant. In 1912 my family emigrated from a town in the Austria-Hungarian empire to the city of Minneapolis, Minnesota. We began as an impoverished family, both in Europe and in the United States. Nevertheless, we managed to embrace the opportunities offered by the land of opportunity. I have long wanted to write the story—my own story—of how this happened.

In a long and busy life, I could recall many incidents, but these did not present a coherent picture; I needed to "connect the dots." So the urge to write my memoirs grew until, in 1996, the project reached top priority. I elected to do the job myself. I had an interesting story to tell, I do love to write, and writing one's memoirs is a logical last hurrah to a busy life. So I set out to race the clock—to finish the project while I was still in the land of the living.

I approached the task with the same doubts that must have troubled other writers of memoirs. A major concern was whether I could be objective when relating the events of the past. Had I written the memoirs in earlier decades, my objectivity would have been suspect; my own behavior was often the source of my problems. I was always truthful to my premises, but some of the beliefs of my life (not those relating to quality!) were warped.

The passing of decades then tipped the scales. My formative years were grim; I endured many trials and indignities. Yet the final result has been a happy ending. That luxury has enabled me to forgive the fates for their early cruelty. It has also enabled me to reexamine my views and to discover why I had been a misfit in society.

Related to doubts about objectivity are doubts about perspective. There was a time when I could not see the forest—too many trees were in the way. I had an engineering degree, but I was ignorant about the humanities. My time was dominated by day-to-day needs; my long-range goals were vague or nonexistent. These and other limitations were yoked to an aggressive mind, one that resembled de Toqueville's comment on the American Constitution—"all sail and no rudder." Despite this unpromising background, I've made a substantial contribution to the science of managing for quality, a science now critical to human affairs. These memoirs have enabled me, at long last, to learn how this happened.

Thus, this book retraces a journey through the twentieth century and a quest for human purpose, closely linked to an activity vital to society—managing for quality. Those who would relish a tale of how a confused, destitute youngster groped his way to the open road, follow me!

Joseph M. Juran
Rye, New York, U.S.A.

Acknowledgments

I began these memoirs late in life (at age 92). By that time my family elders had passed on. I was, however, able to draw on the recollections of later family generations, especially my siblings—my sisters Betty and Minerva, and my brother Nathan. All were generous in their responses.

I owe thanks to the leaders of Juran Institute—Joseph DeFeo, Blanton Godfrey, and Howland Blackiston—for their assistance during my research within the Institute's database.

I owe a major debt to the executives, managers, and other personnel in numerous institutions world wide for so unstintingly sharing their knowledge and experience with me. Their inputs, derived from facing the realities, are reflected in the case examples.

I am grateful to Larry Frey and his colleagues in the Minnesota Chapter of the American Society for Quality for their research into the archives of the city of Minneapolis to find many details of my family's years in that city.

Thanks also to Stephen B. Adams, co-author of *Manufacturing the Future, a History of Western Electric,* for his help in securing useful inputs relating to Western Electric.

Special thanks are due to my assistant Laura Sutherland. Her mastery of the computer enabled her to produce the entire text and all figures in book format. In addition she conducted much of the incidental research.

Finally, I am thankful to my wife Sadie for enduring my years of seclusion while I was occupied with these memoirs. She also graciously allowed me to read her mini-memoirs, which provide some fascinating insights into how I was viewed by her and her family while I was courting her.

Q

Part One

An Immigrant's Story: 1904–1924

1

Old World Roots: Romania, Judaism, and Poverty

My knowledge of my ancestral tree goes back only as far as grandparents; even that is sketchy. My paternal grandfather's given name was Naftuli; I don't know his original family name. As a young man, he fled czarist Russia to escape military service. He and a companion—one Mordecai—crossed the Carpathian Mountains and came to Gura Humora, a village in the then Austria-Hungarian empire. They probably arrived sometime during the 1830s. Weighty reasons as well as courage were required to make that journey; those mountains harbored both animal and human predators.

In Gura Humora the young men found refuge with an elderly, childless couple named Juran—a *melamed* (a teacher of Hebrew) and his wife. The young men then adopted the family name of their benefactors, and Naftuli became Naftuli Juran. He died in 1881 in Gura Humora.

My paternal grandmother was Rifka Richtwalt, daughter of a traveling rabbi. She came from Gorlice, now a part of Poland. She died in 1893, also in Gura Humora.

Naftuli and Rifka were married in Gura Humora. They had eleven children. Two died in infancy; six girls and three boys survived. Jacob, my father, was born in 1874. He was the second youngest child and was the youngest boy.

Naftuli may well have escaped military service, but many of his descendants did not. His second son, Avram, was killed in Bosnia during one of the imperial wars. One grandson—my nephew, Julius Kliffer—was a tail gunner in the United States Air Force. During World War II he died while on a bombing mission over Germany. (His plane, hit by gunfire, returned safely to England, but he bled to death en route.) A great grandson—Peret Leker—died in a mine clearing operation during the Israeli War of Independence (1948). In my immediate family, I was an officer in the U. S. Army Signal Corps Reserve for fifteen years. My brother Nathan was on active duty as a U. S. Navy officer during World War II. My three sons all did military service following World War II. Many of Naftuli's descendants emigrated to Israel. We may be sure that they were called up for military service in that garrison state.

My maternal grandparents were Josef Goldenberg, who died in 1880 in Izmail, Bessarabia, and his wife Mindel, who died in 1884, also in Izmail. That is all I have learned about them.

Levites

The sole exception to my ignorance of early ancestors is Levi, son of the biblical Jacob and patriarch of one of the tribes of Israel. I am a Levite. How is it that I identify with Levi but not with later generations until that of my grandparents?

Years ago, I asked my dad, "To which tribe of Israel do we belong?" He answered, "Levi." I persisted. "How do you know?" I asked. His answer: "My father told me."

At the time I was an engineering student. My training had already begun to reinforce a childhood skepticism of traditional beliefs.

Science rejected hearsay; it demanded hard evidence, not beliefs adorned by centuries of embroidery. Yet faith triumphed over reason. At that moment, I accepted his assertion that I am a Levite.

The matter did not end there, however. In the summer of 1970 my youngest son, Donald, visited Israel with his bride of a year. Of all my children, Don has been the most drawn to Judaism the religion and Israel the race. As part of that visit, he stood exalted at the Western Wall and there clasped hands with his ancestors across the millennia. Not until his return had we ever discussed the matter of the tribes of Israel. I volunteered it. "We are Levites," I told him. There was no challenge. A new generation had embraced this belief on faith and stood poised to convey this same belief to generations yet unborn.

Parents

Dad was born in Gura Humora and so became an Austrian subject; the year was 1874. At the age of seven, he lost his father and was then raised chiefly by his sisters, especially his beloved Chaye. At the age of eleven he'd already had four years of schooling and had shown an aptitude for learning. The family hoped that he would continue his studies and become a scholar, even a rabbi, but he rebelled at the idea. Instead, he skipped classes to spend time at the shop of the bagel baker.

His mother then put it to him: "I can't support you; you must learn a trade." She apprenticed him to a gentile shoemaker named Gail. Under Gail's discipline, Jacob learned the trade rapidly and became an excellent shoemaker.

My mother's name was Gitel Goldenberg. She was born in Braila, Romania, in either 1877 or 1880—there is a conflict in dates. She was orphaned at the age of four and was reared by her grandmother. Her marriage marked the beginning of a life of toil and unhappiness, sweetened only by her love for her children and her God.

My parents went through two marriage ceremonies. The religious ceremony came first; that mattered most to the Jewish community. I don't know the date, but it must have been about 1900. At the time my dad would have been 26 years old and my mother 20. Then on

July 15, 1903, they were married in a civil ceremony. I have a copy of the official document—the original is in the 1903 marriage register of the city of Braila, Romania. The document concludes, "After the record had been read aloud to all the parties present, it was signed by them in their own hand. The bride, being illiterate, signed by affixing her fingerprint thereunto."

My Birth

I was born in Braila, Romania, on December 24, 1904. On that date, the front page of the Los Angeles Times carried this story:

BY THE ASSOCIATED PRESS—P. M.

KISHINEFF, Dec. 23—(by Atlantic Cable.) Sentences were pronounced today on the persons found guilty of participation in the anti-Jewish riots here in May 1903. Seventeen of them were sentenced to 180 days imprisonment, two to eighty days, and eleven were acquitted.

Kishineff is within 150 miles of Braila. News of that riot almost certainly reached Braila and sent shudders through the Jewish community there. Such riots were not isolated local acts of violence. Over the centuries, anti-Jewish riots had recurred often enough, and in enough localities, to have earned the status of a separate criminal species with a distinctive name—"pogrom." They were infrequent, but the threat was always there. So the fear of pogroms hung over European Jews as a permanent, hellish black cloud. As a child I heard much about this threat.

Braila

From 1904 until 1907, my family lived in the city of Braila. It was then, as now, a part of Romania. I have no recollection of life in Braila; when we moved away I was no more than three years old. However, from tales handed down by family elders and from later visits as a guest of the Romanian government, I have been able to reconstruct some aspects of our life there.

The house in which I was born still stands at 134 Boulevard Cuza; I saw it during my 1972 visit to Romania. It is one of several tiny, contiguous one story masonry houses surrounding a courtyard. In 1904 it had dirt floors and no amenities. That is literally where I was born, at three o'clock in the afternoon. At the time it housed my parents and their three small children.

Dad's shoemaker shop was also on Boulevard Cuza, just a few doors away. Directly across the boulevard was the more spacious house occupied by affluent relatives—the Dankners. Josef Dankner was a merchant; his wife, Sprinze, was one of dad's older sisters. Dad tended to live within easy range of affluent relatives.

Gura Humora

My family moved to Gura Humora in about 1907. Gura Humora was then within the boundaries of the Austrian empire. Today it is a part of the Romanian province of Bukovina and is called Gura Humorului. By the year 1904, it had a population of more than 4,200 people and had attained the status of a city. The neighboring region has remained rural. To this day, farmers use horse drawn carts to deliver their produce and dairy products to the town markets and households.

Early in the twentieth century, the residents of Gura Humora were free from many of today's quality problems. Lacking electricity, gas, or running water, they never had outages in these utilities. Lacking household appliances and automobiles, they had no field failures. They traveled on foot and they used wood for fuel and candles for light. Men, women, and children drudged. What they did have was high mortality rates from diseases, infections, accidents, and general lack of health care. Those were "the good old days," a term invented by people who never lived in Gura Humora in those days.

The unpaved streets and sidewalks of Gura Humora turned to squishy mud during the rains. Here and there, wooden planks crossed the open sewers that drained into the river. I well remember those wooden planks. One rainy day, I slipped on one of them, dislocating my right hip. (I was thin, with frail legs; one of my nicknames was "the spider.") No one in the town was qualified to reset that hip, so a team of men carried me, screaming, to a bonesetter—a hermit who lived in the hills. His hut had a low ceiling; everyone had to stoop to enter. He did reset the hip, but the town had no facilities for keeping the leg in traction. I ended up with one leg a bit shorter than the other, plus a slight curvature of the spine—a condition known as scoliosis.

When my dad was born, he automatically became a subject of Kaiser Franz Josef of Austria. (Franz Josef ascended the throne in 1848. He would reign until 1916—a remarkable 68 years.) In those days the Austrian empire dominated central Europe.

The Austrians were clearly in charge. The official language was German; official proceedings and documents were in German; and classes in the public schools were taught in German. To my knowledge, however, the regime made no effort to suppress use of the many other ethnic languages.

The region harbored numerous ethnic groups, including Romanians, Ukrainians, Germans, Jews, Magyars, Poles, Turks, Bulgars, and still others. Romanians were the most numerous. Jews composed about five percent of the regional total, but they tended to live in the towns, where they were usually tradesmen and merchants. As a result, when the population of Gura Humora reached 4,200 people, Jews were about one fourth of the total. This was enough to support a synagogue, a Hebrew school, and still other Judaic activities.

Our diet was the food of peasants. One staple was *mamaliga*—cornmeal mush. Its bland taste was made more palatable with milk or cottage cheese. Beans were another staple. When mashed up with fried onions and chicken fat, they were a favorite dish. We had bread—sturdy peasant's bread—and the favorite spread was prune paste, called *povdil*. In New York the Hungarian shops sell it as *lekvar*.

The Jewish Community

In Gura Humora, we were part of a close knit, self-sealing Jewish community. The community ties, including religion, held all in a tight embrace. Racial purity was a high priority goal; I was told that without racial purity, Jews could not survive as a race. It was a cardinal sin to marry a Gentile. Such marriages were rare enough to be scandalous, resulting in virtual expulsion from the Jewish community.

The community was also a social system. Through its synagogue, Hebrew school, rituals, and social activities, it provided means for members to meet, to know each other, to exchange information, and to help each other. Expulsion from such a social system was a disaster not limited to the guilty parties—it struck their children as well.

Mother was devoutly religious and remained so for life. Dad was already a rebel, however, and I had begun to develop doubts of my own. I questioned the biblical assertion that we were God's "chosen people." If this were true, why did God allow his chosen people to endure all those calamities? My doubts also extended to some of the beliefs that are central to many organized religions.

Terror

There were deep suspicions between Jews and Gentiles—*goyim*—and these were passed on to the children at early ages. Our elders told us of pogroms, indignities, discrimination, and other injustices long endured by Jews at the hands of Gentiles. There was also the dreaded conscription of young men to serve as cannon fodder in the imperial wars. These men were torn from their families and marched away, not to return for years or perhaps not to return at all.

Central to this hostility was the virus of hatred for the Jews—anti-Semitism. It had existed even before the Christian Era and had erupted throughout the centuries with devastating effects—during the Egyptian captivity, during the Crusades, in medieval Europe, during the Spanish Inquisition, in the numerous pogroms of Eastern Europe.

No one dismissed the anti-Semetic tales as ancient history that was no longer relevant to life in Gura Humora. The orderly Austrian regime frowned on riots of all kinds, but that record did not convince the Jewish community. They knew of too many examples in history in which long periods of peace were shattered by grisly pogroms. Fire had always lurked in the ashes.

Such tales of horror had a profound effect on me; *I was terrified.* I became convinced that I was surrounded by enemies. This conspiracy was confirmed whenever I encountered Gentile bullies. When they demanded my trinkets, I had to surrender them.

My fears followed me night and day. They invaded my nightmares as well as my waking hours. I was even afraid of the *galakh*—the Gentile priest. I cringed whenever one of the priests strolled by while the Gentile boys came up to kiss the hem of his dusty black robe. Our elders assured us that priests played a leading role in infecting each new generation of *goyim* with the virus of anti-Semitism.

Other Jewish boys heard the same tales I did. They shared many of the same experiences. Yet, to my knowledge, none was as terrified as I. My nightmares seem to have been the most vivid. I accepted the conclusions of my elders that anti-Semitism was a fate—a plague to be endured because there was no known remedy.

In time I would discover that in the world of the intellect, I had no such fears. In that world I was well armed. Not only could I defend myself; I could take the offensive.

Hebrew School and Public School

I attended two schools while in Gura Humora. One was the public school run by the town authorities; the other was the Hebrew school, run by the Jewish community. The former was a model of discipline; the latter was the precise opposite.

Hebrew was taught in a ramshackle room in the synagogue. My class consisted of about ten students of various ages and sizes. The *melamed* (the Hebrew teacher) was a harassed individual. One of his major challenges was maintaining order; the students were a rowdy lot. I learned rapidly. By the time we left for America, I could read the Hebrew texts and write the script.

Going to the public school became my favorite activity in Gura Humora. I was an eager learner. I also found that school provided me with an opportunity to compete successfully against others. My aptitude for arithmetic fed my ego; I came up with correct answers as quickly as the best.

My classes were in German, and they were all taught by the same teacher, *Lehrer* Hoffman. For me that was a stroke of luck. Hoffman was a superb teacher, and to this day I retain respect for his competence.

In contrast to the harassed *melamed* in the Hebrew school, Hoffman maintained discipline with ease. His way of dealing with rowdies was swift and unvarying. The culprit was ordered to hold out his hand, palm up. Then down would come the *stock*—a flexible stick that left an enduring, memorable sting. As I recall it, every such punishment was richly deserved, including my own.

I learned in short order to read and write German, including the cursive script. By the time we emigrated to America, I could speak, read, and write in both German and Hebrew. I was also fluent in Yiddish, which we spoke at home, but I had only limited knowledge of Romanian, which was the language of most town residents. From all this, there now remains only a modest capability in German and Yiddish.

Emigration

Our emigration followed a commonly used sequence. The father went first, leaving the family behind. Once in America, he established himself with the help of relatives who had emigrated previously. He then accumulated the money needed to bring the family over. This could stretch out to several years; in our case it took three years.

Dad's passport is dated January 21, 1909. He made the journey to America in that same year. Minneapolis city records show him living with the Kliffers (his sister and brother-in-law) that year.

In 1957 I had a lengthy discussion with my aunt Sisel Kliffer about Dad's life in Minneapolis while his family was still in Europe. Her version was as follows:

> While he lived with us, he would sleep until ten in the morning. I had to nag him for not working. I wrote regularly to Gura Humora to let his wife know what was going on. When he left us to room elsewhere, I arranged to be kept informed so I could keep his wife informed. His family stayed in Europe, in poverty, because he frittered his earnings away on

The family in Gura Humora in about 1910. They include Mother; Rudolph, 9; Rebecca, 8; myself, 6; and Nathan, 3. Dad had already emigrated to the United States in 1909. My little sisters Minerva and Charlotte were both born in the U.S.

gambling and other vices. I nagged him to a point that he threatened to leave Minneapolis. I then went to the police to set watch on him. My keeping after him was a big reason why he finally got the tickets to bring his family to America.

Sisel told me this with evident relish, and it was clear that she despised Dad. (The feeling was mutual.) Yet much of her account matched my own observations of Dad's later conduct in America.

Mother's passport is dated May 20, 1912; we made the journey in August of that same year. When we left Gura Humora, mother was 32 years old. She set out on that journey with four children, ranging in age from eleven to five years.

From Gura Humora our train lurched its way north and west, terminating at the Belgian port of Antwerp. None of us had ever set foot on a ship, so the sea voyage became an exciting adventure. We were in steerage, the lowest class. The passengers were segregated—men on one side of the ship, women and children on the other. We slept in bunks that were stacked like bookshelves. The top bunks held an unexpected hazard—hellishly hot steam pipes.

We were not greeted by the Statue of Liberty; our ship did not land at Ellis Island. Instead we sailed north to Canada and down the St. Lawrence River to land at Quebec City. There Mother's money ran out. We were quartered in some hotel for two or three days until Dad sent us money for the train trip to Minneapolis. In the hotel we encountered for the first time two marvels of the new world. One was ice cream, which we had for dessert. The other was an inside flush toilet. We had a merry time testing it out.

From Quebec we traveled by train, entering the United States at Sault Ste. Marie, Michigan, on August 22nd. From there we went by train to Minneapolis. Dad was waiting for us at the train station. For him it was a joyful occasion as he repeatedly embraced and kissed us. I don't recall being drawn to him. To me he was a stranger; after that absence of three years, I was not even able to recognize him.

From the train station we took the streetcar to our new home. Along the way I had my first glimpse of the city that would shelter me during twelve formative years. I was awestruck by the sheer size of the city, the tall buildings, the streetcar system, the automobiles, and the other wonders of modern civilization. Yet on arrival at our new home, we discovered that it had much in common with what we had left behind. We would live for years in a tiny house and, except for the streetcar, in an area devoid of modern civilization's wonders.

Worrisome Baggage

I was unaware when I arrived in Minneapolis that I had brought to America a load of deep resentment. I resented the terror I had endured, the bullying and indignities. The old world had been mean to me. I was also unaware that my baggage included an itch for revenge. In time I would take revenge, but on innocent people. I would thereby inflict much damage, especially on myself.

Those We Left Behind

Our emigration saved us from the Holocaust. In the late 1930s, the rise of the Nazi regime in Germany stimulated a sharp rise of anti-Semitism in Romania. (By this time Gura Humora had become a part of Romania.) On October 11, 1941, the Gura Humora Jews were collected, locked into cattle cars, and transported across the Dniester River to concentration camps in Transnistria. There, about a third of them perished before they were liberated by the advancing Russian army. The survivors found their way back to Gura Humora, where they found no welcome. They reached a consensus:

There is no hope of rebuilding our lives under an anti-Semitic regime and amid anti-Semitic neighbors. Their hostility will never end. Our diminished numbers are no match for the forces arrayed against us. We must leave this cursed land and rebuild our lives elsewhere.

Most tried to emigrate to Palestine, but their ships were intercepted by the British and rerouted to camps in Cyprus. Following the Israeli War of Independence (1948), the refugees finally were permitted to go on to Palestine.

Q

2

An Immigrant's New World:
Same Problems, Same Fears in Minnesota

We had come to Minneapolis, Minnesota. In the fall of 1912 it was a busy, thriving city on the banks of the Mississippi River. The state of Minnesota was at the northern edge of the great Midwestern farm belt, and farming was a major industry. Minneapolis was an important center for grain storage, processing, and distribution. Manufacturing was a growing industry, as were service industries such as banking, insurance, and transportation. Its twin city, St. Paul, located directly across the river, was the state capital and housed numerous government offices.

The Shack: Our New Home

Our new home was a tarpaper shack set in a wooded area. The address was 3445 Central Avenue Northeast. The term "tarpaper shack" derives from the absence of siding on the outside. Instead,

The "shack" in 1917. At the time it housed our family of eight.

protection against the elements consisted of sheets of tarpaper held in place with lath strips. The inside walls were likewise unfinished, so the vertical support beams—the two-by-four studs—were visible. We used to hang our clothes on nails pounded into those studs.

The shack was a rectangle of about 360 square feet. It was partitioned into three areas without doors. In the rear was the kitchen, which included a cast-iron stove that was the sole source of heat for the entire shack. The middle area provided sleeping quarters for the children. On one side the three boys slept crosswise in one bed; the girls slept on the other side. The front area held the curtained bed for the parents. The remaining space was reserved for "company," who never came. Eight people would soon be crowded into that little shack.

There were also two other buildings. One was the outhouse. In the summer it buzzed with flies and was disgustingly malodorous. In the winter it was brutally cold while the wind howled outside and in. A chamber pot under one of the beds served to spare us a journey to the outhouse during foul weather. The other outbuilding was the woodshed, where we stored wood for the kitchen stove's ravenous appetite. The shed also held our various tools as well as the galvanized tub that served for laundering and baths.

Our new home had no amenities—no running water and no sewer, gas, or electricity. Kerosene lamps provided light. The streets were not paved with gold—they were not paved at all. The outward evidences of technology consisted of the Central Avenue streetcar tracks, the overhead trolley wires, and the arc lamps at occasional street corners.

The kitchen stove was a cast-iron monster. It had four removable lids on top and an oven below. At full heat, those lids glowed a dull red. The stove served many purposes. It warmed the shack, baked bread, cooked meals, heated water for baths, and still more.

Despite the demands on her time, Mother kept the shack clean and neat. Oilcloth covered the kitchen shelves and table. The children were trained to keep their respective areas orderly. This neatness did not extend to the outside, however. There the woodcutting, the chickens, the mud, and other aspects of life on a limited budget converged to provide an image of squalor.

By the time we left the shack in 1918, Central Avenue had been paved and amenities had begun to arrive. One was the telephone; another was city water.

In winter our water supply had come from snow, melted on the kitchen stove. In summer, water had to be hauled from the well at the Aaron's farm nearby. The coming of city water was pure joy. The city dug trenches on our side of Central Avenue and laid down hefty water mains. The water was oily at first but soon ran pure and sweet.

Contrast with Gura Humora

Our move to America made no notable change in our physical living conditions. We still lived in squalor and would do so for some years to come. In other respects, however, we were indeed in a new world.

We soon felt a sense of liberation from the hereditary rule of monarchs like Kaiser Franz Josef of Austria, along with their supporting casts of hereditary noblemen. In the Minneapolis schools, we did not start the day by singing a hymn to President Woodrow Wilson. He had not inherited his job; he had been elected to it by the people. There were policemen in Minneapolis, but we soon sensed that they were on our side.

To me the most obvious difference was the comparatively low level of aggressive, organized anti-Semitism. Anti-Semitism was present, but in greatly subdued forms. I ran into some of this in grammar school, where it took the form of ethnic name-calling—I was called kike, sheenie, and occasionally Christ-killer.

The Neighborhood

Within a radius of several blocks, we had only three neighbors. The Aarons had a dairy farm at 36th and Central Avenue. We had an easy relationship with them. Our water came from their well. One agreeable ritual was the exchange of our mother's freshly baked bread for creamy warm milk, fresh from their cows. The friendly Wilsons lived at 35th and Tyler. They were a childless couple, and Mrs. Wilson visited with mother regularly, especially after our little sisters were born. The unfriendly Harrises lived at 34th and Central, near the swampy bottom.

In our broader neighborhood, our fellow immigrants provided a classic example of the melting pot in action. One of the ingredients in the melting pot is language. In Minneapolis there were enough Scandinavian immigrants to support a Swedish newspaper. However, the public schools were taught only in English; government and private business were all conducted only in English as well. Thus English became the language of the children, and parents learned English from their children.

No laws were enacted in Minnesota to make Swedish an official language; bilingualism never took root. Instead, within two generations, Swedish virtually disappeared as a widely used language. The Swedes and other ethnic groups were keenly motivated to become American citizens, thereby making their children citizens, so my generation avoided a potential source of divisiveness.

Winter in Minneapolis

Minneapolis winters were snowy, long, and brutally cold. Temperatures were consistently below freezing and sometimes far down on the Fahrenheit scale—too often minus twenty below zero. Mercifully, at such times the wind was usually calm. When it was not, the wind chill made it dangerous to be outside for long; ears, noses, fingers, and toes were in danger of being frostbitten.

I sometimes did need to be outside for long periods. Within a few years I would occasionally have to walk to and from Dad's shop in downtown Minneapolis. That was over four miles one-way, a full hour's walk and a serious threat to a poorly dressed boy. I learned to walk briskly, and this became a lifelong habit.

The cold weather overwhelmed the shack. During a storm, a fine mist of snow managed to enter the shack. The windows developed a coating of ice, thick at the bottom and thin at the top. The most striking feature of this coating was the beauty of Jack Frost's designs, especially the soaring trees and cathedral spires.

Subsistence

Dad never discussed his financial problems (or much else) with any of his children. Yet we soon realized that these problems were severe. When we arrived in America, he had no shop of his own; he was employed by someone else, at sweatshop wages. I never knew how much he earned, but his wages were simply not enough to support the family. We bridged the gap by using natural resources and child

Dad (in apron) while employed in a sweatshop, about 1910.

labor. The children worked solely outside of school hours; schooling was sacred.

Food

Our major natural resource was the vegetable garden. Vacant lots surrounded our shack, and we claimed land for our garden. The virgin soil responded with enthusiasm. Potatoes were our chief crop, but we also grew cabbages, carrots, corn, beets, beans, onions, cucumbers, radishes, and still other crops. We ate heartily of those vegetables in the summer and preserved much to be eaten in winter.

Raising vegetables is labor intensive, requiring digging, raking, planting, watering, weeding, fighting insect pests, and harvesting. Most of the garden work was child labor. Interestingly, while we children grumbled about many of the chores assigned to us, this did not extend to work in the garden. We seemed to sense that this work was related to survival, so it got done without protest.

Our daily diet consisted mostly of cheap, nourishing staples. In the morning we ate oatmeal or cornmeal mush—the *mamaliga* of the old country. For lunch at school we took sandwiches—bread (baked by Mother) spread with jam. The evening meal was mainly potatoes and beans. Mother baked bread frequently, but cakes and other luxuries were limited to high holidays.

Despite our poverty, we ate meat quite often, because it was free. In those days the beef butchers discarded certain parts, including the brain and liver. These were given away to anyone who was willing to take them away. Mother was a superb cook, and she made tasty dishes from the brain and liver.

We raised chickens in our yard. Mostly they raised themselves by scratching for the numerous worms in the soil. A sack of feed provided supplemental nutrition. The chickens roosted in the shed and sat on the glass eggs that were intended to urge them to get busy and lay their own eggs. In any event, we were well supplied with eggs. Some of those eggs were allowed to hatch into fluffy little chicks.

Fuel

We needed fuel throughout the year, especially during the Minneapolis winters. Our main resource was the surrounding woods. The trees were mostly oaks of modest girth, with plump acorns. We salvaged fallen trees and felled others. A long crosscut saw, with a boy at each end, served to cut the trunks to stove length. The ax, wedge, and sledgehammer then split these lengths into firewood. Woodcutting was a year round chore due to the endless demands of the kitchen stove.

We had another source of fuel—coal. Periodically Mother would take a gunnysack and walk to the railroad tracks at the city limits, two long blocks away. There she would collect the lumps of coal that had fallen from locomotive coal bins. I accompanied her on some of those trips. Our gleanings were usually meager, but sometimes we returned with bulging sacks. Such occasions arose only when a locomotive was resting on the tracks, waiting for orders. Some crews, witnessing our plight, heaved large lumps overboard. We gratefully waved to our benefactors to acknowledge their largess.

Money

Our most acute need was for money. Once again, the family resorted to child labor, and this began shortly after our arrival from Europe.

The morning newspaper—the *Minneapolis Tribune*—was using various means to increase its circulation. One idea was to sell newspapers to men on their way to work. To this end, the *Tribune* teamed up with the streetcar company and local newsboys. Under this arrangement, the earliest morning streetcar dropped off a bundle of newspapers at our corner—Central Avenue and 35th Street. Brother Rudy and I recovered the papers, divided them up, and then stationed ourselves at two of the streetcar stops, he at 37th Street (the end of the line), and I at 33rd Street. There we sold the papers to the men who came to take the streetcar to work.

At the time, the daily morning newspapers sold for one cent each. Of this amount, half went to the *Tribune*; the other half was ours. Rudy and I probably sold about thirty papers each, so our combined net income was close to thirty cents a day—about a ten percent increase in the family cash income. We turned this money over to Dad.

Gaining that extra ten percent required that two boys—then eleven and eight years old—be awakened at five o'clock and sent out into the savage Minnesota winter. Neither of us protested; evidently we were aware that our family was in crisis and that it was our duty to help out.

A shattering blow to my faith in humanity was struck while I was selling those newspapers. One morning, one of my customers "bought" a paper but said he had no change; he would pay me tomorrow. I gave him the paper—my first experience with extending credit. The next day was the same, as was the third. By then the awful truth was dawning on me: this could go on forever. On the fourth day I mobilized enough courage to tell him, "No more papers until you pay me the three cents you owe me." He never paid up. It took time to recover from that blow. I had not dreamed that grown men existed who were willing to cheat an eight-year-old boy out of three cents. After the incident I saw that man day after day, and I silently cursed him for not paying me and for undermining my faith in human integrity.

Living in Poverty

We lived in poverty during most of my entire twelve years in Minneapolis, yet there was little complaining. In my case, it didn't even occur to me to complain. I seem to have assumed that poverty was for us a natural state of life. We had lived in poverty in Gura Humora, as did so many of our neighbors. When we came to Minneapolis, it seemed that our entire neighborhood was poor. So poverty was the natural state; affluence was unnatural.

Then in the schools, and especially in high school and at the university, I met classmates who were well dressed, had bicycles, knew how to use knives and forks, went to parties and dances, and played musical instruments. When I had a job delivering packages for a downtown boutique, I got to see the interiors of some spacious, well furnished houses. When I became a college student, I saw that the homes of some of my classmates were so spacious that each child had his own room! So I learned that in some neighborhoods, poverty was not a natural state.

Most people are offended by seeing young children engaged in child labor. Yet judging by the children in our family (a small sample to be sure), our exposure to child labor gave us some enduring benefits. We grew up with no fear of long hours or hard work. We learned to seek out opportunities and to use ingenuity to gain from them. We accepted the responsibility for building our own safety nets. By enduring the heat of the fiery furnace, we acquired a work ethic that served us well for the rest of our lives.

I have dwelt on the details of our years in poverty simply because I lived through them. The experience belongs in my memoirs. Yet our escape from poverty was not unique—millions of other immigrants to America did the same thing. Early in the twentieth century, a large majority of Americans were poor. By the end of that century, only a small minority were listed as living below the poverty line—a line that is envied by untold millions in developing countries. It has been a stunning transformation. It supports my conviction that during the twentieth century, the United States was indeed the land of opportunity for millions of its citizens and immigrants.

3

Early Years in Minneapolis

Our early years in Minneapolis were lived in virtual isolation. Opportunities to meet and know others consisted of rare visits to relatives (or from relatives). Of course, we children did meet other children in school, but this did not result in social activities after school. Dad insisted that we not mingle with Gentiles. (Dad made himself an exception to the rule about not mingling with Gentiles; he associated with Gentiles more than with Jews.)

During those years of isolation I built a refuge, a world of my own. That refuge was the world of books, which I found at the public library. We had no books at home, but now I could borrow books to be read at home. Amazingly, all this was free.

I became a voracious reader. I tended to favor tales of fantasy. I read widely in mythology and legend—Greek, Roman, Norse, King Arthur and the Knights of the Round Table, Homer's *Iliad* and *Odyssey*. I read adventure stories by authors such as Jack London and Alexandre

Dumas, as well as the Sherlock Holmes stories of Sir Arthur Conan Doyle. The librarian guided me to still other authors that I found enjoyable: Mark Twain, O'Henry, Robert Louis Stevenson, Edgar Allan Poe, Rudyard Kipling, and Victor Hugo. She also led me to classics in poetry. I especially liked Tennyson and the rousing verses of Kipling.

Reading books served its intended purpose, for during my hours of reading, I was indeed in a world of my own. I was also acquiring habits and skills that would serve me well in the years to come. Those authors not only had tales to tell; they also provided examples of the craft of writing at its best, demonstrating how to choose—precise phraseology and to use the tools of the trade (analogy, irony, humor, and so on) to stir the reader's emotions and orchestrate his or her response. Some of this rubbed off on me, and my own writing began to improve.

World War I

The First World War began in 1914 and soon engulfed most of Europe. The sinking of the Lusitania (May 1915) then became an important stimulus for United States involvement, first as a supplier to the Allies and then, in April 1917, as a combatant.

The war had little effect on our lives. Dad had already applied for citizenship, and this was granted in September 1917, thereby making all members of his family citizens as well. Nevertheless, we children were subjected to minor harassment. With the entry of the United States into the war, the loyalty of all German-Americans became suspect, especially the noncitizens. Of course we were not Germans, but our classmates knew that we were immigrants and that when we arrived, our language had been German.

The person most affected by the war was brother Rudy. When the United States entered the war, he was almost 16 years old. He itched to enlist, but he was rejected—he was under age. He found an outlet for his fervor by learning and singing the many patriotic songs that emerged to inspire recruitment. At the time of the armistice in November 1918, he was still under age. He never did see military service.

From Shack to House

In 1918 we moved out of the shack and into a more conventional house. The address was 2916 East 25th Street. It was located in a working class neighborhood that was mostly built up; there were few vacant lots. We now had many close neighbors. Children of our ages abounded. There were sidewalks and paved streets. The utilities included water, sewer, and gas. For us this move was a dramatic change. The new house was more spacious than the shack, though hardly generous for eight people. The ground floor included a kitchen, dining room, and living room. As before, Mother and Dad slept in a curtained off area in the living room. The two upstairs rooms provided sleeping quarters for the children.

We welcomed the conveniences of the house. The kitchen stove was heated by gas, and the living room had a "self-heater" stove—it burned coal briquettes. Suddenly we were rid of woodcutting. Gas also provided the brilliant incandescent lighting from the Welsbach mantles. A welcome luxury was indoor plumbing and its array of services: hot water from the gas-fired boiler; hot baths in the second-floor bathtub; and waste disposal from the indoor toilets—two of them.

Judaism

My isolation from Judaism extended into my high-school years. Even though South High did have a small percentage of Jews, they lacked any organized means for meeting with each other. My knowledge of Hebrew continued to decline. Even my knowledge of Yiddish declined as Mother learned to speak English, and English increasingly became our language at home.

Beyond this isolation from Judaism, I had become increasingly skeptical about its teachings. I was unable to accept many of the Old Testament's assertions. To me they were beliefs not supported by a factual base. I was not convinced that the Jews are God's chosen people, that the Jews of the Old Testament had held discussions with God, or that there is a hereafter.

While I had no idea how many people shared my views, I knew that many intelligent people did not. That troubled me. I had no explanation for the difference in views, but I knew that I must find one.

Fears

By the time I was a high-school senior, some sources of my fears had dried up. My classmates were now older and facing sobering realities. Upon graduation most would be entering the workforce; the others would be entering college. Either way, horseplay and bullying were becoming declining priorities.

My fears about poverty had also declined. After all, our family had survived years of it, and we had become experienced survivors. I'd held enough jobs to give me confidence that I was employable and that I could make good at any job I was thrown into. My modest wants could be met, even by the prevailing low wages. I disliked living so close to the edge, but I thought that the end was now in sight. My college education would qualify me for a steady job with steady pay, and *voila*— farewell to poverty forever. So it seemed.

My deep-seated fear of active anti-Semitism was now dormant. I cannot recall an instance in Minneapolis of the formation of hate groups that targeted Jews or other minorities. In contrast, I was increasingly aware of the existence of a *passive* anti-Semitism. There did exist organized groups whose members intentionally but quietly avoided association with Jews by excluding them from their clubs, fraternities, and the like. At the time I thought such groups to be harmless—they seemed to pose no threat to me.

Meanwhile, a new and serious fear had emerged. Our parents' marriage was under threat. By the year 1916, Mother was openly hinting that life with Dad was no longer tolerable and that the solution was divorce. I became alarmed. If the family were to break up, what would happen to all of us? What would happen to me?

4

Tragedy

The year 1920 witnessed the tragic end of a train of events that was set in motion by the circumstances of my parents' marriage. Here is what happened. My parents' marriage was unhappy from the outset. I was unaware of this until years later, when my sister Betty shared with sister Minerva some things that Betty had learned from Mother and from Aunt Sisel:

When mother's mother died, her father then remarried. The stepmother treated Mother roughly, so Mother went to live with her grandmother, who raised her until she was of marriageable age. Mother had no dowry but was a very pretty girl, and Dad fell in love with her. Her family thought Dad was not good enough for her, but lacking a dowry, they had no bargaining power. Dad had a mean streak, and he struck Mother even on the night of their wedding. She became scared of him.

In those days, Jewish customs were heavily biased in favor of men. Education for girls had low priority, and few women could become self-supporting. Marriage was overwhelmingly the station in life available to most women. Divorce was difficult to obtain; even if obtained, it could leave the woman without means of support, for it was a man's world. To make matters worse, divorce was a social disgrace and could end up separating the woman from her precious children. So most unhappy marriages were endured because the alternatives seemed worse.

Mother's Tribulations

During all those years in Europe, Mother was unhappily married to a man she disliked and feared, yet she was locked in by her love for her children and by the Jewish customs relative to marriage. In addition, her life was one of endless toil as a result of living in poverty and lacking the resources needed to care for all those children.

In America matters became worse. Within ten months after our arrival in 1912, our sister Minerva was born. Eighteen months later, our sister Charlotte was born. I learned from Betty that Mother had tried to abort both pregnancies by use of traditional, crude methods: lifting heavy loads and the hatpin. Those efforts failed; the latter sent Mother to the hospital with a dangerous infection. Then, when the little ones were born, she took them to her heart.

Mother lived for her children; her own needs never had priority. I can recall Mother at rest only on Friday nights at sundown—the beginning of the Sabbath. Mother would put a shawl over her head, light two candles, kneel, and quietly recite her prayers. During that solemn ritual, Mother's thoughts were far from the site of her drudgery. She was alone with her God, and her angelic face shone with "the peace that passeth all understanding." We children watched in respectful silence as she performed that ritual. Her prayers were never answered, but her faith never wavered. I am convinced she drew renewed strength from it. She would need it; for her, the worst was yet to come.

Dad as a Provider

Dad was in financial trouble most of his life, yet it seemed that he shouldn't have been. He had learned a trade in an era when tradesmen in America were able to support their families. Most of those who came here as immigrants early in the century were able to do so.

Dad was an exception, not because of bad luck but because he was unwilling to give top priority to his family's needs. Aunt Sisel once gave me an account of Dad's conduct on his arrival in America—his unwillingness to go looking for work, his inclination to waste his time playing cards, and the like. My own observations after coming to America verified Aunt Sisel's account.

Dad came to America in 1909. By the time his family arrived in 1912, he was 38 years old but had not yet managed to set up a shop of his own. Our relatives who had emigrated before him—the Kliffers and the Wolds—were well established and affluent. Dad was still in poverty, working long hours at sweatshop wages. This disparity must have gnawed at him, for he was a proud man.

Within a few more years (probably about in 1915), he did have a shop of his own. This might have made him affluent but it didn't. Dad was an excellent shoemaker, but he attracted few customers. His shop locations (behind the post office building and later on Washington Avenue North in the red-light district) were poor choices. In addition, he managed badly. The shop was disorderly, dusty, and unsightly. Often several of his German pals were seated near the stove playing cards. Customers were not attracted to such an environment.

Nevertheless, from about 1919 to 1924, Dad's fortunes improved. This was unrelated to repairing shoes. It resulted in part from his selling liquor illegally and in part from his lawsuit against the streetcar company for the injuries sustained by my sister Charlotte. In his final years, when his children were grown up and gone, he occasionally asked me to help him out financially. At the time of his death he was widely in debt; his estate yielded less than a hundred dollars.

Dad as a Parent

At home Dad established a strict code of conduct for his children. He believed in corporal punishment, and he dealt this out with his leather belt or a handy stick. These punishments were usually deserved, but on occasion they were acts of fanaticism.

One such incident involved our sister Charlotte when she was still an infant, just learning how to talk. She had made some mistake—had spilled something or whatever. Dad questioned her, but her grasp of the language was too limited. He mistakenly concluded that her action was willful. He punished her by slapping her with a stick; her little behind became covered with angry welts. All of us watched that spectacle in horrified silence amid the pitiful screams of the bewildered little one.

I have since tried to understand Dad's conduct in the light of the severe problems he faced. His childhood had been unhappy and possibly traumatic. By the time he had a family, his burdens were overwhelming him. He would have little patience with children whose behavior added to his problems.

His tyranny was not due to irrationality; he was no alcoholic. Rather, he seemed to want a system of justice that would deter the children from adding to his problems while keeping them on the path of righteousness. His approach alienated us from him, however, and his efforts to serve as our guide to proper behavior had little effect. Our real role model was Mother, who hardly ever laid a hand on us.

As the years wore on, Dad continued to cling to his authoritarian ways, so the tensions grew. There were clear signs that Mother's patience was giving out but no signs that her health would soon give way. We children resented Dad's ways. We had no affection for him; the predominant feeling was fear.

Talk of Divorce

By 1916 Mother was openly talking of divorce. She was strongly encouraged by Aunt Sisel, who had been facing domestic problems of her own. Sisel was not one to suffer in silence—she was quite willing to do battle.

In Mother's talk of divorce, two things were clear. She felt she could no longer go on living with Dad. She also felt she could not live without her children. The rest was uncertain. Meanwhile, the very talk of divorce signaled an alarm to the rest of the family.

Dad was terrified by the talk of divorce. He seemed to see his world collapsing, and he made belated efforts to endear himself to his wife and children. He pleaded with us. He offered affection. He tried to create experiences of togetherness. It was almost too late. For years Dad's actions had given him the image of a distant, stern disciplinarian, lacking in compassion and incapable of loving his family. That image had become virtually indelible. Nevertheless, the divorce never took place.

It is unlikely that Dad's pleadings convinced Mother that he would mend his ways. What did take place was the move from the shack to the East 25th Street house. That move wiped out much of the toil associated with life in the shack. In addition, Dad engaged a housekeeper to relieve Mother of still other chores.

How Dad financed all this remains a mystery to me. I suspect his brother-in-law, Herman Kliffer, helped him to buy the 25th Street house. Having his own shop was no doubt giving him a better income than working as a sweatshop employee. His bootlegging activity, though on a small scale, also made a useful contribution to his income. Whatever the sources, he managed to make the move.

Mother's Health Fails

By 1918 all those years of drudgery and abuse had taken their toll, and Mother's health was failing. Soon we would learn that she had contracted tuberculosis. At the time, it was an incurable disease; antibiotics were not yet available.

Even in illness Mother was not protected from a traumatic shock. It came when my sister Charlotte was injured by a streetcar. Charlotte was then about four years old and was playing on a mound of sand that was piled up next to the car tracks. Just as a streetcar was passing by, Charlotte slipped down the pile and under the streetcar. The cries of the passersby alerted the motorman, and he stopped the car. Charlotte was brought to Mother's bedside, bloody and screaming. Mother's reaction was a pitiful cry, in Yiddish, "*Siesser Gott, nem mekh zie.*" ("Dear God, take me to you.")

I was there. I heard that cry, and I sobbed uncontrollably. Today, as I was writing the preceding passage, I sobbed again. I always do when I recall that agonized cry.

Charlotte survived. She bravely endured weeks in the hospital, her head shaved, her wounds stitched up, and her broken leg in traction. The experience did not prevent her from becoming an excellent golfer in later years.

Dad took revenge on the streetcar company. An ambulance-chasing lawyer emerged out of nowhere and urged him to sue the company for negligence. The suit was successful, but I never learned how much he collected.

In May 1920 Mother was moved to the Hopewell Hospital in Minneapolis. An affluent patient could have gone to a fresh air sanatorium to prolong life, but that was hopelessly beyond Dad's means. Mother was now failing rapidly—she had only four more months to live.

I visited her regularly. She awaited death with dignity. She did not talk of herself. Her mind was on her children, especially her little girls. Who would take care of them once she was gone?

She died in September 1920 at the age of forty. She was buried in the Minneapolis Jewish Cemetery at 70 1/2 Penn Avenue South. Her gravestone shows her name as Gertrude Juran, an anglicized form of Gitel Juran. I don't know how this came about.

Remembering Mother

She was a beautiful woman, tall and stately, with determination shown in the cut of her chin. Her hair was jet black; it hung to her waist when she was combing it, but she wore it pulled straight back and neatly knotted up in a bun on top of her head. While we were living in the shack, her teeth, rotted by lack of dental care, all had to be extracted. For a time her shrunken cheeks made her look like an old woman. Then, to our relief, a set of dentures restored her good looks.

She was ever at work. When we children woke in the morning, Mother was already dressed and working. She was still at it when we went to sleep. Meeting her duties always took priority over her need to relax.

Her love for her children knew no limit. For our sake she endured an unloved husband and grinding poverty. Her personal needs were always secondary to ours. During one winter, a savage blizzard came up while I was at the Prescott School, over a mile away from home. Mother showed up at the school, having trudged that distance on foot. She then presented me with five cents to take the streetcar home, after which she again trudged through that blizzard on foot.

During brother Rudy's effort to become a movie actor in Hollywood, Mother secretly sent him help from her meager funds. Then, when she became too weak to be doing laundry, Dad gave her money to send the laundry out to be done. Instead Mother sent that money to Rudy and did the laundry herself.

Her love was not expressed by showering us with embraces and kisses. It was expressed by her deeds: by the endless ways in which she protected us; by her boundless devotion to our needs; by the example she set for us.

She stood in awe of educated people such as doctors and teachers. It was her respect for education that kindled the lamp of learning for her descendants. Collectively they generated a long list of college degrees, including numerous masters and doctorates. Ironically, she, the least educated, led the family into the halls of learning and higher education.

She was deeply religious, and her religion was that of the Old Testament. She believed in a personal God, in a hereafter, and in divine rewards and punishments. Within the limits of her resources, she observed Jewish customs. She observed the prayer ritual at the beginning of the Sabbath but not the admonition to keep the Sabbath as a day of rest.

For me, what has endured most is the image of Mother as a role model. This has not been limited to education; it has extended also to the entire range of ethical conduct—honesty, compassion, a sense of responsibility. In my earlier years I would consciously pause and ask myself, "What would mother have done?" Such pauses gave me useful guidance.

What Might Have Been

There was something grossly unjust about Mother dying at so young an age. Surely she deserved to be repaid for all that toil and sacrifice, to live long enough to see what became of her children and to see her hopes for them fulfilled. Had she lived, she would in fact have seen many of her dreams become realities. But it was not to be. She would never see her children emerge as educated, useful, and respected citizens. She would never meet my young bride or any other of her children's spouses. She would never have the joy of embracing her twelve grandchildren. How they would have welcomed the love of someone so unselfish and devoted! She would never be free to relax and reap the fruits of all those years of suffering.

It may be that Mother did not view matters as I do. I know well that she had a fierce love for her children and that she derived deep satisfaction from seeing them live and grow. It may even be that she considered herself well rewarded—I will never know. Nevertheless, I say it was unjust for her to have died so young.

In my moments of grief, I have asked *Why?* I have received no convincing answer. Many theologians assert that God is all knowing, merciful, compassionate—"His eye is on the sparrow." I am aware that this concept gives comfort to myriad grieving people. Yet such concepts conflict with the fact that my mother died at so young an age. I say it was unjust, not merciful or compassionate.

5

Life with Dad: Bootlegging, Bums, and the Red-Light District

Mother had been the cohesive force in the family; with her gone, the family disintegrated rapidly. For about a year we all remained at the East 25th Street house and had a housekeeper to do most of the chores. Then several dismal events scattered us forever. Within a few years, we children were all gone, leaving Dad to live alone.

My little sisters went first. They were placed in an orphanage and remained there through adolescence. My older sister Betty was next. She was expelled from the house for violating Dad's curfew.

With Betty gone, Dad sold the 25th Street house. The males—Dad, my brothers, and I—then moved into the upper half of a duplex at 2823 Grand Avenue North. Rudy left next, voluntarily. He was instinctively and fiercely independent—he wanted to be in control. Because he was already employed full time, he was no longer dependent on Dad.

After Rudy was gone, we moved again, this time to the rear of Dad's shop. There Nat and I shared a bed until he, like Betty, violated Dad's curfew law and was ordered out.

So Dad and I ended up as the sole tenants in the rear of his shop. By then I was within several months of graduation, so I endured those wretched quarters until the bitter end. When I left for my job in Chicago in 1924, Dad remained as the sole occupant. He was still there at his death in 1931.

Dad's Shops

Dad acquired a shop of his own in about 1915. Although the shop was always located in downtown Minneapolis, it moved from time to time. I recall the last two locations. One was behind the (then) main post office; the other was on Washington Avenue North, in the Minneapolis's "red-light" district.

Dad's fortunes were helped by an activity unrelated to shoe repairing—he sold whiskey. He probably began doing this in 1915, when he first set up his own shop. He had no liquor license, but he did have a small clientele. Most of the customers were Dad's German friends, whom Nat and I derisively called the "bums." Others included a few characters who plied their trade in the red-light district.

National prohibition became effective in January 1920, making it a federal crime to sell liquor. The law improved the economics of illegal sales but increased the risks. Dad had a source of supply, however, and continued to sell the booze. To my knowledge he never got into trouble with the authorities. They may have suspected what was going on but his operation was small relative to the speakeasies of that era.

The Bums

The bums were a loose band of Germans that used Dad's shop as one of their hangouts. They came and went at unpredictable times. In some respects they made the shop a part-time den of thieves. The ringleader for joint projects was probably Goldzahn (Goldtooth), although each man was a freelancer. For relaxation during winter, they would sit near the stove playing pinochle. In summer they would often be behind the shop, rolling dice on the stone slab.

The bums gradually became accustomed to my presence and seemed to regard me as harmless. In any event, they would openly discuss their methodology even when I was within earshot. On several occasions I overheard Goldzahn explain to others some of the methodology of the trade.

To my knowledge Dad was not directly involved in thievery, but he must have known (as did I) that thievery was afoot. Dad probably didn't even know the real names of the bums—they always referred to each other by their nicknames. In addition to Goldzahn they included Willy the hunchback—he of the powerful hands, der Bayer, who evidently hailed from Bavaria, Pigust der Waldspecht (Woodpecker), Heisel, and several others who showed up now and then.

Without doubt Dad liked having the bums around. He enjoyed playing pinochle and drinking with them. He seemed to be their political mentor; they were a ready audience for his socialistic beliefs. He clearly preferred their company to that of most of his relatives or other members of the Jewish community.

On one occasion, Dad may have come close to crossing the line. It was a time when Goldzahn languished in the city jail, and a large coil of rope mysteriously appeared in the shop. Then, according to Nat's account,

> … a few of the bums drove up to the shop in a big Winton Six touring car and borrowed a long rope from Dad. On the following morning, the *Minneapolis Tribune* carried a picture on the front page showing the severed bars of an upper-floor jail window with Dad's rope still dangling from a remaining stub of the window bars.

Dad may not have known the intended use of the rope, but he might have had trouble convincing the authorities.

Life in the Red-Light District

As mentioned before, soon after Rudy moved out of the Grand Avenue duplex, the rest of us—Dad, Nat and I—moved to live in the rear of Dad's shop. The move took place early in 1924. The address was 205 Washington Avenue North, in Minneapolis's red-light district. It was the last and worst of our joint living quarters.

Life in the shop was wretched. The place was infested with rats and cockroaches. Sanitation and ventilation were not even marginal. Once each week, Nat and I went to the Turkish bathhouse for a hot tub bath. Every morning it was a relief to get out into the light and away from that depressing atmosphere. One saving feature gave me hope—within a few months I would be on the way to the new job. So long as there was an end in sight, I could endure it.

The end came sooner for Nat. Here is his account:

I was about sixteen years old and totally innocent about girls and social gatherings when I was invited to my first party. Dad said I could go provided I was back in the shop by ten o'clock.

At the party, there were refreshments and we all stood around the piano singing "Marquita" and other popular songs of the day. I was having a great time when I happened to notice that it was already eleven o'clock. I frantically called the shop, and Joe answered. I said, "Tell Pa I'm coming right home." There was a pause, and Joe said, "Pa says don't bother. Just come in the morning and get your things." I spent the night trying to sleep on the screen porch of one of the girls, who was a classmate. The next day I left home, never to return.

Conditions outside the shop were no better than those inside. The area harbored shady characters, along with good Samaritans and the forces of law and order. Pimps and their prostitutes warily plied their trade. The prostitute Margaret—she of the broad-brimmed hats and broader derriere—occasionally visited the shop. It may well be that while Nat and I were at school, she and the bums made use of our bed.

Winos retched and urinated into doorways. The sight of those derelicts made me a lifelong total abstainer. On some days a pitchman would set up his collapsible display, attract a crowd, deliver his spiel, and swindle the gullible.

Diversions in the red-light district served the baser instincts of man. In the block next to ours, the Gaiety Theatre offered risqué jokes and a chorus line of painted girls. Even earthier were the furtive "stag party" entertainments featuring nude women. The police raided these when they could, and the newspapers collaborated by publishing the names of those caught in the police net. On a loftier plane, the Salvation Army came out on some evenings to sing hymns and offer salvation to the denizens.

1924: My Views on Religion

By the year 1924, I was a confirmed unbeliever. Those who like to label people based on religious beliefs would classify me as a deist. This label is valid as applied to my views on those religions (including Judaism) that base their origins on supernatural events. I was suspicious of organized religious institutions generally—their claims of infallibility, their intolerance of the views of others, and their brutal record of dealing with unbelievers, apostates, and (especially) heretics.

I marveled at the immensity of the universe—the vastness of space, the incredible numbers of galaxies and stars, the relative insignificance of our own earth and solar system, the mystery of time. I was convinced that the universe exhibited an amazing degree of order and that this must be the result of some profound Design by an awesome Intelligence. Most people gave the name "God" to this Intelligence, but their definition of God included supernatural elements that I was unable to accept.

To me a stunning example of this amazing order was the structure of the physical world. The myriad different molecules in that world are all composed of combinations of about a hundred chemical elements. In turn, these elements are made up of combinations of a relative few incredibly tiny physical components—electrons, protons, neutrons, and such. Seemingly, these elements and particles were a part of the original Creation by that same awesome Intelligence.

In Europe, both in Braila and Gura Humora, the Jewish community had in place a structured "package" featuring a system of religious
beliefs, a code of ethical conduct, a social organization, a language and
literature, and so on. This package was designed to "imprint" the very
young so indelibly that they would follow in the ways of their ancestors.
Failure to follow would in effect deny them membership in the social
organization and thus leave them all alone in a hostile environment.

Our coming to America had created a discontinuity. When we
lived in the shack, our physical separation from any convenient Jewish
synagogue eliminated our access to the associated Jewish social organization. I did not realize it at the time, but I had thereby lost one of
the important benefits conferred by being a member of a structured
social organization. That same discontinuity terminated my lessons in
Judaism. I soon lost all ability to read, write, or speak Hebrew. The discontinuity also forced me to build my own system of beliefs, starting
with a virtually blank slate. I did so subconsciously, using self-challenge
as I went along. My most troublesome problem was to explain away a
hard fact: many people of undoubted intelligence believed many
things that I had rejected. As of the year 1924, I had no satisfactory
explanation for this contradiction.

While groping for a new set of beliefs, I puzzled about the long-
standing survival of Jews as a race apart. Their concept of racial (and
religious) purity and their intense opposition to intermarriage no
doubt contributed to that survival. Yet their insistence on racial purity limited their assimilation into their host countries of residence. This,
in turn, conflicted with the concept of nationalism in the host countries, thereby contributing to anti-Semitism.

In our family, assimilation relative to religious beliefs has proceeded rapidly. My parents' six children contracted nine marriages: six were
to Jews; three were to Gentiles. My parents' twelve grandchildren contracted nineteen marriages: six were to Jews; thirteen were to Gentiles.
Within two generations, only a third of the marriages were to Jews!

I have also puzzled about the pros and cons of assimilation. In the
United States, assimilation of *national origins* has proceeded apace and
has blurred the national origins of immigrants' descendants. My great

grandchildren claim descent from numerous countries of origin. I see nothing wrong with this—it diminishes one of the divisive forces in our society, yet with minimal damage to any nation. The descendants of Swedish or Irish immigrants may become fully assimilated in the United States, but Sweden and Ireland remain as nations with populations of Swedes and Irish.

With Jews it has been different. Assimilation was a clear threat to the continuity of the Jewish race, so I could not say, "I see nothing wrong with this." That was before the founding of the state of Israel in 1948, an event that has dramatically changed the equation. Now, even if Jews in host countries are assimilated, Jews as a race can still survive so long as the state of Israel survives.

Myself at Launch

When I left for the job at Western Electric, I was nineteen-and-a-half years old, of medium height (five feet, ten inches), and underweight (125 pounds). I was poorly dressed and indifferent about my appearance to an extent that was conspicuous to others. I also had a sharp tongue that could offend. I could have been labeled in many unappetizing ways: uncouth, sarcastic, tactless, ill-mannered. My years as a loner had contributed to my being a misfit in society.

Exposure to a full social life might have prevented these unpleasant traits, but I lacked such socialization. My life had largely followed a triangular path—from home to school, school to job, job to home. During all my years in Minneapolis, no classmate ever came to visit where I lived. Not only did Dad frown on our having visitors, I was too ashamed of our living quarters to invite anyone.

From twelve years of experience on many jobs, I had acquired the precious habit of self-reliance. I did not fear hard work or long hours. I was confident that I could in short order learn any new job.

My brief exposure to the red-light district was enough to inoculate me against the habits of its denizens. They smoked; I never acquired the habit. They drank alcohol; I became a lifelong total abstainer. They regarded loose women as an acceptable element of society; I followed Mother's admonition to keep my distance.

My chief fears were largely on hold. Anti-semitism in America was mostly passive and not at all on the scale prevalent in the old country. I still carried an accumulation of resentments—the world had been mean to me. I had been the victim of physical bullying. This had receded over the years but the memory had not.

I now realize that in 1924 I might have avoided many future miseries had I reasoned thus:

> You are about to enter a new world. People in that new world have never offended you. You haven't even met them. So it is time to leave those past resentments behind you and wipe the slate clean.

That concept never occurred to me. I was not even aware that I housed those resentments and that they would finally break out, like the imps in Pandora's box, causing much damage all around, especially to myself.

I did have the benefit of one wonderful breakthrough. My activities in chess had brought me self-respect and the respect of others. Lacking self-respect, I might well have emerged as an embittered, self-pitying person. Happily, I did find a basis for self-respect, and I thereby avoided a potentially dismal fate.

On to Western Electric Company

With graduation behind me, it remained to take the train to Chicago, the site of Western Electric's Hawthorne Works. I decided to simplify matters by sending most of my worldly possessions on ahead of me. They fit readily into a cardboard suitcase, which I addressed to the Training Department. (It would have been interesting to witness the recipient's reaction when this arrived). I closed out my bank account and now had eleven dollars to sustain me until my first payday. My farewell to Dad was short—neither of us had much to say. His last words as we shook hands were: "You should be a good boy." I then left for the train station to face whatever awaited me.

This thread of the story will continue in Chapter 8. The following two chapters recount some of my more colorful childhood jobs and my education during the Minneapolis years.

Q

6
The Icehouse, Snake Oil Sales, and Breaking a Strike

During my twelve years in Minneapolis, I had about sixteen jobs. I worked at three of them during the years 1912 to 1916. My early morning job of selling newspapers on the corner of Central Avenue and 33rd Street made me highly visible and led to my being employed by two neighborhood businesses—the grocery and the icehouse.

The Grocery

Early in our century, food distribution to city consumers was done mostly by independent neighborhood grocery stores. Another name was "corner grocery." Our neighborhood had such a corner grocery on the ground floor of a two-story house, one block from my newsboy site. The upper floor served as the living quarters for the owner,

Mr. Oscar J. Walker, and his family. He had no employees, and he invited me to become his clerk. The year was probably 1914 or 1915.

My duties were to wait on customers and to take care of matters during Mr. Walker's absence. I made short work of learning where everything was, along with memorizing the associated prices. I also learned how to operate the soda fountain, the coffee grinder, and other equipment.

I worked at the grocery for three hours each afternoon during weekdays, plus all day Saturday—a total of about twenty hours a week. For this I was paid one silver dollar, which works out to about five cents per hour. At the time, the prevailing wage for laborers was in the range of twenty to thirty cents per hour. Of course, I was being exploited, but I didn't fully realize it, and I cheerfully accepted the weekly silver dollar.

The Icehouse

I was hired away from the grocery job to become the bookkeeper for Peter Corbin's icehouse. It was located on the very intersection where I sold the morning papers. Again, my visibility had been influential. The change of jobs may have involved some agreement between Mr. Walker and Mr. Corbin. In any case the new job paid a bit more, but I was still being exploited.

The icehouse was a storage facility. In winter, ice was cut from the frozen Mississippi River and transported on horse-drawn sleds to the icehouse. In summer the transport was reversed. The ice moved out in horse-drawn wagons to fill the iceboxes of commercial customers and householders.

Although I was hired to keep the books, my ignorance of book-keeping was total. My predecessor had been a professional bookkeeper. In her beautiful handwriting, she had maintained precise records in two books: *Journal* and *Ledger*. I had no idea what those words meant. I also knew nothing of the ingenious concept of double-entry bookkeeping. What saved me was the fact that Mr. Corbin's ignorance was more abysmal than mine; to him, bookkeeping was an awesome mystery.

Mr. Corbin's formal education had ended at a primitive level. I quickly learned that he needed to know the state of his sales, costs, and customer balances, as well as the state of his bank accounts. I had no trouble keeping him at bay while I devised a record system to produce this information. I did not produce balance sheets or profit statements—I was unaware that such things existed. Had I produced them, they would have been irrelevant, for Mr. Corbin would not have understood them.

Mr. Corbin also had a contract to sprinkle some of the city streets. In those days most streets were unpaved, so in the summertime a good deal of dust would blow around. It became my job to drive the sprinkler wagon, a large horizontal wooden tank mounted on wheels. Somebody who knew about horses would hitch the horses to the wagon. I would then climb to the driver's seat perched high above, and off we would go. I had no problem driving the horses; they knew the way, and they probably were aware that I was an amateur.

During my high-school years, I continued to be fully employed (afternoons, weekends, summers) outside of school hours, but the location of the jobs and the size of the employing companies changed. There was an abrupt end to neighborhood jobs; now I was working in downtown Minneapolis. In addition, my employers were much larger than the local grocery or icehouse.

M. W. Savage

One of my summer jobs was at the M. W. Savage warehouse. It was really a discount department store. In part it bought distress goods from manufacturers and sold these at bargain prices. I was hired as "bundle boy" to wrap packages for the shoe department. I discovered that there is an art to wrapping packages and tying them up; I mastered some of this art. Even better, I soon was promoted to salesman. Now I needed to learn about all the various styles of shoes, the prices, the paperwork, the system of sizes and how to fit the shoes, and above all, making the sale. The base pay for salesmen was low, but there was a welcome commission supplement.

I enjoyed that job. The department head was a knowledgeable manager, a competent teacher, and a friendly human being. I was grateful to him for promoting me and for treating me with respect. I was sorry that the company was in the process of closing that warehouse.

Root & Hageman

Root & Hageman was a women's apparel store. It sold in the medium-price market, but its label was respected. A multi-story building housed its various departments. To my recollection, all the full-time employees were women except the two owners for whom the business was named. Among those employees were the head of the shipping department, who was also my boss (Lambert "Lam" Hallgrain), and the elevator operator. My job was variously that of shipping clerk, delivery boy, and janitor.

I disliked janitor work and its association with dirt—sweeping the carpeted floors, wiping up dust, baling up papers and cardboard in the basement baler, and so on. (Happily, cleaning the washrooms and toilets was done by the night charwomen.) Janitor work was the lowest-caste job in the company hierarchy, which made me the lowest-caste employee.

Delivering packages was higher-caste work. Valuable goods had to be delivered on time; money needed to be collected for COD packages; diplomacy had to be exercised upon entering people's premises; and routes needed to be planned for efficient delivery to a series of addresses. I developed an encyclopedic knowledge of the streets of Minneapolis, the streetcar system, and the time required to get around.

During my employment at Root & Hageman, the advocates for child labor reform successfully pushed through a city ordinance requiring that children under sixteen years of age not be employed in shops or offices after six o'clock in the evening. This directly affected my situation. Root & Hageman found an ingenious way to comply with the letter of the law. Shortly before six o'clock, they loaded me up with two sacks of packages to be delivered. It often could be eight, nine, or even ten o'clock before I would get home.

The State Prohibition Committee

One of my jobs provided me with a mini education in political campaigning. I was employed by the state Prohibition Committee. The Prohibition Party had a slate of candidates running for state office in an upcoming November election; the Committee had the job of helping those candidates get elected. This involved sending speakers (including candidates) to various towns to speak at political rallies and drum up interest in the Prohibition ticket. Our office had the job of sending campaign literature to the towns in advance, so that the information would be on hand when the rallies took place.

We had a generous supply of political giveaways—posters, banners, badges, and more. We also had the itineraries of the various speakers. I printed add-ons to the posters (names and themes of the speakers, locations, dates, and so on) so they could serve as local announcements. There were standardized assortments of materials to send out; I bundled these up and got them shipped to their proper destinations so they would be waiting for the speakers when they got there. The office was well equipped to get all this done.

That job stretched out beyond the summer and into the fall, until election time. Those loyal supporters then suffered a cruel blow. The entire Prohibition ticket was slaughtered at the polls.

The enactment of national prohibition (1920–1933) gave rise to a poetic gem:

> Ten thousand Jews are selling booze
> Without the state's permission
> To fill the needs of a million Swedes
> Who voted Prohibition.

Standard Press

Standard Press was a printing shop owned and managed by a Mr. Swenson, a capable, no-nonsense Swede with a flair for philosophic utterances. His son, a senior at the University of Minnesota, served as the after-school bookkeeper and accountant.

The shop equipment included several Linotype machines, a large rotary press, a few small job presses, a folding machine, a guillotine, some lesser machines, and many wooden "job cases" holding fonts of type. I had no experience with any of this equipment, but Mr. Swenson was a patient teacher. I learned to operate the job presses and the stitching (or stapling) machine. I also learned how to distribute used type back to the job cases. This required memorizing where all the letters belonged. (At first I botched some of this). I delivered finished work to various destinations around town.

I developed a profound respect for the skills of the tradesmen— Mr. Swenson, the typesetters, and especially the pressman who presided over the large rotary press. Getting that press to print a huge sheet with uniformity required a patient, gentle mastery of the many variables in the process. That pressman was very much in command.

Making deliveries for Standard Press had tragicomical aspects. Some of those printing jobs resulted in bulky, heavy deliveries that required using a cart to trundle them to their destination. The cart was housed in a nearby blacksmith shop where horseshoes were fitted to horses. The resulting accumulation of horse manure, urine, and burnt hooves made it as fragrant a place as I can recall. I learned to take a deep breath before I entered and to hold my breath as much as possible until I was safely out of there.

My early jobs served to supplement our family income. During our years in the shack and while I was in high school, I turned all my earnings over to Dad. This arrangement changed as Dad's fortunes improved and his expenses declined with the disintegration of the family. With his permission, I opened a savings account at a bank and began to accumulate what would become my college funds. During my final four years in Minneapolis, my earnings from jobs met virtually all my college needs and my living expenses.

The Medical Institute

In the summer of 1921, I found a job with a "medical institute" that I will call MED. MED was an enlightened employer. The people were friendly and the pay was generous, as were the amenities. The money I saved that summer financed my school and living expenses for the following school year.

The image MED presented to its employees was that of a benevolent Dr. Jekyll. In contrast, its image to the outside world was that of a predatory Mr. Hyde. MED practiced mail-order medicine.

With one notable exception, MED had no physicians, nurses, pharmacists, or other licensed specialists. It had no facilities for dealing with walk-in patients. It had no reception room, examination rooms, or diagnostic equipment. There wasn't even a clinical thermometer in the place. Yet MED was busily occupied diagnosing and treating patients for real or pseudo ailments.

MED's plan of operation can be summarized as follows: secure the names of men with a prior record of having responded to mail solicitations relating to sexual matters; persuade them to fill out a symptom form; offer to treat those who are diseased; deceive the rest into believing that they too are diseased; take advantage of their ignorance to sell them harmless, worthless remedies at high prices; and keep this up until the customers' credulity or their money is exhausted.

My job was in the pseudo pharmacy. I was trained by my boss (a vulgar, voluble chieftain I will call Abe) to produce and package one of the pseudo medications that accounted for a healthy share of MED's income.

I was well aware of the ongoing quackery, but I rationalized that I was merely a foot soldier obeying orders. In fact, when another school summer vacation loomed, I foresightedly revisited MED to discover if another summer of employment was available. It wasn't. State legislators, prodded by medical associations and reformers, were prying into mail-order medicine. Field investigations were under way. Although none had as yet struck MED, its turn was inevitable. A widespread gloom had descended on the entire MED senior staff.

New legislation was soon enacted, and it closed the mail-order clinics. The medical associations triumphed, and thereby extended their monopoly over the practice of medicine.

Mose Rosenstein

By the spring of 1922, it was becoming difficult to find a job; a recession was setting in. After much anxiety I became the after-school shipping clerk for Mose Rosenstein.

Mose was in the Army-Navy surplus business. During World War I, the military services had overbought certain goods—blankets, folding cots, tents, and so on. At the end of the war the government sold the surplus at bargain prices to entrepreneurs like Mose. He had a warehouse in Minneapolis from which he filled customers' orders. He also had a few retail stores in Minnesota, Wisconsin, and the Dakotas. My job was to bundle up goods for shipment to the outlets and take the bundles down to the delivery trucks on the street below, or even to the railroads or post office.

Mose was a friendly boss. He respected my efforts to get a college education, but this did not extend to paying me a decent salary. His business was flourishing; he soon agreed to employ me full time during the upcoming summer. Yet I saw trouble ahead. At my level of pay I would not be able to finance the next school year. I searched for a job that paid better but had no luck. Jobs of any kind were scarce—the 1922 recession had begun to grip the country.

The prospect of losing a school year gnawed at me, as did the associated uncertainties. It seemed as if only a miracle could save me. Then, out of nowhere, came that miracle; the railroad shopmen's union went on strike.

The Burlington Railroad

Shopmen are railroad employees who keep the locomotives and other equipment maintained and in running order. Their role is vital to human safety, meeting schedules, and so on. Despite that vital role, it was a monumental blunder to strike during a recession. The railroads decided to fight it out. They secured an injunction relating to overaggressive picketing and sabotage. They also hired strikebreakers and finally broke the strike.

I was drawn by newspapers advertisements offering railroad shop jobs to machinists, electricians, helpers, and others. I could not qualify as a tradesman, but I certainly could qualify as a helper. The pay for helpers was forty-seven cents per hour—a level notably higher than mine. Even more important was the opportunity for overtime, which was paid at time and a half.

I applied to the Chicago, Burlington, and Quincy railroad (the Burlington) and was hired as a helper. The pay was indeed as advertised, with much opportunity for overtime. The regular work shift was twelve hours, but overtime started after eight hours. I now realized that salvation was at hand, and I responded by working long hours. On several occasions, I even worked a consecutive thirty-six-hour stretch—my regular shift, the nightshift, and then my regular shift again. At my age that was easy.

Suddenly I was earning the royal sum of forty to fifty dollars a week. On top of that, my expenses were at a minimum. The company provided a dormitory and meals; except for Sundays, I lived on the premises.

The most interesting feature of that summer job was the workforce. It was a strange mixture of humanity.

One category of workers comprised Burlington shopmen who did not go on strike; they remained on the job. I learned that while they had grievances against the company, they had even greater grievances against the union. Evidently the union leadership had become remote and dictatorial. The men seemed to trust the company more than they trusted the union leadership.

A second category consisted of union shopmen employed by other railroads who had gone out on strike and *who then became strikebreakers* by signing up with the Burlington. I was astounded at this subterfuge, which was widespread. It was a way of showing solidarity with coworkers while meeting their own family needs. These strikebreakers seemed to be accepted by the Burlington employees without rancor. They shared common bonds: membership in their trades and distrust of the union leadership.

A further category was workers who had no railroad experience but who, like myself, were in poor-paying jobs and wanted to seize an opportunity. Most were mature men with families to support; I could understand their plight.

Finally, there were those who gave me much discomfort—ne'er-do-wells, drifters, and opportunists. Generally they were noisy, vulgar, shifty, abrasive, or all of the above. They were easy to identify, and I tried to keep my distance. I was drawn into only one fight—with a big slob who had taken to pestering me. As usual, I lost, but at least he stopped pestering.

By the time school reopened, I had several hundred dollars in the bank, and I was financially safe for the school year ahead. When I left to return to school, the strike was still in progress. My recollection is that it collapsed soon after.

Despite having resolved my financial crisis, I look back on that job with a feeling of guilt; I had been a strikebreaker, a scab. Of course, I could rationalize my actions: I needed the money badly. If I hadn't taken that job, somebody else would have. Nevertheless, the stain hasn't washed out.

It was rotten luck to be forced to choose between two such wretched alternatives. I was in agony until I made the decision, after which there was no turning back. It has now been eighty years since I took that job at the Burlington. During all those decades I have been ashamed of having been a scab. I am still ashamed.

Chess Column Editor

One of my jobs in 1923–1924 was created out of thin air. From my activities in the Minneapolis Chess League and in the world of correspondence chess, I came to realize that while chess players had low visibility, there were a lot of them. An idea hit me: why not a newspaper column for chess players?

I propositioned the sports editor of the *Minneapolis Star*, and he accepted my idea. My being the university chess champion helped to sell it. I was to provide a weekly column, for which I would be paid five dollars a week. It was a bonanza. It would take only a few hours to prepare a column, yet in those days I could eat all week on five dollars.

The *Star* bought two sets of the special type fonts needed to show a chess position on a board. In each column I included news of the goings-on in the local chess clubs and in the Minneapolis league. I analyzed interesting games. I included problems to be solved and set up a "ladder" to be climbed by sending in correct solutions. The column was well received. About twenty readers undertook to climb the ladder. Some readers sent in news items or fan mail. It was gratifying to become a sort of communication center for chess devotees.

Kinney Shoe Stores

Kinney was a chain of shoe stores. I was hired as a salesman based on my experience at M. W. Savage. I worked there weekday afternoons and Saturdays at a low salary and in my ROTC uniform. The personnel numbered no more than ten people. There were two bosses—a manager and his assistant. There was also an invisible, impersonal management. Corporate procedures governed most of the activities: customer relations, employee relations, pricing, forms to be filled out, and so on. As a company, Kinney's people were warm but the institution was cold.

Reflections on Jobs

Between 1920 and 1924 (except for the recession year 1922), my ability to secure and hold jobs had become easier. I had grown in physical size enough to be accepted as a man instead of a boy. My being a college student was regarded favorably by employers. I was no longer a novice—I had a background of experience.

My perceived purpose in getting jobs was to meet basic human needs. I was unaware that a by-product of employment was education. Working in several key industries—transportation, health, trade, politics—was educational. My contacts with coworkers gave me a broader understanding of the problems of raising a family on the then existing levels of income. Those workers shared their experiences with me, and I learned from them. They also shared their ignorance with me; they knew some things that weren't so.

Q

7

How I Became the First Juran to Go to College

Within days after arriving in Minneapolis, we children were enrolled in the Prescott Grammar School. Prescott was about one and a half miles from home, at 25th Street and Taylor Avenue. We walked to and from school. School buses did not exist, and riding the streetcar was a prohibitive expense.

Because we spoke no English, we were all placed in first grade. (Based on age, I belonged in third grade.) We learned English quickly and were soon reassigned to higher grades. In my case, based on proficiency in arithmetic, I was put into fourth grade. That placed me a year ahead of my age group. I was proud of this recognition, but I was unaware of the negative side effects. Now I was smaller than most of the students, and this difference widened as I skipped additional grades.

That difference in size, along with my sharp tongue, made me the target of bullies. I got into a few fights and lost all but one. The exception was Frank K. He had pestered me until one day I flared up and charged into him. Suddenly the tiger turned into a pussycat. He had been bluffing—he was actually a coward.

As immigrants, we were the objects of much curiosity. This declined as we became fluent in English. We may have been the only Jews in the school. In any case, we met virtually no evidence of open anti-Semitism. One exception was an Irish boy who was preoccupied with the slogan "Kill the Christ-killer."

I was one of the star pupils in arithmetic. I had a natural aptitude for adding long columns of numbers and for multiplying numbers in my head, all with speed and precision. But I did not enjoy homework assignments consisting of practice problems in arithmetic. I was bored by such work and tried to avoid doing it. As a result I fell into the habit of not studying. In the primary school I could get away with it—I got excellent grades even with minimal study. That didn't work in college.

I graduated from grammar school in January 1917, a few weeks after my twelfth birthday. I was two years ahead of my age group but quite immature, physically and socially.

High School, 1917–1920

I began to attend East High in January 1917 and graduated from South High in June 1920. As in grammar school, I had good aptitude for learning, especially in math and science. I received excellent grades, sometimes all A's. I qualified for the honor roll and was proud to receive the coveted "E" that East High awarded for scholarship. I never received a letter for athletics—I never even tried out for any team.

The Dawn of Universals

During my studies of algebra and geometry, I stumbled across two broad ideas that I would put to extensive use in later years. One was the concept of "universals"; the other was the distinction between theory and fact.

My study of algebra exposed me for the first time to the use of symbols to create generalized models. I knew that three children plus four children added up to seven children and also that three beans plus four beans added up to seven beans. Now, by using a symbol such as x, I could generalize the problem of adding three plus four and state it as a universal:

$$3x + 4x = 7x$$

This universal said that three plus four adds up to seven, no matter what x stands for—children, beans, or anything else.

To me, the concept of universals was a blinding flash of illumination. I soon found that universals abounded, but they had to be discovered. They had various names—rules, formulas, laws, models, algorithms, patterns. Once discovered, they could be applied to solve many problems.

Magic Squares

An early example of such discovery was a universal for constructing "magic squares." In high school I discovered the three-by-three magic square—numbers arranged in a pattern so that all the rows, columns, and diagonals added up to the same total—fifteen.

$$
\begin{array}{ccc}
2 & 9 & 4 \\
7 & 5 & 3 \\
6 & 1 & 8
\end{array}
$$

My discovery was actually a rediscovery. The original likely took place thousands of years ago.

As I studied this magic square, I saw some patterns in it.

- Two numbers in the bottom row (one and eight) are followed by two and nine, respectively, in the top row but in the column to the left.
- Two numbers in the left-hand column (two and seven) are followed by three and eight, respectively, in the right-hand column but in the row below.
- Two numbers (four and five) are followed by five and six, respectively, in the diagonal space directly to the left and below.

From all this I derived a set of rules—universals—to be used to construct any odd-numbered magic square. I tested those rules for a five-by-five square and a seven-by-seven square. I found that each was indeed "magic"—all rows, columns, and diagonals added up to iden-

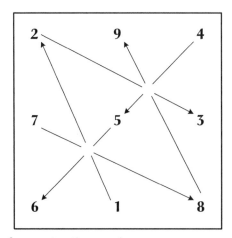

Figure 7-1. Rules for constructing magic squares

tical sums. I was quite pleased with myself for having developed these rules from so small a starting point, but as was typical of my insights, I did not share my discovery with anyone else.

Theory and Fact

My exposure to geometry provided a second flash of illumination. In geometry every theorem is an assertion that has to be proved before being accepted as valid. To be sure, there are starting points called axioms—self-evident truths that are accepted without the need for proof. Everything else is a theory—an unproved assertion.

It struck me that this distinction between theory and fact was the key to many riddles. I had already run into numerous unproved assertions; the Old Testament is full of them. Some seemed far-fetched in light of new knowledge uncovered by the advance of science. Yet I had been urged to accept such assertions on faith. In effect, I was given two options:

1. **Accept the assertions on faith.** I was unable to do this. Faith had not been imprinted on me during early childhood.
2. **Deny the validity of the assertions.** I had already discovered that such denials brought me into confrontations with those whose faith had been imprinted on them during early childhood. For them, denial of the unproved assertions was not possible with-

out bringing into question the credibility of the entire social structure into which they had been born.

Now I had a third option:

3. **Avoid confrontation.** Take the position "I am not convinced. These are just unproved assertions—theories."

During my years as a consultant, this new option became invaluable for making progress. Time after time I faced an impasse that had its origin in conflicting theories. I was usually able to break the impasse by proposing that we list all theories and then agree on the sequence and manner in which they should be tested.

South High School

Our moving to the 25th Street house required that I transfer to South High School. Rudy avoided the transfer somehow. He graduated from East High with the June 1919 class and so became the first Juran to earn a high-school diploma.

At South High I continued to get good grades. I was on the honor roll and third in the graduating class. I also engaged in some extracurricular activities. I served on the school paper—*The Southerner.* I also did some reporting. For example, I visited the city's small claims court and wrote a report on it.

During my years at South High, I was regarded as bright but immature. Some of my quirks are documented in the 1920 yearbook, which shows my nickname as "Bolshevikee." I was ignorant about the nature of communism, but I welcomed the overthrow of the czarist regime that had so often tolerated and even encouraged pogroms. My support for the Bolsheviks was my way of supporting the "enemy of mine enemy."

The yearbook also shows opposite my name the comment, "His second name should be 'work.'" I am sure that many boys had after-school and summer jobs, but I was probably among those who worked the longest hours. In any case, my perseverance was conspicuous enough to be noticed by the yearbook editors.

Higher Education

Our parents wanted good educations for their boys. They sacrificed their own well-being to make this possible. Dad told me more than once, "I don't want you to be a laborer all your life." He also urged us to study hard. The time even came when he offered a dollar to anyone who brought home a report card containing nothing but A's. His boys were good students, but getting all A's was not easy. I did collect, but not always.

Mother's urging was more subtle. She had a profound respect for learning; she knew first hand the handicaps of the uneducated. Her method was to point out examples, such as teachers and doctors. In a curious, inverted way she, the illiterate one, became the role model.

By the time I was well into high school, I already knew I wanted to go on to college at the University of Minnesota in Minneapolis. I wanted to break out of poverty, out of our hand-to-mouth existence. I had already noticed that one's level of education was influential during job hunting. Most employers seemed to favor the better-educated applicants.

My jobs had all been temporary. I thought a logical goal was to qualify for "a steady job at steady pay." A college education seemed to be a key element for getting such a job.

A college education had no precedent in our family. Rudy graduated from high school a year before me but showed no interest in spending four more years preparing for life. He wanted to graduate from poverty now. Sister Betty had been denied the opportunity to attend even high school. I would be the family's first college graduate, provided I could finance it.

Financing a College Education

Financing my education at the University of Minnesota proved to be a precarious balancing act year after year. I hoped that while school was in session, I could meet my living expenses by working after school and weekends. I also hoped that my summer vacation earnings would enable me to pay for the next year's school expenses: tuition and fees, books, equipment, and so on. Such was the budgetary plan.

Actually, I ran a small deficit in two of those years, but Dad was able and willing to rescue me—I was never forced to go into debt.

What to Study?

During my senior year in high school, I puzzled about what to study at university. I was strongly influenced by the advice of Mr. Fisher, my high-school physics teacher. He suggested I consider engineering. He reasoned that I was well qualified to study it since two of its basic elements were science and math—subjects in which I had always excelled. Mr. Fisher also suggested I consider electrical engineering, which was newer than most of the engineering fields and was also undergoing rapid growth, a state that usually offered good opportunities for young graduates. I followed his advice.

Meeting Expenses

From the day I first set foot on the University of Minnesota campus, I ran into the grim realities of the costs of a college education. My assets, so painfully hoarded week by week, seemed to just melt away. Each year had three terms, and the tuition for just one term demanded more than two weeks' worth of summer earnings. So did a slide rule—the engineer's portable calculator. A set of drawing instruments ate up even more. Beyond tuition there were added fees for this and that.

I was stunned by these frightening realities, which clarified why so many boys went into the job market after high school or even after grammar school. Education ate up past earnings and precluded full earnings for the present. It often demanded sacrifices from parents—a denial of comforts they had earned.

Courses and Grades

My grade point average during my four years was 2.02, which is just barely above a C average. I had only one A (in a math course). In two courses I flunked the final examination (but in each case I successfully passed the repeat exam). These grades were a far cry from my performance in grammar and high schools. Looking back it is easy to see why:

- I hadn't acquired a habit of studying. In the primary schools things were too easy; I received excellent grades with minimal study. In college the courses were more demanding, and competition was much stronger.
- My time for study was limited; my jobs had high priority and ate into my time.
- My school schedule did provide some hours for study, but I played chess instead. (As it turned out, chess provided me with invaluable benefits.)
- The atmosphere at home was not favorable for study.

Not all courses were attractive to me, but some captured my imagination because of the elegance and sheer majesty of the concepts: the calculus, differential and integral, descriptive geometry, and infinite series. I was in awe of the equations that governed the behavior of electricity. They seemed to be part of some Master Plan.

My engineering education was largely devoid of courses in the humanities. I had no problem with that emphasis on technology and had an amused contempt for some of the courses taken by my friends in the Science, Literature, and Arts (SLA) curriculum. I could not understand how time spent on courses such as philosophy could possibly be of help on any future job. Not until years later, when I studied law, and still later when I was drawn into problems of national and international importance, did I learn how ignorant I had been.

Reserve Officers Training Corps (ROTC)

During registration, I learned that the campus housed a unit of the Reserve Officers Training Corps (ROTC). It was an arm of the U. S. defense forces, and its aim was to recruit and train college graduates to become reserve officers in the armed services. One inducement was an opportunity to serve the country in the event of an emergency. That struck a responsive chord in me. Another inducement was that I would be issued an army uniform. I welcomed that bonus, especially the warm overcoat. I wore the uniform often, even on days when there was no drill.

Being in the ROTC involved obligations. Most electrical engineering students were assigned to the Army Signal Corps, and their training included classes in communication—telephone, telegraph, and the newly emerging radio. ROTC training also included a summer camp, which I attended at Camp Custer in Battle Creek, Michigan, in 1923.

One of the lecturers at camp was William F. Friedman, the leading Army expert on codes and ciphers, a subject that had intrigued me for years. Following Friedman's lecture, I talked with him at length; it seems that I was the only student who had a keen interest in the subject. As a result, when I received my commission I was assigned to what came to be known as the Signal Intelligence Division. In the years that followed, Friedman and I developed a close rapport that became a lifelong friendship.

Chess: a Source of Respect

It was exciting to enter college, yet my spirits were low. My family was beginning its slide into disintegration. I was working long hours, and I had no social life and hardly any fun. In addition, I still harbored fears and resentments (albeit dormant) that I had accumulated since childhood. Of course, I contributed to these problems by my behavior as a loner and an angry young man.

It would have helped had I acquired some basis for being respected by others. Here and there I had exhibited sparks of creativity, such as my plan for constructing magic squares. Such feats gave me a feeling of accomplishment, but they brought me no respect from others. Those around me were not aware of what I had done or weren't interested. I hungered for respect. The game of chess satisfied that hunger.

In 1920 or 1921, I learned the game from our next-door neighbor, Mr. Soderberg. He was most patient with his eager student. He himself was not a strong player; to him the game was a pastime. Within a few weeks I was winning regularly, and he suggested that I seek out other opponents. He told me, "There's nothing more I can teach you."

I found new opponents at the University of Minnesota. In the men's union, one of the rooms was filled with chess tables. Soon I was spending my study hours playing chess, and I became addicted to the game. For me it was an ideal form of recreation. It required analysis of complex problems, which I relished. It also involved no expense, a feature well suited for one who was perpetually broke. I progressed rapidly, and in 1922 I entered the campus chess tournament. I emerged as champion, after which I defeated the "Ag campus" champion to become the all-university champion. I then successfully defended that title during my junior and senior years.

Becoming the university chess champion had a dramatic effect on my outlook. News of the event was published in the campus newspaper. It became known to my professors as well as to my classmates. The effect was magnified in the academic atmosphere, where mental achievement can outrank the physical. My status followed me around. It was common for me to be introduced to a stranger as the chess champion. I became a celebrity and I lapped it up.

My interest in chess stimulated me to blossom out as an organizer for the first time. I visited the chess clubs in Minneapolis and proposed creating a league so that teams from the various clubs could play each other. The idea was well received, and the end result was the founding of the Minneapolis City Chess League. It consisted of six clubs, including those from the University of Minnesota, the YMCA, and the Minneapolis Athletic Club.

Chess greatly influenced my well-being, mostly for the better. I acquired self-respect and the respect of others. I enlarged my world and contributed to organizing useful events. And I also established contacts with many people who would have been of help to me had I remained in Minneapolis.

Social Life
Classmates

Until I entered the University of Minnesota I had hardly any social life. Our family belonged to no organized social group. We were a family of loners, and I was the loneliest of the lot. The university changed all that. It teemed with formal and informal social groups.

My class of 1924 classmates consisted of about fifty electrical engineering students. That class became an informal social group into whose membership I was accepted. We had the common goal of higher education; getting our degrees was serious business. We also faced common problems relating to grades and money. Those of us in the ROTC attended summer camp and literally lived together. Togetherness also emerged from those experimental engineering projects that demanded the intimacy of teamwork.

My classmates tolerated my quirks, and they seemed to take into account my immaturity. My prowess at chess may have surprised them, but they respected it all the same. Some liked the idea of having one of their own as the university champion.

The Chess Players

The chess players were a loosely organized social group. Although there were officers and committees, most activity was highly informal. As champion, I had a special relationship with the players, but they also elected me secretary in my sophomore year and president during my junior year. For me it was a first. Never before had I received formal election to office in a social group.

Two of my closest lifelong friends came from among the chess players—Archie McCrady and Charles (Chuck) Milkes. McCrady was in the 1924 civil engineering class. Chuck Milkes was in the 1924 chemistry class. We met at the chess table and also had occasion to work together in the chemistry laboratory. We became close friends and remained so for life.

The Menorah Society

As a young boy I had been shy around girls and was abysmally ignorant about them. I became a firm believer in Mother's views on relations between the sexes. She never discussed such matters in detail, but her meaning was clear: women were either pure or loose, and she hoped her boys would keep their distance from the loose ones.

During my first three years in college, my social life did not include women. The campus teemed with women—they made up nearly half of the student body. Yet I had no way to meet them. There were none in my engineering classes, and none ever entered the men's union.

Then, in my senior year, a Jewish chess player friend told me about Menorah. It was a society organized "for the study and advancement of Jewish culture and ideals," and its members included women as well as men. (Menorah was also a hunting ground for Jewish women on the prowl for mates.) I attended some Menorah meetings and was introduced (as the chess champion) to a few of the women. They were cordial and relaxed, so my shyness began to melt away.

I managed to have several dates, but they were fleeting encounters. When I left Minneapolis my views on women were blurred. Mother's influence had caused me to worship womanhood, but I was not focused on specific women. I did hear indirectly that in some quarters I was regarded as an eligible bachelor. Two of Dad's friends had daughters who needed husbands; a college graduate would be suitable. None of such overtures aroused my interest. My priorities were elsewhere.

Preparation for Future Social Life

My life at the university did little to prepare me for social life after graduation. I was an alien in the prevailing culture, and this had its effect on my classmates. I was also lacking in social graces to a conspicuous degree. Very likely some of the students, both men and women, regarded me as a "chump" rather than as an alien.

Recruitment

Until my senior year, I gave little thought to the problem of getting a job after graduation. I did know, from an "orientation" course, that during February and March of the senior year, men from various companies would visit the campus to recruit engineering graduates. As the time approached, the excitement heated up. Spontaneous bull sessions emerged to discuss the merits of the visiting companies, how to behave during the interviews, and much else. I participated eagerly in such sessions.

I was interviewed by recruiters from about six companies and received offers from three—General Electric, Western Union, and

Western Electric. The offers had much in common. I would first undergo a training course, and then I would be assigned to some department based on further interviews.

Western Electric was a part of the Bell System, the national telephone monopoly. Bell sent a team of three recruiters, one from each of its companies: Bell Telephone Laboratories, the research arm; Western Electric, the manufacturing arm; and Northwestern Bell Telephone, a part of the marketing arm.

I signed up with Western Electric. In this case I was influenced by a judgment from the bull sessions. The telephone industry was still in its early growth stages but was already competing briskly and successfully against the telegraph industry. The past belonged to Western Union; the future belonged to the Bell System. Such was the conclusion of the bull sessions, and they were right on target.

The offer from Western Electric—dated March 12, 1924—offered a starting salary of $27.00 dollars per week, with an increase to $35.00 per week during the first year. It added that, "The increases thereafter depend entirely on the ability and initiative shown by the individual, increases being given at regular intervals to all deserving employees."

I read that passage more than once; I thought I could live comfortably under such a statement of intent.

I accepted the job offer as of April 2, 1924. At long last I would reach a major milestone—I had a steady job at steady pay. Or so I thought.

Graduation

During my senior year, the pressures on me seemed to subside. My financial crisis was behind me. My grades improved, reaching an average of 2.4+. This was still well below my capabilities but the best ever. The door to social life had opened enough to give me a glimpse of what was possible. My college degree was now clearly in sight. I had an assured job waiting for me. At long last the sun was shining and I would have the luxury of basking in its warmth.

I did not attend the commencement. The schedule for the event would have meant a week's delay in starting my new job, with loss of a week's pay. For my classmates, attending commencement was as important for their families as for themselves. In my case I was now living essentially without a family—only Dad and I were living together. I don't know if he would have attended. I didn't ask him.

Reflections on Life and Education in Minneapolis

Despite my own personal hardships, I have fond memories of my years in Minneapolis and especially my years at the University of Minnesota. Minneapolis was dedicated to the well-being of its people. It insisted on law and order but provided opportunities to pursue the American Dream. I was nourished by those opportunities in its schools and libraries. I was inspired by the work ethic it encouraged. I am grateful for the bounty it bestowed on me, and I am proud to call Minneapolis my hometown.

I owe a great debt to the University of Minnesota. More than any other institution, it accepted me and made me welcome. I am eternally grateful for the warmth it extended to me. During occasional return trips to Minneapolis, I have revisited the sites where I lived, worked, and studied. Of these, none inspires such deep feelings of affection and gratitude as the university.

Once Mother was gone, the university became my foster home. It filled my needs for acceptance, respect, and inspiration. I wish I had done my scholastic best and regret deeply that I did not. I trust I have atoned in part by becoming a useful citizen of the world.

Q

Part Two

My Early Career in Quality

8

Western Electric

During the overnight train ride to Chicago, I sat up in a coach seat. I was not apprehensive about what lay ahead. The Bell System recruiters had been friendly, and the follow-up correspondence had been informative. In Minneapolis I had tackled numerous jobs, and the least of my problems had been learning how to do the work.

In Chicago my friend Chuck Milkes met my train, and I spent Sunday night at his home. I was up early Monday morning and went on to Hawthorne. I was directed to the office entrance and escorted to the Training Department. There I began to meet some of the other newly recruited college graduates who were arriving that same morning. Before the week was over, more than fifty graduates had arrived from numerous colleges in many states.

On that first day we were told what would be happening during our first week and in the weeks ahead. We would receive our physical examinations, and then we'd be briefed on what Hawthorne and its branches did and how they fit into the overall mission of Western

Electric and its parent, the American Telephone and Telegraph Company (AT&T). Then we would spend a day or two at each of the major branches to receive briefings in greater detail.

Following the briefings we would be assigned to a branch that would become our employer. At that branch we would be put into a training course, after which we would be assigned to some department to begin our work. We were also given entrance passes and provided with information on local services such as transportation, lodging, and meals.

Crisis

On the third day I received terrifying news—I had failed the physical examination! The doctor had detected an incipient hernia—a hernia waiting to happen. He recommended that it be corrected (by surgery) before my being hired. Suddenly my world had collapsed around me. I didn't have enough money even to feed myself until payday, let alone to undergo surgery. The dream of a steady job at steady pay seemed to evaporate.

After some agonizing hours, I was rescued. My savior was A. P. (Pope) Lancaster, head of the College Training Department. He managed to get the doctor's recommendation overturned, so I was added to the Hawthorne payroll after all. (In a way, the doctor was proved right. The hernia indeed happened twenty-nine years later, in 1953, at a most inconvenient time.)

Orientation

My orientation consisted of some high-density lectures supplemented by reading material. We recruits also filled out numerous forms, including a sale to the company of our rights for our future inventions. The consideration was one dollar; each of us was handed a dollar bill then and there. We also visited various offices. I learned that Western Electric was divided into various major functions, each called a "department." Hawthorne was a part of the Manufacturing Department, and its job was to make the hardware that enabled

AT&T's customers to talk to each other by telephone. Hawthorne was virtually the company's sole manufacturing facility, but planning was in progress to build a large new factory in Kearny, New Jersey.

Hawthorne was, in turn, divided into seven major functions, each called a "branch": Clerical, Industrial Relations, Production, Operating, Technical, Development, and Inspection. In addition, Hawthorne served as landlord to some sizeable detachments from other departments, notably Installation and Merchandise.

The Inspection Branch Training Course

At the end of the week's orientation period, all college recruits were assigned to the branches that would become their employers. Fifteen of us were assigned to the Inspection Branch. We came from a total of twelve different universities. (In recent decades I have often been asked, "How did you happen to choose managing for quality as a lifetime career?" My response has always been, "I didn't choose it. It was chosen for me by the powers that be.")

Now we embarked on a training course to learn what the Inspection Branch did. We had been told that Inspection was "the guardian of quality." Its job was to see that products made by Hawthorne met their quality specifications. To this end it inspected and tested the products before they were shipped to Hawthorne's customers—the regional Bell Telephone Companies.

Inspection and testing took place at all stages of product progression: raw materials, work-in-process, and finished goods. The Inspection Branch also had laboratories to calibrate and maintain the accuracy of the many mechanical gages, electrical meters, and other kinds of testing equipment. It took a large force to be the guardian of quality. At Hawthorne's peak in 1929, the Inspection Branch employed about 5,200 people of the total Hawthorne population of more than 40,000.

The Inspection Branch was subdivided into thirty-six departments. Nineteen of these were "line" departments—they did the actual inspection and tests. The remaining departments were "staff"; they developed methods for inspection and testing, ran the measurement laboratories, and did extensive planning and analysis related to quality.

The training course ran to several months. We recruits spent a day or two in each of those thirty-six departments. Each department assigned an employee to serve as instructor. We were required to submit written reports on what we had learned from each department visited.

During that training course I learned a great deal. Much inspection work was simplicity itself, such as sorting mechanical parts with a "go/no-go" gauge. Other work was fiendishly complex and required extensive training beforehand. For example, one of the circuits used in machine switching was the line finder. When a subscriber lifted his or her receiver off the hook, the line finder made a search, found an idle line, and then used a "dial tone" to inform the subscriber that all was ready for dialing. The electromechanical apparatus of those days took eleven seconds to do all that, but it took thirteen weeks to train a tester to understand what went on during those eleven seconds.

Inspection Fallibility

In one of the departments I made a discovery that would later stun the entire Inspection Branch. The departmental instructor was a young woman whose regular job was inspecting sandblasted metal parts prior to their receiving a black japan finish. I watched closely while she "detail inspected"—inspected every piece. As part of my training, I was required to inspect several pans of those parts, after which she reinspected the same parts to assure that I had made no mistakes. To my surprise, she found several defective parts that I had missed. I thought I had done a thorough job, yet the evidence said I had not.

I was embarrassed at having made those mistakes, and I looked for some explanation that might restore my honor. I came up with a theory: human beings are simply unable to maintain attention 100 percent of the time. It was a far-fetched theory; during the training course, I was told over and over that "detail inspection finds all the defects." To the department heads that was an article of faith, yet I had just learned that it did not apply to me. In self-defense I set up an experiment to see whether my instructor was also an exception.

When she was momentarily away, I slyly took one pan of parts that she had just inspected and moved it to the area of pans awaiting inspection. On her return, she inspected that pan (again), and, sure enough, she found some parts to be defective. A few were borderline cases, but the others were undoubtedly defective. She had made mistakes during her original inspection.

Now I had the beginnings of support for a theory of human fallibility as applied to inspection. Within a few years I generated enough proof to support the theory and destroy the article of faith; I proved that human inspection does not find all the defects. In later decades, that same proof would profoundly affect planning for quality in any application that demanded perfection.

The Inspection Departments were all located adjacent to the departments that made the products. As a result, the training course exposed me not only to the many products being made but also to the processes used to make them. Collectively those processes were a journey to a technological wonderland. Routine inspections held little interest for me, but I was fascinated by the technology. I raised many questions and stored the answers in what was then a highly receptive memory.

My reports on the departments I visited were factual and blunt. I recall one report in which I expressed my admiration for the mastery exhibited by the men who could test those complex machine-switching circuits, then find and remedy the causes of any failures. In another report I noted that at some stations, the inspection had been "listless." I thought my reports were forthright, and it did not dawn on me that others might regard them as tactless.

Another Crisis

As the training course was drawing to a close, there was much excitement among the college recruits as they wondered to which department they would be assigned. Without exception, all were assigned to staff departments to do planning, devise inspection methods, and conduct investigations or analysis. My assignment was to the Complaint Department.

I was unaware that I had meanwhile survived another crisis. I didn't learn about it until early 1964, forty years later, when I talked to A. P. Lancaster—the same "Pope" Lancaster who had rescued me from the "incipient hernia" crisis. Lancaster told me (in 1964) that at the end of the Inspection Branch training course, there were no bids for me; no department offered to hire me. He then went to A. T. Wood, head of the Inspection Branch Personnel Division, and A. B. Hazard, head of the Process Inspection Division, to urge them to find a job for me, describing me as "one of the brightest of the college recruits." He succeeded in getting me placed with the Complaint Department.

As I write these memoirs, I suspect that the bluntness of my reports contributed to my being rejected. My lack of tact may well have become a topic of discussion among the department heads. In any case, it is evident that at the time I had not yet learned the importance of stating my views in ways that carried no gratuitous bite. It would take me decades to learn that.

A Steady Job at Steady Pay

With my assignment to the Complaint Department, I had reached a major goal—a steady job at steady pay. During my college years I had only a vague idea of how a college education could be so transforming. That became clear only during my senior year when I was being interviewed by the recruiters. There, men from prestigious companies talked to me about *a career, not a job*. The idea of a career with an industrial giant was for me an alien concept, but I welcomed it.

The career concept was reinforced during my early weeks at Hawthorne. I was treated with courtesy. I was rescued from a terrifying crisis. I learned about the company's employee benefits (health services, after-hours recreation, vacations, pensions). These were more liberal than the prevailing market levels, yet the company had established them voluntarily. So the concept of a lifetime career looked attractive, especially a lifetime career with Western Electric. I had no trouble concluding, "I want to spend the rest of my working life with this company."

The Complaint Department

Thanks to Lancaster's persuasion, I became a "troubleshooter" in the Complaint Investigation Division. It consisted of two departments. I spent a year in the Complaint Department, investigating shop complaints and then spent a year investigating field complaints for the Investigation Department. Both jobs were fascinating.

The customers of the Complaint Department were mostly shop foremen. (Without exception, all shop foremen were men). A shop foreman ran one or more shop processes and presided over as many as several hundred shop workers. Now and then a foreman would run into a quality problem that he was unable to solve. For example, one of his processes was suddenly unable to meet the quality specifications; components intended to mate with each other suddenly could not be mated; or a batch of components received from a storeroom bore no resemblance to what had been requisitioned.

Each such case required that someone collect and study the facts, theorize about possible causes, and then test the theories—follow the trail until the cause was discovered. A further step was to find a department able to provide a remedy for the problem. In addition, it was necessary to dispose of any defective material and take steps to prevent a recurrence. The shop foremen and their assistants lacked the time, mobility, and (in most cases) the training to do such troubleshooting.

The Complaint Department consisted of about thirty men who were available full time to do troubleshooting. They were authorized to follow the trail—to enter any area not specifically restricted. Each had years of experience in the shop and in troubleshooting as well. During my time in the department, it had only two college-trained engineers—me and another college recruit, also from the class of 1924.

"Following the trail" took me to many departments, both shop and office. I met many supervisors and learned about their processes and methods. In those days my memory was excellent, so I soon acquired an encyclopedic knowledge of what went on at Hawthorne: the products, the processes, the methods, the department functions, and so on. There was a great deal to be learned, but my memory seemed to have a boundless capacity.

Troubleshooting included doing the paperwork. A report was written to summarize the investigation, set out the conclusions reached, and recommend the action to be taken and by whom. Work orders were written to pay for any extra costs involved, such as scrapping defective goods. The reports also "charged" the departments found to be responsible—a conclusion that might be vigorously contested.

The Complaint Department was headed by Frank Merritt and consisted of two sections. One was the Complaint Investigation Section; it included the troubleshooters. The other section was "Returned and Scrap Material Inspection," which was responsible for disposing of scrapped material as well as material returned from the field.

What little contact I had with Merritt was on a high level of courtesy and ethical conduct. In contrast, Elmer Smith, the section chief, was of a different breed. He spent little time on complaint investigation and much time on gossip and intrigue. I soon learned to minimize my exposure to him.

Happily, my immediate boss was the subsection chief Max Swan, the departmental workhorse. Max seemed to be the direct supervisor of all the troubleshooters. He was of middle age, compactly built and with a square jaw to match. His was a no-nonsense approach to the job and to the men. He wielded a large fountain pen whose business end was ground at an angle. The resulting broad, dark blue script heralded authority. Like the master sergeant in the military, Max got things done.

I responded readily to the leadership of this stern boss. His experience and competence made him surefooted when pondering the causes of shop troubles. He readily shared his experience with the men and so spared them hours of time rediscovering what he already knew. In later years, our positions were reversed—I became his organizational superior. That change made no difference in our basic relationship, which from the outset was one of mutual respect and trust.

The Investigation Department

The Investigation Department dealt with quality complaints from the field. These originated chiefly with the regional Bell Telephone companies and were sent to Bell Telephone Laboratories' Inspection Engineering Department. That department determined where in the Bell System the problem had originated. Problems that had their origin in the Manufacturing Department were routed to the Investigation Department, whose troubleshooters then proceeded much as their shop counterparts.

The troubleshooters in the Investigation Department were mostly college-trained engineers. The atmosphere here was more relaxed than in the shop Complaint Department—field complaints seldom posed any threat to meeting shop delivery schedules.

The department head was Otto Sternberg, a practical thinker who had risen from the shop ranks based on his keen analytical ability. He was widely respected for this. He was also the subject of merriment—he was a slob in dress and demeanor.

My immediate boss was the section chief, Walter Cobelli. Like Max Swan, he had risen from the shop ranks, but unlike Max Swan, Cobelli kept loose hands on the reins. Under him, productivity was low but the comfort level was high.

I had no difficulty adapting to investigating field complaints. By now I was familiar with life at Hawthorne and with its products and processes. I was also familiar with the cultural code for conducting investigations. I had no idea what my future assignments would be but I was not worried. I was safely aboard a sturdy ocean liner that would protect me from storm and sea.

The Hierarchy: A New Goal

Soon after my arrival at Hawthorne, I discovered that the telephone directory showed, for each person listed, the name and code number of his/her organization, the telephone number, the building location, and the person to whom the employee reported. From all this I was able to map out the management hierarchy, from the works manager down to any foot soldier. During my assignment to the Investigation Department, that hierarchy was as follows:

Works Manager	C. G Stoll
Assistant Works Manager	C. L. Rice
Inspection Branch Superintendent	W. L. Robertson
Assistant Superintendent	M. E. Berry
Chief of Investigation Division	G. E. Hildebrandt
Chief of Investigation Department	O. Sternberg
Section Chief	W. K. Cobelli
Engineer	J. M. Juran

From sources outside the telephone directory, I soon learned that the fastest road to higher salaries and more perquisites ("perks") was through promotion—climbing the hierarchical ladder. AT&T followed a strict policy of promotion from within. Whoever joined up had to start at the bottom of the ladder. In addition, the merit system was in force; all had equal opportunity. (There were exceptions; some were "more equal" than others.) One exception was in my favor. College graduates were a minority of the employees, but they held the bulk of the top jobs.

All this was exciting stuff. The way was open to me to climb each of the seven steps of that ladder and claim the goodies along the way. Not only that, I was at an advantage; my engineering degree was a passport to the fast track. So there emerged the outlines of a new goal—climb that ladder all the way to the upper reaches of Hawthorne.

Although my degree was an asset, my Jewish origins were a liability. I soon learned that in all of Hawthorne, there were only three Jewish managers: the two Berman brothers were division chiefs, and Hyman Glicken was a department chief in the Inspection Branch.

There was more. The hierarchy did not end with Mr. Stoll, the Works Manager. There were five additional rungs of the ladder beyond him, as follows:

President, AT&T
Executive Vice President, AT&T
Vice Presidents of AT&T
President, Western Electric Company
Vice President, Manufacturing Department

The scope of the opportunities was now clear. To reach the top of the Hawthorne ladder required seven promotions, from engineer to works manager. To reach the dizzying heights of AT&T then required five additional promotions. I became increasingly intrigued with the idea of climbing those ladders and gave little thought to the handicap of my Jewish origins.

The Taylor System

Hawthorne operated under a system of separating planning from execution. This system is traceable to the advocacy of an American engineer, Frederick W. Taylor. Taylor began his career by learning the machinist trade and running a lathe in a machine shop. Meanwhile he took engineering courses at night and received a degree in mechanical engineering. He then received successive promotions to foreman of the lathe "gang," superintendent of the machine shop, chief engineer, and plant manager.

From all this experience Taylor concluded that the foremen and shop workers of those days (the late 1890s) lacked the technological literacy to plan their work or to set standards for what was a fair day's work—how many units should a worker produce in a day. Taylor's solution was to *separate planning from execution.* To this end, he employed engineers to establish methods for doing work and to set standards for a day's work. He also used piecework incentives to stimulate workers to use the methods and to meet the productivity standards.

Having attained great increases in productivity in his plant, Taylor became a forceful advocate for his system. Many companies, especially during World War I, tested it out, and most made gains in productivity. As a result it was widely adopted in the United States, and it became the dominant system used during most of the twentieth century.

At Hawthorne, the most intensive application of the Taylor system was in the factory shops. The Planning Departments (in the Technical Branch and elsewhere) prepared the product specifications, set the quality standards, published the drawings, established the work methods and published them in "layouts," set the piece rates, and so on.

Each shop department was headed by a foreman, whose responsibility was limited to executing the plans: following the prescribed work methods, meeting the schedules, meeting the quality standards, and maintaining the workers' piecework earnings. One result of all this separation of planning from execution was that in the main, *the foremen were supervised impersonally.* These impersonal supervisors included the specifications, drawings, layouts, schedules, personnel manuals, and budgets.

The Caste System and Formal Perks

The published Hawthorne organization charts showed jobs arranged in two dimensions. The vertical groupings separated the various functions from each other. The horizontal rows separated jobs by rank in the hierarchy. I soon learned that such charts told only part of the story. There was also in place a caste system, informal as well as formal, that provided differences in perquisites (perks) to the respective caste members.

Shop work was lower caste than office work. Shop work was also classified into "labor grades" based on such factors as the extent of education and experience required, the degree of responsibility, the working conditions, physical demand, hazards, and so on. For each labor grade, there was a range of hourly pay rates. Employees newly entering a grade would receive the minimum of the rate range. The rest of the range was then available for increases later. Most shop workers also had opportunities for increasing their earnings through the piecework system.

The workweek for all employees was five and a half days—the weekdays plus a half day on Saturday. The shop workers' day began at 7:30 AM and ended at 4:30 PM, with a half hour allowed for lunch. That resulted in an eight-and-a-half-hour day, but the last half hour was paid at time and a half. The Saturday schedule was from 7:30 AM until 11:30 AM, all being paid at time and a half.

All shop workers were "on the clock." Each worker was given a clock card number and he or she punched in before starting work and punched out before leaving. The clock recorded the times in and out, using black ink except for latecomers, whose tardiness was recorded in red ink to alert the payroll clerks. There were penalties for being late as well as for unauthorized absence. Punching someone else's clock card could result in dismissal.

Most office workers were also "on the clock" but were paid weekly salaries. Their day began at 8:30 AM and ended at 5:30 PM, with a half hour for lunch. (Saturday hours were from 8:30 AM to 12:30 PM).

Quitting time at Hawthorne, 1922 (Property of Lucent Technologies Archives; reprinted with permission of Lucent Technologies.)

Beyond the hourly and weekly payrolls, there was the monthly payroll—the highest caste payroll. It was attained by anyone whose weekly salary exceeded the equivalent of three hundred dollars a month. Those who reached that exalted state were automatically "off the clock"—they no longer had a clock card and so were freed from its discipline. All employees looked forward to going off the clock, but the great majority never reached that goal.

To my recollection, for identical grades, women were paid the same as men. Women were seldom assigned to the higher grades of work, however. Women engineers were a rarity, as were women in managerial posts.

Length of service was a critical factor in some important decisions. The length of vacations was geared to length of service. So was retirement pay. One's annual pension was determined by this formula:

$$\text{Pension} = \frac{\text{Highest salary x Years of service}}{100}$$

For example, a person retiring with forty years of service would receive an annual pension equal to forty percent of his or her highest annual earnings.

Rank in the Hierarchy

The most important factor governing powers and responsibilities was one's rank in the hierarchy. Those powers and responsibilities were set out in writing. Some powers related to matters of utmost importance to the employee body: hiring and firing of people, assignment of work, approval of transfers, or increases in pay. Other powers related to approval limits for expenditure of money—the higher the rank, the higher the limits. Still other powers related to perks that served also as symbols of power. An example was the space and furniture allotted to employees. The higher the worker's rank was, the greater was the allotment of space and furniture.

There were other ways in which Hawthorne awarded perks based on rank in the hierarchy. Entrance passes varied widely. At one extreme was the simple shopworker's identification card (ID) allowing entry at a designated gate. At the other extreme was the photographic ID that admitted the bearer plus guests to any Western Electric facility.

Division chiefs and up were entitled to attend the annual (free) weekend golf outing at the Nippersink Country Club. Assistant superintendents and up were permitted to park their cars in the company garage. Superintendents and up were entitled to make use of the company's chauffeur-driven limousines to drive them to a meeting in Chicago, to meet their train on their return from a business trip, and so on.

During my years at Hawthorne I qualified for most of these and other perks. I had no difficulty getting used to them.

Ethnic and Religious Differences

One element of culture that was *not* set out in writing was the influence of ethnic or religious origin in hiring, promotion, and the like. Nevertheless these things were influential. Most obviously, in 1924 there was not a black face to be seen at Hawthorne despite the fact that Chicago already had a significant black population.

Most Hawthorne employees were American-born, but a sizable minority were immigrants from areas of mid-Europe, notably Poland and Bohemia. In the 1925 Hawthorne telephone directory, names that suggest such origins are well represented in the lowest levels of supervision but are less numerous in the higher levels. This confirms the then-prevailing belief that the system of promotion carried a bias in favor of WASPS—White Anglo-Saxon Protestants.

College Degrees as Prerequisites

For many nonmanagerial jobs, especially those in science and engineering, the prerequisite education was "college graduate or equivalent." This requirement was not the result of some unwritten bias in the Hawthorne culture; the requirement was set out in writing and so became a mandate to all in the recruitment process.

For managerial jobs, the education requirements were not clearly set out, so the practice varied. In functions employing many scientists and engineers, all the managers were graduate scientists or engineers. In contrast, virtually all shop foremen lacked college degrees, as did many general foremen. In other major functions—clerical, materials management, industrial relations—the higher managerial jobs were mostly held by college graduates.

The grapevine consensus was that there were two tracks to promotion in the hierarchy. Entry to the fast track was limited to college graduates. For them the major basis of promotion was merit, and there was no ceiling. The slow track was open to all others. For them the pace of promotion was closely linked to seniority, and in any case there was a ceiling. It was all summarized for me by one cynical realist: to get ahead in this company, be born a WASP, get a college degree, and don't be born a woman.

■   ■   ■

Appendix: The Hawthorne Experiments

During the late 1920s, Hawthorne became the site of groundbreaking research in industrial sociology. The innocent beginning was a study to test the effect of illumination on factory productivity. Some advocates had asserted that an increase in illumination would result in increased productivity of factory workers. The cognizant official (G. A. Pennock) listened but insisted on experimental proof before authorizing the large expenditure required.

To test the assertion, a "laboratory" was created in one of the assembly departments by erecting partitions around one of the assembly benches. The ceiling of this little room was fitted out with various types of lighting fixtures, and means were provided for varying the illumination. Care was taken to make the remaining physical working conditions in the lab identical with those in the main room.

Experiments were then conducted by varying the illumination while recording the productivity both in the lab and in the main room. The records soon presented a puzzling phenomenon. As expected, when illumination in the lab was increased, the productivity rose. However, when the illumination was then decreased, *the productivity in the lab continued to increase.* (All the while there was no change in the main room.)

To help explain this surprising result, Pennock brought in some behavioral scientists, notably Professor Elton Mayo of Harvard University. The scientists created a new source of data—*they interviewed the assemblers working in the lab.* Those interviews made it clear that to those workers, the working conditions in the lab differed remarkably from those prevailing in the main room.

In the main room, the workers were largely considered to be nameless clock numbers; in the lab, they were flesh-and-blood people and were treated as such by the engineers managing the project. In the main room, the workers were forbidden to talk to each other on the grounds that the distractions interfered with productivity; in the lab, there was no such prohibition. In the main room, the workers were subject to various other petty disciplines; in the lab, they were not.

As viewed by the engineers and managers, the working conditions in the lab were identical to those in the main room; as viewed by the workers in the lab, there were remarkable differences.

Awareness of these differences led the managers to conduct a number of studies to discover more broadly how employees viewed their working conditions. Those studies turned up new and surprising disclosures. For example, there existed informal worker organizations within the factory departments; these informal organizations established rules of conduct that sometimes conflicted with those of the formal organization. Also, some long-standing managerial beliefs about what motivates workers' behavior were invalid.

Such disclosures caused the managers to undertake a massive program of worker interviews to learn what was on the workers' minds. The findings were analyzed and became the basis for a broad program of supervisory training.

Collectively, these activities came to be known as "The Hawthorne Experiments." They were a milestone in the field of industrial sociology, consisting of the convergence of several essential elements. They were conducted not in the psychological laboratory but in the workplace, where the subjects were workers and supervisors living their normal lives. While they were initiated by the factory managers, the cast of characters included behavioral scientists who participated in the design of the studies and who analyzed the resulting data using scientific tools of analysis. The Hawthorne Experiments were pioneering large-scale research studies embodying the convergence of those essential elements. For elaboration, see *Management and the Worker* by F. J. Roethlisberger and W. J. Dickson, Harvard University Press, 1939.

Q

9

First Job
in Quality

y mid-1926 I had two years of troubleshooting under my belt. During that time, I had learned much about the anatomy of the industrial organism in which I was a living cell. My employment contract was with Western Electric, but my ultimate employer was the huge American Telephone and Telegraph Company (AT&T), which owned Western Electric. (Another name for AT&T was the Bell System; its generous employee benefits stimulated the more endearing term "Ma Bell.") During those same two years, my job of troubleshooter took me to the far corners of Hawthorne and beyond. From all those contacts, I began to understand how AT&T was organized to provide its subscribers with a telephone service that was second to none.

AT&T's Strategic Plan of Managing for Quality

One basic concept at AT&T was that any person in the United States should be able to talk by telephone to any other person. This concept suggested that provision of telephone service should be a monopoly. To this end AT&T formed regional telephone companies to provide telephone service within their regions—New York Bell Telephone Company, Pacific Bell, Northwestern Bell, and so on. Through these companies, plus the acquisition of independent companies, AT&T did end up with a virtual monopoly on providing regional telephone service in the United States. In addition, AT&T created a Long Lines Department to provide long-distance service between regions.

Provision of telephone service on a national scale required a huge array of facilities. Subscribers needed the means to make and receive calls. They also needed a connection to their central office, which in turn needed a switching apparatus to make the interconnections. Cables were needed to connect central offices and regions to each other. Giving commands to all this hardware required intricate circuitry plus versions of what today we call software.

When AT&T set out to build those facilities, it faced an array of familiar quality problems (precision, interchangeability, standardization, reliability, and so on) but on a scale without precedent in human history. It solved those problems by innovations in organization and in managing for quality.

- It created an elite corps of scientists and engineers to carry out research and development of the hardware and circuitry. This corps later became an AT&T subsidiary known as Bell Telephone Laboratories (Bell Labs).
- It created a captive source of supply—Western Electric Company—to build the hardware.
- It established measures of the quality of service provided to its subscribers.
- It established a system of data feedback on quality of service and on field quality failures.
- It established means for measuring the quality of products produced by Western Electric.
- It created a "quality survey"—an audit—to review the effectiveness of AT&T's entire system of managing for quality.

Hawthorne's Strategic Plan of Managing for Quality

My job as troubleshooter had exposed me to virtually all functions at Hawthorne. That exposure confirmed the Inspection Branch's claim of being the "guardian of quality." I learned, however, that other branches also had roles that were essential to producing quality products. One of these essential roles was played by Hawthorne's Development Branch.

AT&T's basic product research and development was done by Bell Labs. The resulting engineering requirements were passed on to Hawthorne's Development Branch, which further developed Bell Labs' concepts into product designs suitable for manufacture. These designs were published as specifications that defined the materials to be used and the resulting end products. Those same "specs" served as Hawthorne's quality goals—a body of industrial law to be obeyed by all.

In addition, the Development Branch devised many of the numerous processes to be used for making the products. The resulting process specifications likewise had the force of industrial law.

Hawthorne's Technical Branch also played a critical role. A major function was to produce and publish the shop drawings (blueprints) describing the products and including the quality tolerances. These drawings also had the force of industrial law.

The Technical Branch had the added job of planning for manufacture. For each piece part and end product, it listed the tasks (operations) to be performed and in what sequence, along with what tools and gauges to use, safety precautions, and so on. The resulting plans were published in the form of written layouts—likewise a body of industrial law.

The most visible role of attaining quality was played by the Operating Branch. It employed most of Hawthorne's population and in it the hands-on work of making the hardware was done. It was responsible for obeying Hawthorne's industrial laws: performing the tasks set out in the layouts, using the prescribed machines, tools, and gauges; and making the products meet the tolerances demanded by specifications, blueprints, and other quality standards.

Conflict in Priorities

The quality strategies designed by AT&T and Hawthorne were effective. The end products were of high quality, but that result was achieved by brute force and at high cost. Part of that cost was the army of inspectors as well as their support services. Far greater was the cost of redoing prior work. I estimate that in the mid-1920s, about a third of Hawthorne's efforts consisted of redoing: scrapping or repairing defective products, finding the defects, resolving field failures, troubleshooting, making up for shipping delays, and so on. (Such wastes were common to most industries.)

Those wastes were largely traceable to conflicting priorities inherent in Hawthorne's strict functional organization. This organization form has considerable merit: it provides employees with a visible career pattern through climbing the hierarchical ladder, and it also fosters development of expertise within the function. On the negative side, it gives priority to functional goals that lead to "suboptimization." For example, a major goal of purchasing managers has been to buy at the best price. Pursuit of this functional goal has resulted in many purchases of low-quality products that have generated extra costs far greater than the price difference.

At Hawthorne no one was against quality. Life for all was more agreeable if nothing was defective. Yet during the mid-1920s, the top priority of managers in the Operating Branch was not to attain product quality; it was two other things.

The highest priority was to meet schedules. AT&T's business was expanding, and the demand for more telephone equipment was intense. Hawthorne was virtually AT&T's sole source of supply, so it was under pressure from higher management to meet the demands. In response, it set production schedules, and the entire Operating Branch hierarchy was under pressure to meet these schedules. That pressure persisted until the Great Depression.

The Operating Branch's second top priority was to maintain piecework earnings. AT&T's policies encouraged friendly, enlightened human relations plus generous employee benefits. Under Hawthorne's application of those policies, shop workers were paid by the hour but with an added piecework supplement that enabled workers to earn more than their basic hourly rate, depending on how much they produced. The emphasis on piecework earnings no doubt stemmed from Hawthorne's dread of labor unrest and, worse yet, labor unions. The darkest nightmare was the threat of work stoppages and the resulting failure to meet the intense demand for more and more telephone equipment.

As shop troubleshooter I ran into many cases in which quality suffered because of the higher priority of meeting schedules and maintaining earnings. Here are two examples:

An inspector sampled a load of machined rubber parts and found a high percentage to be cracked. As it turned out, the milling machine operator had reported to his supervisor that many parts were cracking when they were clamped in the fixture. The supervisor called the maintenance department, which estimated that it would take several days to repair the fixture. Upon receiving this news, the supervisor told the operator to run the job anyway in order to meet the schedule.

An assembly department complained of numerous electrical short circuits in its final product caused by metal chips from one of the piece parts. I traced the chips to a tapping operation (it cut threads into the copper bushings of that piece part.) The workman had made an ingenious chute to enable the chips from the tapping operation to drop into the bin of finished parts. Those chips added to his piecework earnings, since the counting of the amount of work produced was done by weight.

The Guardian of Quality

The Inspection Branch was proud to be the guardian of quality. To play that role, it relied almost exclusively on a single approach—inspection. That word "inspection" had meanings beyond visual examination; it included making measurements with mechanical gauges as well as testing of all kinds—electrical, chemical, metallurgical, and others.

Hawthorne's system of materials management included a "move ticket" that accompanied each "lot" (batch) of product as it journeyed through the shop. The move ticket provided information about identity, destination, and so on. In theory, only the truckers were authorized to move goods from one department to another. The truckers, in turn, had orders not to move material unless the move ticket bore an inspection stamp.

Despite these precautions, some unauthorized moves did take place. Some batches of material, though rejected by the inspectors, managed mysteriously to reach the next processing step. The guilty unseen hands and feet may have belonged to a shop supervisor seeking to avoid blame. Another usual suspect was a "chaser" from the so-called Production Branch.

The Production Branch had the job of determining how much product to make, ordering the materials, scheduling the work, following-up to assure that the schedules were met, managing and storing the process inventory, providing internal transport, and keeping the associated records. The "chaser" was a lobbyist assigned to the follow-up role. If overzealous, a chaser would slyly carry out illegal transport. (The name "Production Branch was a misnomer"; its functions were more usually called by names such as "Production Control." Today a popular name is "Materials Management.")

The cases of bypassing inspection stamps may have been few, but there were enough to arouse resentment among the inspection supervisors. To make matters worse, some shop foremen regarded such illegal conduct as mere misdemeanors. Such attitudes created wide mistrust. In the view of some inspection supervisors, a shop foreman was not to be trusted until he had earned that trust by extensive good behavior.

The Benefits of Inspection

The Inspection Branch was a costly guardian of quality. It had thousands of employees, occupied much floor space, required expensive facilities, and delayed the flow of work. Nevertheless it was an essential function. Like the human immune system, it identified and removed defective elements from Hawthorne's products.

The Inspection Branch provided additional benefits to Hawthorne. Its laboratories maintained the precision of measurement. Its decisions helped to establish quality standards in areas where the specifications were nonexistent or silent. A proposal to abolish the Inspection Branch would have been rejected out of hand.

The Limitations of Inspection

With the benefit of hindsight, it is easy to see that Hawthorne's reliance on inspection contained weaknesses that would take decades to remedy. The weaknesses were numerous.

- The chronic waste resulting from defectives was huge, yet Hawthorne was not organized to reduce this waste.
- Planning of manufacturing processes was mostly done empirically; concepts such as quantifying process capability were waiting to be invented.
- Most production workers did not have a say in controlling their own work.
- Inspection gauges were designed to separate good product from bad, not to provide data feedback to those who could make use of it.
- There was no awareness that inspectors are unable to maintain attention 100 percent of the time and that inspection is a fallible process.
- In most sampling inspections, the Inspection Branch tolerated the presence of defects in the product up to some acceptable level.
- Early in our past century, such weaknesses were common to factories, including progressive factories.

Sporadic Waste and Chronic Waste

All inspection departments kept records showing the inspectors' findings. For mass-produced piece parts, the records showed the results of batch-by-batch sampling (the sample size and number of defects found, broken down by defect type). For detail inspection of finished goods, the records showed the number inspected and the number of defects found, again broken down by defect type.

During my weeks in the training course, I had seen many such records. I soon learned that there were certain commonalities. Each product was subject to multiple defect types, just as humans are subject to multiple diseases. No product was immune; all had diseases. The resulting waste was huge. No one knew how much it was costing, however; the books were not kept that way. As a result, the waste remained hidden in the overheads.

The inspection managers regularly reported the frequency of defects to the general foremen and foremen in the Operating Branch. Those reports did not lead to action unless a sudden (sporadic) rise in the defect level became a threat to meeting the delivery schedule or the earnings level of the workers.

There was some resort to exhortation. ("It costs less to do it right the first time." "You can't inspect quality into the product; you must build quality into the product.")

Such slogans had no effect. Reducing the continuing (chronic) waste level was not high on Hawthorne's priority list. The responsibility for taking action was vague; in addition, a way to diagnose and remedy such wastes was not well understood.

Process Capability: The Heat Coil

During 1926, one of my assignments concerned the "heat coil," a tiny circuit breaker that Hawthorne made by the millions. The sensing element was a wire-wound coil. A circuit overload would overheat that coil and cause the circuit to open. The inspectors regularly scrapped about 10 percent of the finished product because electrical resistance was out of specification limits. The local production supervisor and I became a team trying to reduce that waste.

The wire from which the coils were made was bought from outside suppliers and came in reels, each having enough wire to make several hundred coils. I measured many reels of the supply wire and found that although the electrical resistance was very uniform within any reel, the reel-to-reel variation was considerable. We got rid of that variable by measuring out from each reel a length of wire whose resistance was halfway between the upper and lower specification limits, then cutting the entire reel into pieces of that same length. Now, despite the reel-to-reel variations, all lengths of wire were uniform in resistance. To my surprise, the defect rate dropped only slightly; nearly 10 percent of the product was still being scrapped because electrical resistance was out of specifications.

I next measured the resistance of fifty *finished* circuit breakers. Figure 9-1 shows the resulting "frequency distribution."

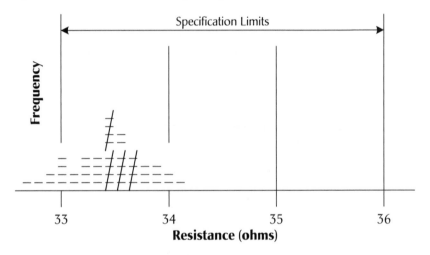

Figure 9-1. Electrical resistance of heat coils compared to specification limits

Figure 9-1 makes clear that the variation in the resistance of the final product is small in relation to the distance between the specification limits. But the average resistance of the finished product is not halfway between the upper and lower specification limits; it is distinctly lower. Why? A close look at the manufacturing process found the reason. The workers were soldering the wire to the units at a point several inches from the end of the wire and then breaking off the excess. The remedy was easy; we added several more inches to the lengths of the wires and *presto*—a defect-prone process became virtually defect-free.

I no longer have the original data from the heat coil project. In my second book (Juran, 1945),[1] I gave an account of the project, recalling the data as well as I could.

I was intrigued by the ease with which we had added nearly 10 percent to the production of heat coils without adding any machinery, workers, or material. I knew from my experience as a troubleshooter that Hawthorne harbored myriad chronic defects. My imagination soared. Why not comb through the factory and get rid of every single one of them?

I discussed the idea with Vacin, my then department chief. He didn't share my enthusiasm, but neither did he reject the idea; he was simply indecisive. He finally suggested I talk about it with *his* superior—S. M. (Smo) Osborne.

Osborne agreed that it would be wonderful to get rid of those wastes, but he pointed out a fatal obstacle. Making the product right in the first place was not the job of the Inspection Branch; it was the job of the Operating Branch. "They don't want us to tell them how to do their job, just as we don't want them to tell us how to do our job." So I found myself blocked by an organizational structure that made no provision for quality improvement.

The heat coil was the first instance in which I had quantified the inherent uniformity of a production process—a property that today we call "process capability." As a byproduct of investigating the heat coil, I had stumbled onto inventing (or reinventing) one of the most useful analytical tools now available to practitioners in managing for quality.

Design of Inspection Tools

During the 1920s, the gauges and test sets provided to inspectors were mainly of the "go/no-go" variety. They were well designed for separating good product from bad, but they couldn't measure process capability or provide information such as the trend of the process.

Most processes exhibit gradual changes that, in turn, keep changing the quality of the product being produced. Machines gradually heat up; tools gradually wear; chemical reagents gradually become depleted; workers gradually become tired. Such trends cannot be detected by go/no-go gauges until the defects are already being produced, which is too late. Detecting trends requires gauges that provide "variables" measurement—numbers along a scale of measurement. Not until the 1950s was there a clear trend to replace go/no-go gauges with "dial gauges."

Allowable Percent Defective

Early in the twentieth century, American industry made wide use of a concept called "allowable percent defective." Under this concept, defects were tolerated as long as they did not exceed some ill-defined limit, usually a few percentage points. At Hawthorne this concept was applied to samples of purchased materials and components as well as to work in process. The presence of a small number of defects in the sample was regarded as "commercial," but the ill-defined upper limit gave rise to endless argument. (For most finished goods, there was no sampling; each unit was inspected and tested.)

Inventions in Managing for Quality

By today's standards, Hawthorne's strategy of managing for quality had serious deficiencies that it remedied by costly inspection and testing. Nevertheless by the standards of the 1920s, Hawthorne's approach to managing for quality was regarded as quite advanced; Hawthorne was a world leader in its field. Its products were a major contributor to AT&T's quality of telephone service.

In common with its counterparts in industry, Hawthorne had no provision for research into managing for quality. The very term "managing for quality" was not yet in use. There was only a vague awareness that over the millennia, numerous inventions had been made to improve managing for quality. The idea that managing for quality would emerge as a new branch of learning—a new scientific discipline—was not yet in incubation. Then, as managing for quality became more and more important, the twentieth century became a virtual hotbed for such inventions. An early example was use of the science of statistics to aid in managing for quality. It took place in AT&T, starting in 1926, and Hawthorne became the test site. I was drawn into that project, and it became a milestone in my professional journey.

Note

1. Juran, Joseph M., *Management of Inspection and Quality Control* (New York: Harper & Brothers, 1945).

10
Enter Statistics

I n late 1925, AT&T's Bell Telephone Laboratories (Bell Labs) set in motion an initiative that would change inspection practices profoundly, first in Hawthorne and later in industry generally. The end result came to be known as Statistical Quality Control (SQC).

AT&T and Use of Probability Theory

The roots of Bell Labs' initiative go back to AT&T's use of probability theory, starting early in the twentieth century. A seminal event was M. C. Rorty's memorandum, "Application of the Theory of Probability to Traffic Problems," dated October 22, 1903.

When any subscriber took the telephone receiver off its hook, he or she needed to be connected to an idle trunk line and given a signal (dial tone) to go ahead and dial. The question then arose: how many trunk lines should AT&T provide for subscribers who might need an idle line? In theory it was possible for all subscribers to need a line at precisely the same time. In practice, only a small percentage of subscribers needed lines simultaneously.

It was clear that some balance must be struck. To provide enough lines for the worst case (all subscribers calling at the same time) would be a huge waste of facilities. To provide only enough lines for average traffic conditions would result in numerous cases of "all trunks busy"—an unacceptable level of service.

What AT&T did was to collect data on actual traffic density, hour by hour and day by day. Those data provided information on peak loads as well as average loads. Then, through use of probability theory, it became possible to calculate how often subscribers would get "all trunks busy" signals at various levels of facilities. Finally, it became possible to make decisions on how many trunk lines to provide for a tolerable level of "all trunks busy" signals.

Bell Labs' Initiative

Bell Labs' initiative came from its Inspection Engineering Department, which had broad responsibilities relative to AT&T's quality of service. The department investigated field complaints and participated in the audits—the "quality surveys." In addition, it received, analyzed, and published data on field quality performance as well as on the quality of Hawthorne's products. Throughout it made use of statistical tools. Its initiative was a proposal to apply the tools of statistics to some factory quality problems: sampling inspection, interpretation of inspection data, and the rating of the quality of Hawthorne's output. Collectively, the subject matter of Bell Labs' initiative came to be known as Statistical Quality Control; the well-known acronym was (and is) SQC.

Committee on Inspection Statistics and Economy

The formal proposal came from R. L. Jones, Bell Labs' Inspection Engineer, to W. L. Robertson, Hawthorne's Superintendent of Inspection. Robertson's response was positive. There was prompt agreement to set up a joint committee—The Committee on

Inspection Statistics and Economy. Its mission was to explore the proposal and to take appropriate action. Its members agreed to meet several times each year and to follow an orderly procedure: agendas were to be prepared in advance, minutes to be published and "homework" to be done between meetings.

Hawthorne soon discovered its employees were woefully ignorant of the tools of statistics. Few employees had training in the subject, and none had knowledge in depth. To fill this vacuum, a young professor from the University of Chicago—Walter Bartky—was engaged to teach an in-house course in statistics. About twenty managers and engineers were selected to attend the course, and I was among those selected.

New Department, New Bosses

The top Inspection Branch managers also decided to organize special-ly to support the Hawthorne members of the committee. To this end they created a new department—the Inspection Statistical Department. It consisted of a department head, Emil F. Vacin, and two engineers, R. J. Bradford and J. M. Juran. The new department reported to S. M. (Smo) Osborne, chief of the Inspection Control Division. It was among the first such departments in industrial history.

My new immediate boss was Vacin. He was a big man, slightly on the fleshy side. His voice was loudly conspicuous. His attention span was short. His assignments to me were sometimes vague, as were his reactions to what I did. I found him to be less than predictable, and we never had a warm relationship.

This coolness with my new industrial lord and master was no obstacle to my getting on with the job. I already knew that industry simply ignored the democratic principle so eloquently set out in the Declaration of Independence: "… governments are instituted among men, deriving their just powers from the consent of the governed."

Part of my new job was exciting. It posed numerous new prob-lems and these required ingenuity for solution. I came up with some inventions that were exhilarating to me and evoked positive comments even from Smo. Other parts of my job were drudgery—such as calculating sampling tables and drawing charts. An example is shown in the "operating characteristic curves" of Figure 10-1.

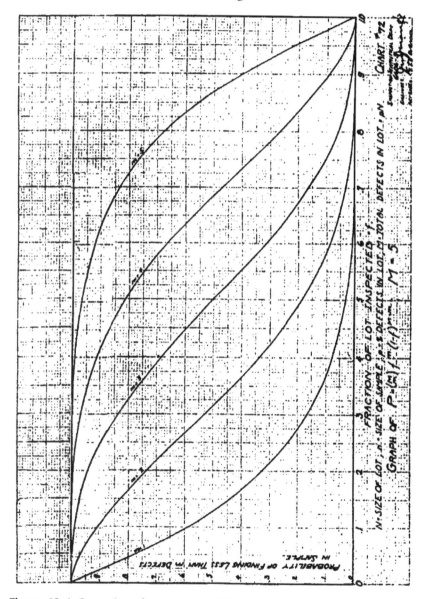

Figure 10-1. Operating Characteristic (OC) curves computed and drawn by J. M. Juran, September 22, 1926 (Turn sideways to read properly.)

The Sampling Tables

The Committee on Inspection Statistics and Economy did a good job of thinking through the subject of sampling inspection. It evolved concepts and nomenclature that have since become embedded into the literature of the subject. It identified the risks involved in the use of sampling and found the mathematical formulas needed to calculate the associated probabilities. It also produced sampling tables that could be applied to a wide variety of practical situations facing inspectors.

Those tables were first used at Hawthorne and then throughout Western Electric. During World War II, a modified version was prepared by Bell Labs for use by the United States Army. That version was then published by the U.S. Government Printing Office as a military standard, MIL-STD-105A. Later the tables were published for general use (Dodge and Romig, 1944).[1]

It took a good deal of committee effort to arrive at the final sampling tables. Some of this effort was technical in nature—designing the mathematical models and then calculating the tables. But most of the effort went to resolving differences in the viewpoints between Bell Labs managers and Hawthorne managers. In turn, those differences had their origin in the managers' different experience backgrounds. (For elaboration on those differences, see my article, "Early SQC, a Historical Supplement.")[2]

No Action on Defect Prevention

To my surprise, the committee never took up the subject of defect prevention. It focused solely on the topics implied by its name—statistics and the economics of inspection. It may be that the committee members, all being linked to the inspection function, were locked into the same self-sealing thought system that I had witnessed when I told Smo about the defect reduction on the heat coil. His response had been that defect prevention was not the Inspection Branch's job; it was the job of the Operating Branch.

I was not a committee member but I was invited to attend the meetings. I knew from the heat coil case and from my experience as a troubleshooter that defect prevention offered a huge opportunity for waste reduction in many forms—labor hours, facilities usage, and material usage. Nevertheless, it didn't occur to me to raise the subject in a committee meeting. I may have assumed that my lowly status doomed me to silence, or that I had already received the final word from Smo. Whatever the reason, I didn't bring up the subject, and I've often wondered what would have happened had I done so.

Training

Once the sampling tables were completed, it was decided to train all Inspection Branch supervisors in how to use them. Bradford and I prepared a training course, and between us we did the training. To my relief, I was comfortable in my new role as a teacher. I had lost my fear of speaking in public, probably because my work for the committee had given me mastery of the subject matter.

Meanwhile, personnel changes took place in the Inspection Branch hierarchy. Mr. G. A. Pennock became Superintendent of Inspection, replacing Mr. Robertson. In addition, my department was transferred to the Inspection Results Division, so I had a new division chief, Charles A. Melsheimer. Vacin remained my immediate boss.

It was also decided that the senior managers of the Inspection Branch (division chiefs and up) should take a training course in sampling and other matters that resulted from the activities of the committee. Vacin and I designed this course, which he assumed he would be teaching. To my surprise (and his), I was assigned to teach it. (I later learned that Vacin was rejected on the grounds that he was a vague communicator.)

Teaching that course gave me exposure to all the top managers in the Inspection Branch, including Pennock and Melsheimer. I relished the opportunity of meeting at length with such influential men on a subject with which I was completely at ease.

The Control Chart

One of the major proposals of Bell Labs' initiative was that Hawthorne adopt the "control chart" as a means of detecting significant changes in product quality.

At Bell Labs, the Inspection Engineering Department published numerous reports, including charts showing how the performance on quality varied from month to month. Managers receiving those reports faced the problem of judging the origins of those variations— which of them were due to chance and which were the result of some "findable" cause.

This problem of judging the origin of variations is widespread. Human beings soon learn that variations abound—in their body temperature, golf score, electric bill, and so on. Some variations are not "significant"; they are the result of minor fluctuations in the numerous variables present. They are "noise in the signal." Other variations *are* significant; they are the result of some cause that may be findable by analyzing the surrounding circumstances—by finding the answer to the question, "What has changed?"

Dr. Walter A. Shewhart was a member of Bell Labs' Inspection Engineering staff. His duties included analyzing the reports on quality performance. He came up with an elegant and useful invention—a perpetual test of significance now known as the Shewhart Control Chart or, simply, the control chart (shown in Figure 10-2).

Figure 10-2 shows a typical control chart. The horizontal scale is usually time or some time-related variable. The vertical scale is performance. The plotted points show successive performances over time.

The chart also exhibits three horizontal lines. The middle line is the average performance over some earlier span of time. The other two lines are "limit lines." They are drawn to separate false alarms from real changes, based on some chosen level of odds (e.g., 20 to 1).

Point A on the chart differs from the historical average, but this difference could be a result of chance variation (at odds of less than 20 to 1). Hence it is assumed that there has been no real change. Point B also differs from the historical average, but now the odds are heavily against

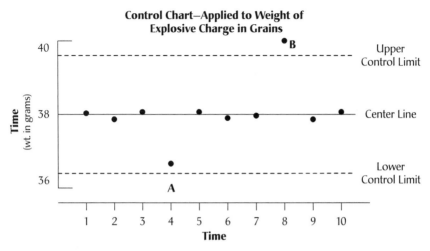

Figure 10-2. The Shewhart Control Chart (from *Making Quality Happen*, 1991, page F-18)[3]

this having been caused by chance—more than 20 to 1. Thus it is assumed that there was a real change and that the cause is findable.

The control chart was a brilliant invention; today many such charts are in use worldwide. Nevertheless, the Inspection Branch managers made virtually no use of the control chart. At the time it was one of my responsibilities to "sell" the chart to inspection supervisors. I rarely made a sale, and I was puzzled by their reasons for rejection; they seemed illogical and even irrelevant. Today the real reasons seem clear. The inspection supervisors saw no way in which control charts could help solve their chief problems. Shop foremen's top priorities were to meet schedules and maintain piecework earnings. Quality was no higher than third on their priority list.

Many production processes continually spewed out unacceptable chronic levels of defects, yet there was no effective provision in place for defect prevention through process improvement.

The Inspection Branch faced a serious internal morale problems. Under Hawthorne's piecework system, production workers could increase their earnings through higher productivity. Inspectors had no such opportunity; piecework for inspectors was nonexistent.

Rating the Quality of Manufactured Product

A third Bell Labs proposal was to refine the "check inspection" process then being used for rating the quality of Hawthorne's products. Bell Labs had made a thorough analysis of this process, and its recommendations were adopted with little revision.

The Effect on Juran

A byproduct of Bell Labs' initiative was its effect on my life journey. It plucked me out of Hawthorne's grass roots and set in motion events that became milestones on that journey, with luck playing a role at every turn.

I was selected to attend Bartky's course on probability theory. I was then selected to become an engineer in the new Inspection Statistical Department. The new department became actively involved in a high-visibility project led by senior managers. I pulled my weight during that project. Then I was assigned to train the senior managers of the Inspection Branch in the new subject matter and thereby was directly exposed to them at length.

Such fortuitous events lifted me out of obscurity and placed me on a fast track.

Notes

1. Dodge, H. F., and H. G. Romig, *Sampling Inspection Tables.* New York: John Wiley and Sons, Inc., 1944; second edition, 1959.
2. Juran, J. M., "Early SQC, A Historical Supplement." *Quality Progress,* vol. 30, no. 9 (September 1997), pages 73–81.
3. Juran, J. M., *Making Quality Happen*, sixth edition. Juran Institute, Inc.

Q

11

From Experienced *Engineer* to Completely Inexperienced *Manager*

y 1928, the work of the Committee on Inspection Statistics and Economy was winding down. The key decisions had been made, and the cleanup was under way. Meanwhile, other matters had been rising to the top of the Inspection Branch priority list. Among these were the interrelated problems of inspection costs, inspectors' productivity, inspectors' accuracy, and inspectors' pay.

Inspection Costs

The size and costs of the Inspection Branch had long been the targets of widespread criticism. More than one in eight of Hawthorne's employees were in the Inspection Branch.

No one advocated cost reduction by arbitrarily cutting the inspection force; such action would have increased the number of defects going to customers. The focus of the criticism was on inspector productivity, which was notoriously low. Senior managers walking through the shops were struck by the obvious difference in work pace between production workers and the inspectors in adjacent areas.

The inspection managers were well aware of this difference, but they pointed out that for identical grade levels, the production workers were better paid than inspectors. To be sure, the base rates were identical, but production workers could earn productivity supplements through the piecework system. There was no piecework system for inspectors.

No one was satisfied. The inspectors emphatically complained about their low pay relative to that of production workers. The Inspection Branch managers were unwilling to place inspectors on piecework, fearing that quality would suffer, because speeding up inspection would cause defects to be missed. Upper management was unwilling to increase inspectors' base pay. "Let them earn it by higher productivity" was their attitude.

The impasse was finally broken by Allan B. Hazard, chief of the Process Inspection Division. Hazard was a towering, well-built manager with a chin that signaled determination and a passion for cost cutting. Hazard skirted around the concept of piecework for inspectors—piecework was regarded as a firm contract between the company and the employees. Instead, he set out to use *informal* productivity goals for inspection work. He encouraged his inspectors to establish their own productivity goals, which came to be known as "bogeys." As it turned out, the goals set by the inspectors were usually about double their previous performance. Then, when they met these goals, Hazard rewarded the successful inspectors by increasing their base pay.

Word of those pay increases soon spread and generated demands from other quarters. Senior managers wanted such cost reductions to be made in other inspection divisions. Inspectors in other divisions wanted the opportunity to increase their earnings through greater productivity.

Measuring Inspector Accuracy

As steps were taken to extend Hazard's approach to the entire Inspection Branch, the inspection managers demanded that there be an adequate measure of inspector accuracy—that is, how well the inspectors did their job of finding defects. There was widespread fear that the emphasis on productivity would endanger quality.

The problem of measuring inspector accuracy was not new, but now it moved to center stage. Some inspection departments did make periodic checks of such accuracy. Their approach was to reinspect samples of the outgoing product and then rate the accuracy based on the number of defects the inspector had missed. This approach made the rating depend partly on luck—whether the product submitted for inspection had come from a defect-prone process or a defect-free process. Inspectors lucky enough to inspect the output from a defect-free process would rate 100 percent on accuracy even if they slept on the job.

I was drawn into the problem of improving inspector productivity by Melsheimer, my new division chief. In his new role, Melsheimer was at the center of the effort to improve inspector productivity. He was well qualified for the job—friendly, calm, and incisive.

Melsheimer gave me two assignments. One was to study the problem of measuring inspector accuracy and to devise a new approach, one that would eliminate the element of luck in measuring accuracy. The other assignment was to examine the payment system and to devise a new approach in order to minimize the risk that quality would suffer. In making these assignments, he largely bypassed Vacin, my official hierarchical boss. Melsheimer and I became an effective team.

We started by measuring the then-existing level of inspector accuracy at Hawthorne. I had told Melsheimer about my discovery while in the training course that inspection by human beings is a fallible process. I now conducted experiments to measure the accuracy of a few inspectors in each of several inspection departments. The results were shocking. *Inspection accuracy at Hawthorne was in the range of 70 to 90 percent.*

The inspection managers were stunned and dismayed by the findings. They concluded that such levels of accuracy were unacceptable, and they demanded that the final approach to improving inspector productivity should improve inspector accuracy as well.

Melsheimer and I also examined the methods then in use for measuring inspector accuracy. In every one of them, the measured accuracy depended partly on luck—on whether the work being inspected had a high or low defect content. We felt that luck should not be a factor in determining employee pay; the measured accuracy should depend solely on matters within the inspectors' control.

We therefore rejected the methods then in use and came up with a new principle: *inspector accuracy should equal the ratio of the number of defects found by the inspector to the number of defects originally present in the inspected product.* Inspectors who found all the defects would have an accuracy of 100 percent; inspectors who found half of the defects would have an accuracy of 50 percent. The inspection managers immediately accepted this principle. Now the problem became one of putting that principle into effect.

We knew how many defects inspectors found, because inspectors kept written records of those numbers. What we did not know was the number of defects the inspectors missed. We decided we must use "check inspectors" to supply this missing information. We also decided that the check inspectors must do their checking at random. All of an inspector's work should be subject to checking, but an inspector should not know which part of his work would actually be checked. To make random checking possible required the inspectors to adapt to a new and annoying procedure: inspectors were not allowed to dispose of any lot of product until their work on the subsequent lot had been completed.

We also found that it was not practical to evaluate inspector accuracy week by week; the sampling errors were prohibitively high. Instead, we proposed that the data on accuracy be summarized over periods of six months each.

Finally, we proposed revisions in the payment system for inspectors. Those proposals included some clean departures from the piecework system used for production workers.

1. The piecework bonus for production workers depended solely on their productivity. For inspectors, the productivity bonus would be based on their accuracy as well as productivity; the productivity rating would be multiplied by the percent accuracy to yield a composite measure of inspectors' performance. The inspection managers liked the fact that quality counted as much as productivity.
2. Production workers' pay changed every week, depending on the productivity attained during that week. The inspection managers were not willing to go that far. Inspectors' productivity could be measured weekly with precision, but their accuracy could not. It was therefore agreed to change inspectors' pay every six months based on the cumulative accuracy and productivity data for the preceding six months.
3. The inspection managers had been shocked to learn that the average accuracy was only about 80 percent. After much discussion, it was agreed to consider 93 percent as a tolerable level of inspector accuracy. The pay plan was then designed to make 93 percent a neutral number for accuracy. Accuracy above 93 percent would add to the pay increase provided by high productivity; accuracy below 93 percent would subtract from the pay increase provided by high productivity.

The new system was put into effect, and it soon proved its merits. Inspector productivity rose dramatically, whereas inspection costs came down, also dramatically. In addition, inspector accuracy rose from its prior level of about 80 percent to over 95 percent. That rise was welcomed by the inspection managers. To add to the good news, the inspectors' morale rose sharply, as evidenced by independent interviews. To no one's surprise, the new system then remained in force for years.

Promotion to Department Chief

Creation of the new payment system also required a force of check inspectors to measure inspection accuracy. Melsheimer asked me to look into this, and I calculated that we would need about forty check inspectors to provide reliable data on the accuracy of the several thousand inspectors then employed at Hawthorne. That was about one check inspector for every hundred inspectors.

Melsheimer reviewed and accepted my figures, as did Pennock, the new chief of the Inspection Branch. They then told me that they were creating a new department—the Quality Inspection Department—to house the check inspectors. They also told me that I was being promoted to chief of that department. The year was 1928.

I was enthusiastic about being promoted. It was actually a double promotion, because it vaulted me over the intermediate grade of section chief. It also held out the promise of good salary increases, since I was below the minimum of the salary range for department chiefs.

Despite my enthusiasm, I didn't realize that my duties were about to change radically. My new duties would be chiefly of a managerial nature rather than of an engineering nature. As a troubleshooter I had drawn heavily on my college subjects—mathematics, electricity, magnetism, and the like. This was also the case with my work for the Committee on Inspection Statistics and Economy. During my work on the new payment system, I had no occasion to draw on what I had learned in college, with one important exception—use of the factual approach to making decisions.

Now for the first time ever, I became a boss. As an engineer I had been utilizing the forces of nature and the properties of materials. As a boss I would be utilizing the forces of people, something in which I had no training or experience. I wasn't even aware that I was entering a new world.

To make matters worse, Hawthorne had not yet set up training courses for newly appointed bosses. I needed such training, even though I didn't know it. Had it been available, it is doubtful I would have taken it to heart, given my background of self-reliance. In any case, I was tossed into a new world to face problems new to me: the use of power, dealing with subordinates, and relations with peers in other departments.

For the short term, I was favored because of my excellent rapport with Melsheimer and Pennock. My occasions to deal with Pennock were few but agreeable in the extreme. He was a gifted listener, capable of understanding complex situations at the first telling. He and I usually talked in half-sentences; each of us could anticipate what would come next. When he was later promoted to Assistant Works Manager—the number-two post at Hawthorne—I knew I would miss him.

Following my promotion, I was faced with recruiting forty check inspectors. My task was simplified because the job of check inspector was given a high grade by the job evaluation system. With help from the Personnel Division, all forty came from within the Inspection Branch. I was younger than any of them. Many were old enough to be my father; some were nearly old enough to be my grandfather.

Promotion to Division Chief

By the time my department was fully in operation, Pennock had been promoted out. He was replaced by J. H. "Jack" Kasley, who came over laterally from his post as chief of the Technical Branch. Soon after that move, Melsheimer was promoted out of the Inspection Branch. (He became deeply involved in planning the "product shops.")

Melsheimer's promotion created a vacancy directly above me. Two weeks then passed before the vacancy was filled. During that time the grapevine was buzzing with speculation about who would be the new division chief. I was drawn into that gossip. In the minds of some, I was a dark-horse candidate despite my youth and my recent promotion.

Before Melsheimer left, I found myself attending a memorable meeting in Kasley's office. Both Melsheimer and Kasley were smiling broadly when Kasley announced, "We've got bad news for you. My reply was, "It doesn't look that way." Then came the "bad" news. I was being promoted to Division Chief, replacing Melsheimer as head of the Inspection Results Division. The year was 1929.

I was not yet 25 years old and had become an important manager at Hawthorne. In the Inspection Branch, I was now part of the inner circle—one of a dozen men managing an organization of over five thousand people.

My new role as division manager brought me prestige along with welcome increases in salary. At the time I was unaware that although

I was well suited for analytical duties, I was not well suited for managerial duties. In time that contrast would force me to change course, but that story must await later chapters of these memoirs.

The "pink sheet" announcement soon appeared, followed by a parade of visitors who came to congratulate me. For a few days, my head remained in the clouds.

I soon informed myself about what was going on in the five departments I now supervised. Collectively these departments provided the leaders of the Inspection Branch with much of the information they needed to do their jobs. For that reason, my division reported directly to the superintendent rather than through one of the assistant superintendents. In turn, this direct access to the top added to my influence, as did my role of official scorekeeper for the performance of all divisions.

Jack Kasley

Kasley was an intelligent and resourceful boss, but he was no intellectual. His extensive experience in planning shop processes made him an authority on the subject. He was also intensely ambitious and was impatient with the glacial pace of promotion that was the norm at Hawthorne. He looked for opportunities to show his organization in a favorable light, and he had no reluctance about biasing his reports. That gave me problems.

On one occasion, he was on a collision course with a fellow superintendent, the issue being whose branch was responsible for a notorious field complaint. He asked me to dig into it, making plain his expectation that I should prove the innocence of the Inspection Branch. When I dug in, I found that the Inspection Branch was the chief culprit. On receiving the bad news, he reacted as though I had betrayed him. With seriousness as well as in jest, he asked, "Why don't you move to the fourth floor?" meaning " Why don't you join the enemy camp?"

Kasley nevertheless learned that he could rely on my reports, though factually unbiased, to show him in the best light. He liked my literary style; he frequently asked me to write his memoranda when negotiations were delicate. He had no objection to passing along my blunt language and even my gratuitous, tactless addenda. He signed the documents, but my initials in the lower left corner identified the knave who had drafted the spicy language.

Salary Increases

With promotions came salary increases. I had started in 1924 at a salary of $27 per week. For a few years, my increases were in step with those of the other college recruits. Then, starting in 1928, the size of those increases accelerated sharply.

That acceleration was likely the result of several specifics: my work of helping the Committee on Inspection Statistics and Economy; my contribution to measuring inspector accuracy and revising the payment system for inspectors; the promotion to department chief; and the promotion to division chief.

Those events all took place between 1926 and 1929. By January of 1930, my salary was $380 per month, or $4,560 per year. In those days that was a respectable salary, the equivalent of over fifteen times that much in 2001 dollars. Moreover, it was likely below the bottom of the salary range for division chiefs. The grapevine estimated that some division chiefs were paid close to $10,000 a year. I could look forward to years of good increases before hitting a ceiling.

Potential Managerial Misfit

During my elation at being promoted to division chief, I was totally unaware that it might have been a mistake. Before those promotions I had been assigned to engineering work, for which I had good aptitudes and training. The promotions then assigned me to managerial work, for which I had poor aptitudes and no training. Why did the higher-ups make decisions that could deprive them of a good engineer and gain them a poor manager? The prime reason was the structure of the prevailing reward system.

My bosses wanted to give me outstanding rewards for what they felt were outstanding contributions. There was no way to provide such rewards to an engineer; the salary range for engineers didn't go high enough, but the range for managers did. In addition, eligibility for perks was based solely on rank, not on performance.

On the face of it, lack of aptitudes and training were not fatal obstacles to becoming a manager. Most men promoted to managerial posts in those days lacked training in how to manage; some lacked aptitudes as well. Yet many became adequate managers; with experience on the job, they acquired training while sharpening their aptitudes. I was a poor prospect for such a scenario because of my deep-seated resentments and my urge to extract revenge—on the innocents. Thus, the stage was being set for someone with my make-up to become a managerial misfit.

My vulnerability was at its worst in my relationship with my peers. All were older than I was, and some were much older. Even though they competed with each other for promotions, their long history of working together had evolved into a culture that included a code of conduct. That code demanded mutual respect and even mutual defense against criticism from on high.

As an individualist, I was, to an important degree, an alien in their culture. I was respectful only to some of them. My bluntness was interpreted as tactlessness and discourtesy. To make matters worse, I was regarded as a dangerous competitor for higher posts.

In a sense, I was not *dis*courteous; I was *un*courteous. As a loner in a private world, I had not grasped the concept of courtesy. (The need for courtesy arises only when one must associate with other human beings.) However, my peers did not recognize that fine distinction; in their view, my behavior was *dis*courteous.

I knew that I was offending some of those peers, but I took no action to change my behavior. I seem to have assumed that my track record (of rapid promotion and generous raises) was proof that I didn't need to change my behavior.

I have often wondered why my superiors did not intervene. They were no doubt aware of the goings-on. They certainly had the opportunity to suggest—even demand—that I mend my ways. But no one did so. I was free to continue in my errant ways while building up a growing, collective resentment among my peers.

Q

12
Winning at Capone's Roulette Wheel

Hawthorne was an immense complex sprawled over nearly 200 acres. Some of this acreage was in Chicago, and the rest was in adjacent Cicero, a bedroom community of Chicago. Many employees lived within walking distance; others commuted by automobile, streetcar, railroad, and the Chicago elevated line (the El). I readily found lodgings with neighborhood families, the most satisfying being the Brandners.

Hans Brandner was a toolmaker at Hawthorne; I had met him over the chess table. He and his wife had recently rented a flat over a restaurant located virtually across the street (Cicero Avenue) from the plant. They had a room to rent, and I did not hesitate. Not only did my commute shrink to five minutes, but I moved in with people who welcomed me warmly. I left them on my wedding day, in June 1926, but meanwhile we established a friendship that would endure for life.

Chess at Hawthorne

Some of Hawthorne's employee benefits were organized through the "Hawthorne Club." The club supported numerous activities, one being the Chess and Checkers Club. I became quite active in chess at Hawthorne. I won the Works championship several times and retired the silver trophy. I played in matches between Hawthorne and other chess clubs. I also joined the Chicago Chess Club in downtown Chicago and competed in tournaments for the Chicago city and Illinois state championships with respectable results. Then, because of the demands of a growing family, I was forced to give up that fascinating but time-consuming game.

Playing chess during a tournament at Hawthorne (1926)

Cryptanalysis and William F. Friedman

As of April 1925, I was commissioned as a second lieutenant in the Army Signal Corps Reserve and was assigned to the Signal Intelligence Division, whose mission included cryptanalysis—the breaking of enemy codes and ciphers. My commission ran for five years, after which I extended it twice, for periods of five years each, reaching the grade of captain. During those fifteen years I was subject to being called up for active military service.

After receiving my commission, I signed up for occasional training courses by correspondence. In addition, I received orders periodically to report to Washington for training. The first of such orders came in 1927, and the company granted me a leave of absence. I went to Washington to spend two weeks with William F. Friedman, whom I had met in 1923 at ROTC camp in Battle Creek, Michigan. It was a privilege; Friedman was a genius at cryptanalysis. In time he would contribute enormously to the American war effort during World War II and would be widely regarded as the leading world authority in the field. Even before I met Friedman, I had an amateur's interest in cryptanalysis. Friedman now led me into the world of the professionals, where the stakes were enormous.

Friedman and I soon developed a close relationship that ripened into a lifelong friendship. I deeply respected that precise analytical mind. Like a laser beam, it penetrated to reach the heart of a problem. He had made a huge contribution to his field by bringing in a mathematical approach, notably the science of statistics. Here I was on familiar ground and could contribute something. We were both unhappy with the limitations imposed by the immense bureaucracies that employed us. On a personal level, we also had much in common—each of us was of Jewish origin, employed by an organization whose upper managers were almost exclusively non-Jewish.

My Dress and Conduct

During my first years at Hawthorne, my dress and conduct attracted attention—the wrong kind. My wardrobe was minimal; what there was showed its age. Yet even after my savings account had grown to a respectable level, I did nothing to upgrade that wardrobe.

My conduct matched my appearance. I spoke my mind and did so bluntly. I equated bluntness with being forthright, but others concluded correctly that I was lacking in tact. I was not aware that their conclusion was perfectly logical, so my supposed virtue of forthrightness was in fact a detriment that became an obstacle to my relations with others.

While writing these memoirs I have tried to discover why I behaved as I did. As to my lack of tact, I have theorized that I was on the prowl for revenge. This theory is all the more puzzling since my revenge was not being inflicted on those who had injured me in the past. *My revenge was being inflicted on innocent people.*

Revenge on the Innocents

In retrospect I marvel that I was so stupid—that I failed to realize I was punishing innocent people. Today I marvel even more at how pervasive is this same form of stupidity.

Some schools tolerate the practice of "hazing." Incoming freshman are subjected to indignities and worse by sophomores and other upperclassmen. This cycle goes on year after year. In a sense, sophomores haze incoming freshmen as a means of avenging themselves for what they (the sophomores) had endured the year before. The most remarkable feature of this practice is that the sophomores do not inflict their revenge on the guilty former tormenters (who are now the junior class). *They inflict their revenge on innocents*—on the incoming freshmen who had nothing to do with the hazing suffered by the present sophomore class.

I was following this same senseless practice of taking revenge on innocents. My Hawthorne colleagues had nothing to do with the abuses and indignities I had suffered during my years in Gura Humora and Minneapolis. The more I ponder this evil of taking revenge on the innocents, the more I realize that it is a widespread practice and is engaged in by people who are otherwise perfectly intelligent and honorable. The practice is at its worst in wars based on hatred handed down through the generations. In such wars, innocents avenge the damage done to their forebears by slaughtering other innocents—the innocent descendants of the guilty.

Beating the Roulette Wheel

Some of the buildings across from the plant were gambling houses with innocent-looking fronts but with entrances in the rear. They were, of course, illegal, but they were located on the Cicero side of the municipal boundaries, and the Cicero political machinery had been taken over by the Capone gang. The gambling houses were less than a hundred yards from the Cicero "El" train station, and so they attracted much of their clientele from neighboring Chicago.

I once visited one of these dens and was fascinated, especially by the roulette wheels. I picked up a brochure that described the game and showed the sequence of numbers around the wheel. I promptly concluded that playing roulette was a losing proposition if one placed bets at random. The wheel had thirty-eight slots into which the ball might roll. They were numbered one through thirty-six, plus zero and double zero. A successful bet on any of the numbers paid thirty-five to one. (The bettor actually received thirty-six chips, since his original chip was returned as well.) However, such success took place (on the average) only once in thirty-eight cycles of play. That meant that for each thirty-eight rounds of play, the house pocketed the wager twice, or about five percent of the amount wagered.

I love to gamble. (I seem to carry a gene that is dominant for gambling.) I itched to play roulette, but I saw no future in gambling against such odds. I also saw that if I could find some consistency in the performance of the wheel, I might be able to offset those odds. So I began to record the goings-on.

First, I studied whether the wheel itself had some bias—a tilt or whatever. The data said no—the ball rolled into the slots at random. I then wondered if the dealer *(croupier)* had some consistent habit pattern that was waiting to be discovered. This time I hit pay dirt.

For each cycle of play, the dealer followed an unvarying series of actions. Once the ball came to rest, he removed all chips from the losing bets. Then he paid the winning bets. Finally, he removed the ball from its slot on the (revolving) wheel and with a sweeping horizontal motion, he released the ball into its groove, where it would spin for a few turns of the wheel before again coming to rest. The challenge was could I predict into which slot the ball would fall on the next cycle? I saw that this was possible, but only if the wheel rotated at constant speed and if the time consumed by the dealer's actions was nearly identical from one cycle to the next.

Once again I recorded the goings-on and discovered the sought-after consistency. On successive cycles, the ball often ended up about fifteen slots clockwise ahead of its previous location. This was enough information to enable me to overwhelm the five percent advantage of the house.

I bought a few stacks of ten-cent chips and began to wager. I placed bets on five adjacent numbers located fifteen slots clockwise ahead of the previous resting place of the ball. The results were delicious. One of my numbers would win about every third cycle of play. This meant that during every three cycles, I was losing ten chips but winning thirty-five. I soon raised my wagers until I was betting a half-dollar per number. My winnings escalated to over a hundred dollars, enough to arouse the attention of a hanger-on who began to proclaim loudly that I had a "system." Indeed I did.

It soon came to an end. The house regularly rotated dealers, and mine was replaced by one who was disgustingly erratic. Now I won only rarely, so I cashed in. I was over a hundred dollars to the good. At my pay of about forty-five dollars a week, that was a bonanza.

I never went back. When I related my triumph to some friends, I learned that the higher-ups at Hawthorne frowned on the practice of patronizing gambling houses. Such conduct might well be recorded in one's personnel file, providing a reason for slowing down one's progress in promotion. Nevertheless, I took smug delight in the thought that I had beaten the Capone gang at its own game.

Smitten

In the fall of 1924, my sister Betty wrote me that she would be coming to Chicago, hoping to find work there. She would be living with friends, and one of them would be meeting her train. She wondered if I also could meet her train.

I did meet Betty's train, and so did her friend, Sadie Shapiro. Then and there I was smitten and have remained so ever since. On the way to Sadie's apartment, I walked on air. Sadie was a truly beautiful young woman. Five feet tall, she was also slender, weighing a mere one hundred pounds. In addition she was quiet and reserved, which I liked and which my mother would have liked.

Sadie's Roots

Sadie's grandparents lived in Kiev, a city in the Ukraine, then a part of Russia. They were wealthy and owned the largest department store in Kiev. They also had thirteen children. Only one was a son, and he, David Shapiro, became Sadie's father.

On his marriage to Sadie's mother, David Shapiro's parents provided the couple with a fully furnished home, including servants. (They did this for all their children as they married.) So Sadie's parents started with a good life, filled with family events, theater, and opera. It didn't stay that way.

During the 1890s, anti-Semitism in Russia once again intensified into savage pogroms. The grandparents feared for the family's safety and sent everyone to live abroad. The grandparents stayed in Russia, and their fate is unknown.

Sadie's parents emigrated to America in 1900. First they settled in Newark, New Jersey, where Sadie was born in 1905. A year or two later, they moved to Minneapolis. In America, life for Sadie's parents was not luxurious at all. They had not been allowed to take their wealth out of Russia. Sadie's father had not learned any trade or profession, and now he was faced with supporting a family. He tried many jobs and ventures but was never successful at any.

For Sadie's mother, the good life came to an end. She had to learn how to do what had always been done by servants—cooking, sewing, and other household chores. In addition, because her husband was a poor provider, she had to supplement the family income. This she did by sewing clothes for other people and by cooking meals for some of the families that rented rooms in her house—a large house deliberately bought with an intention of providing a rental income.

High-school graduation pictures of Sadie and me. I was smitten with her in 1924.

Courtship

Sadie was three months younger than I. She had long been a resi-
dent of Minneapolis. Because her father was unable or unwilling to
finance a college education for her, she entered the job market, moving to Chicago, where one of her brothers lived. There she soon
found work, after which she and her brother rented an apartment
jointly. Their mother left her husband and came to live with them.
They took in boarders to help with the rent. My sister Betty became
their newest boarder.

After I met Sadie, I began to visit her apartment to see my sister
but increasingly to see Sadie. Finally, my interest overcame my shyness,
and I asked her for a date. She took a while to make up her mind.
Here is her recollection of how she felt at the time:

> I was not at all impressed with him. I didn't like his looks, and
> his manner of dressing was rather shabby. But having no bet-
> ter prospects, I agreed to meet him on a Saturday afternoon at
> the Art Institute.

So we had a date, and for a long afternoon and evening I had her to myself. We went to the Chicago Art Institute, to a theatre matinee, and then to dinner. Happily, she enjoyed all of it:

It was quite pleasant, and after that first date I agreed to meet him every Saturday for a similar date. My mother and brother were not impressed with him, and that was quite understandable. His social manners and his appearance were against him. But I continued going out with him every week, and he often came to visit during the week.

On our second date, I had one of those experiences that becomes a milestone on one's journey through life. We had gone to the Art Institute, then to a matinee. (I believe the play was *Sakura*, starring Sessue Hayakawa.) Sadie scolded me gently for my extravagance. "I don't want you to spend a lot of money on me," she had said. Then we had dinner, after which I took her to her apartment door. There I mustered enough courage to ask, "May I kiss you, Sadie?" She tilted her head up. I embraced her and kissed that mouth—a long, lingering kiss. During that kiss a flood of emotion overwhelmed me—a feeling that defies description yet gropes desperately for expression.

Until that kiss I had focused on womanhood, not on some individual woman. My image of womanhood was derived from my mother's views—a good woman was chaste, modest, demure, sincere. My first impression of Sadie had fit that description. My visits and our dates then confirmed my first impression. With that kiss I no longer needed an idealized image of womanhood—I had embraced and kissed a living example.

So the months passed. I looked forward to our dates. We both enjoyed Chicago's museums, and they were free. We also enjoyed the theatre and concerts. (The Hawthorne Club sometimes was able to secure free tickets, which we welcomed.) During those dates it was enough for me to sit quietly at performances while holding the hand of my beloved. I was at peace with the world.

I gradually became possessive. The time came when I asked her not to date anyone else. She wasn't ready for that. Neither was she ready for the day when I would propose marriage, but she was already giving the matter considerable thought.

Gradually my feelings toward him began to change as I began to understand the kind of person he was. He was extremely bright and ambitious, and I felt that he would go far in his chosen field. It was important to me to marry someone who was ambitious. I did not want to have a future like my mother had had.

In the fall of 1925, Sadie received a letter from a former employer in Minneapolis, asking her to come back for six months. She jumped at the chance to go away, to think things over, and to make up her mind. She was gone from November 1925 though April 1926. During that time, she made up her mind:

> I gradually began to realize that he was a diamond in the rough. His social manners and his clothes were things that could change, and I was pretty certain that he was going to be successful in his career.... My temporary job was to end in April, and I had to make a decision before returning to Chicago.... I had just passed my twenty-first birthday and I had to think of my future.... The only courses open to me were office work or marriage, and the only marriage possibility was with the then uncouth young man who had recently turned twenty-one and who was so insistent. By the time I returned to Chicago, my mind was made up, and on the day I came back we were engaged.

Creating a Home

We set our marriage date for June 5, 1926. Sadie found a stenographic job in the stockyards on Chicago's south side. Her employer was Swift & Company's lard department—a curious place for a nice Jewish girl.

We rented space from Dr. Leavitt, a dentist. Our address became 3403 Madison St., just across from Chicago's Garfield Park and quite close to Sadie's former apartment. Dr. Leavitt's offices occupied most of a large apartment, and he sublet the rest to us.

It strained our resources to furnish that space. My accumulated savings during two years at Hawthorne were not nearly enough. We were fortunate to get a loan of two hundred dollars from those wonderful people, the Brandners. Repaying that loan then had top priority, and we repaid it within twelve months.

I still have some of the checks I wrote in the weeks before our wedding date.

17 May	$45.00	to Dr Leavitt, for one month's rent
22 May	$100.00	to Tobey Furniture Company (We also bought some of our furniture on credit, especially from Smyth and Co.)
22 May	$6.00	to Lebolt Jewelry Company (for the wedding ring expense)
2 June	$12.00	for my final week's room and board at the Brandners
5 June	$5.00	to Rabbi L. S. Schwartz for performing the marriage ceremony

Our Wedding and the Reluctant Rabbi

We had scheduled the wedding for a Saturday afternoon, and by necessity it was a spartan event. There was no white wedding dress for the bride and no bridesmaids. Other than ourselves, those in attendance were Sadie's mother, my friend Chuck Milkes, and his friend Bernice. Despite such simplicity, we soon found ourselves in a crisis. When the rabbi questioned me, he concluded (correctly) that by his standards, I wasn't a very devout Jew. He then lectured us on the evils of the reform movement in Judaism, and it appeared that he would decline to go through with the ceremony.

I was stunned. The rabbi seemed unconcerned about the plight of the two young innocents who had in good faith planned to live together legally married but who now faced a crisis. Happily, Sadie's mother and Chuck Milkes interceded for us, and the rabbi finally relented. He performed the ceremony, and I listened intently. I was impressed by the meanings and solemnity of the ancient rite. I had every intention of being a good husband, even if not a devout Jew by the standards of Rabbi Schwartz.

Belated wedding photo (1927) of Sadie and me

Sharing Lives

We had no trouble organizing our time and other details of living together. We willingly shared the chores of maintaining the apartment. As it turned out, we had little time to ourselves. Our jobs kept us busy for five and a half days each week.

But we did have time for recreation during the weekends. We visited with friends, went to movies, and occasionally attended special events. In 1926 we saw Vitaphone's *Don Juan* with John Barrymore. The movies were in the early stages of adopting sound tracks, and in

1927 we saw the first talking picture, *The Jazz Singer*, starring Al Jolson. Radio was still in the crystal-set stage, and television was a few decades away.

Sunday mornings were special. We slept late and then had the luxury of extravagant brunches that included huge cinnamon rolls costing ten cents each, along with juicy navel oranges. We were leading a simple, prosaic life, but our hopes were to make the American Dream come true—a house of our own, children, peace, dignity. Both of us were accustomed to living frugally, so we managed comfortably on our modest income.

Even during our engagement, we talked about family planning. We agreed to defer having children until my income was adequate. In the spring of 1927, Sadie was fired from her job at Swift and Company. She never found out why. We decided that it was no longer necessary for her to continue working. Her modest salary was welcome, but meanwhile my own salary was creeping up.

With Sadie no longer working, it made no sense for us to continue to live where we did. Mine was a poor commute—a ride on the elevated train plus another on the Cicero Avenue streetcar line. So we moved to Cicero, where I would be within walking distance of my job at Hawthorne. Living within walking distance of the plant made it easy for us to participate now and then in the activities organized by the Hawthorne Club. Being within walking distance of the "El" train station enabled us to have an occasional date in downtown Chicago.

The Happiest Year: Robert Arnold Juran

Sadie and I have long believed that the happiest year of our lives was the twelve-month span from June 1928 to June 1929. The prelude to that happiest year came in November 1927, when we learned that we would become parents in June 1928. We were elated. Our first child was born in North Chicago Hospital on June 11, 1928; we named him Robert Arnold Juran. I had scheduled my vacation to greet him on arrival, and he arrived on time. The hospital bill was fifty dollars. We paid it, and the baby was ours to keep.

We were ecstatic when touching or holding this tiny little human, so perfectly formed, with exactly the right number of fingers and toes. During his first winter with us, my morning routine began by firing up the basement furnace. Then off I went to Bobby's crib, where he was awake and expecting me. I changed his wet diaper and then, with his little arms around my neck, I carried him to Sadie to nurse. All this time he uttered not a peep; he was fearless because he knew he was safe. Then I had my reward—viewing the sacred portrait of a mother nursing a child—my Sadie nursing our child.

Week by week we watched in wonder as Bobby became aware of his surroundings. He soon learned to coordinate hands with eyes, to respond to us, to mimic, to smile, to laugh. We were witnessing the beginnings of a miracle—the timeless evolution of an infant into an adult. We marveled at the spectacle. We were sure that our little boy was gifted and that, with his gifts, he would become a respected member of society.

During that happiest year, the world around us wore a benign face. Hawthorne was besieged with demands for its products. My intimate involvement in important projects brought me a dizzying series of promotions. My pay had already reached a comfortable level, with good prospects for more of the same. In a very few years, we would be in a home of our own.

So the happiest year came and passed. We had not the faintest idea that the country would soon undergo a terrifying ordeal that would engulf Hawthorne and ourselves. Neither did we have any idea that the precise mind of our gifted Bobby would in time become confused to a point that would threaten our own sanity.

Sylvia Louise Juran

Our second child was born on January 10, 1930. We had wanted a girl, and a girl it was. We named her Sylvia Louise Juran and promptly took her to our hearts. Soon we were calling her Mitzi; that nickname endured for years.

Immediately after Sylvia's birth, an event took place that received no attention at the time but that later came back to haunt us. When

Bobby first saw the new baby nursing, he was seized with a tiny fury. He pushed over a lamp and then ran out of the room. I didn't see the event; Sadie told me about it many years later when we were desperately trying to understand what change had come over our Bobby to transform him from a safe and secure little fellow into a mischievous, even vengeful, child.

A Chronology of Miscellaneous Events

Beyond life at home and at the plant, I busied myself with many activities. My scrapbooks include mementos of some of these, and my memory has supplied still other recollections. I was fond of sports and games. I tested out golf, tennis, table tennis, billiards, and bowling; I excelled only at table tennis. I enjoyed card games of all sorts and excelled at virtually all of them, notably contract bridge. The following are more events in the early days of marriage.

- February 1925—Sadie and I attended the Hawthorne University Club Dance—the second and last dance I ever attended. When I was courting Sadie, I learned that she enjoyed going to occasional dances. I proceeded to sign up for a few lessons to add to my qualifications as a suitor. It was in vain; I remained unfit to set foot on a dance floor. Then, having acquired a wife, I gleefully bade farewell to dancing.
- April 1925—I completed a course in Carrier Current Systems at the Hawthorne Club Evening School.
- June 12, 1926—I played my first round of golf at a divisional outing. My score for 18 holes was 149. (My best ever was 84.)
- March 1, 1927—Dad wrote (in German) asking me for money. It must have been a blow to his pride to do so. Evidently he had exhausted his credit with friends and other relatives. Because of his past relationships with my brothers, I was the only one he could turn to. I sent him what he asked for, the first of several such checks.
- April 14, 1927—We repaid the Brandners the $200 loan they had made to help us set up housekeeping. It was a relief to repay those wonderful people.

- May 24, 1927—Charles Lindbergh flew the "Spirit of St. Louis" nonstop across the Atlantic, arriving in Paris 33.5 hours later. Within days, his framed picture was seen on the desks of some Hawthorne stenographers and secretaries.
- 1927—Babe Ruth hit 60 home runs during the season, a record that would stand for decades. I never saw him play.
- November 1928—I was now eligible to vote in the elections for president, and I voted for Herbert Hoover.
- 1929—We bought our first automobile, a Model A Ford. Our Ford lacked many features that became available in later models, but it never failed to take us there and bring us back.
- May 1929—I was ordered to active duty with the Army Signal Corps in Washington, D.C. My mentor again was William F. Friedman, with whom I had already developed an excellent rapport. During that tour of duty, I was a guest at a dinner hosted by the Friedmans. Another guest was H. O. Yardley, whose later book (*The American Black Chamber*) infuriated Friedman because it disclosed much information that would have best been kept secret.
- Summer 1929—We vacationed in Minneapolis. While there, I took Sadie and Bobby to Dad's shop to meet him. Dad got up from his pinochle game to greet us; he also enjoyed playing a bit with the little fellow. It was the only time Dad ever saw Sadie or any of our children.
- 1929—I became Hawthorne Chess Champion for the third time running and retired the championship trophy. It was also the last time I competed in that annual tournament.
- October 28, 1929—This was "Black Friday." The stock market crashed, ushering in the Great Depression.

Charles Edward Juran

In the late summer of 1930, Sadie and I learned that we were to become parents for the third time. This time the event was unplanned and, to Sadie, unwanted. It was a severe shock to her, and she wept bitterly at the prospect of having to care for three little ones, each of them under three years of age. Nature then took its course; the idea of abortion never entered our minds.

Charles Edward Juran, the unplanned one, was born on April 17, 1931. At birth he sported a thick crown of jet-black hair and a chin that augured determination. We immediately took him to our hearts. His nickname became "Chuck," and this has endured.

The Family in 1930

By the end of 1930, the uncertainties of the Great Depression were already sending out alarm signals. At the outset, none of this affected us directly. I was still fully employed at a comfortable salary. The economic climate was clearly changing for the worse, however; the benign face of the outside world was becoming grim.

I was no longer alone. I now had a wife and three small children, and I was their sole provider; they depended on me to keep them out of poverty. At the plant I was an important manager, but I was only 26 years old and had only six years of service. Would I continue to hold a steady job at steady pay? I didn't ask; I knew that the answer would be distressingly vague.

Meanwhile, a second worrisome problem had arisen—a change had come over our little Bobby. Sadie worried about the burdens of caring for our mischievous first child and about the new obligations she would face with the birth of our third child. I worried about the deepening Depression and the threat it posed for all of us. We were unaware that we would survive the Depression essentially unscathed. We were also unaware that the mischievous pranks of our gifted little Bobby would multiply and intensify to become our dominant preoccupation.

Q

13

Layoffs, Law, and the Great Depression

On October 28, 1929, prices on the New York Stock Exchange plunged precipitously from their historic highs. That decline was to continue for several years, during which time the country endured what came to be known as the Great Depression.

Soon after the stock market crash, the country entered what seemed to be a recession—a temporary downturn in the business cycle. Unhappily, in this cycle, "temporary" went on and on. The decline in stock prices persisted and continued to make headlines, contributing to an atmosphere of fear. A downward spiral set in, gained momentum, and finally reached terrifying proportions. By early 1933, the number of unemployed had soared to about a fourth of the workforce; some estimates were as high as a third. The resulting drop in incomes greatly reduced consumer purchasing power as well as the ability to meet mortgage payments, resulting in extensive foreclosures on homes and farms. The effect on business was equally devastating. Bankruptcies soared in numbers, as did bank failures.

By March 1933, the threat of financial collapse became national in scope. Averting such a collapse became the first priority of the newly elected administration of Franklin Roosevelt. They succeeded admirably.

Layoffs

By mid-1931 the economy was roaring downhill at a reckless pace, bringing layoffs and ruin to the lives of millions. Hawthorne was already being affected; orders from the telephone companies were drying up and falling below production capacity. The first step taken was to reduce work hours. In part, this was done by eliminating Saturday work—a move cheered by managers and workers alike. A further reduction in hours came from eliminating overtime. Now the workweek consisted of five eight-hour days, a far cry from the six twelve-hour days I had worked at the Burlington Railroad. It was still not enough. Within months the plummeting rate of incoming orders was again out of balance with production capacity, and layoffs became necessary.

The senior managers set up quotas for numbers of people to be laid off and guidelines for choosing those to be laid off. Length of service weighed heavily; then came job performance and family obligations. I had never laid anyone off, so those guidelines were most helpful.

At first, long-service employees were safe. Then, as layoffs grew and grew, anxiety escalated into a terror that engulfed more and more victims. The dreaded truth burst into full view: no one was secure. In the final stages of the Depression, the layoffs reached employees with more than twenty years of service. The Hawthorne population had peaked at over 40,000 employees. It hit a bottom of about 7,000 before the recovery set in.

Those laid off suffered in multiple ways: the anxiety of looking for work; the time lost in pursuing leads that led nowhere; the shame and stigma of being unemployed; the despair that set in following repeated disappointments; the feeling of helplessness against powerful forces that lacked compassion. Those who did find jobs were forced to settle for pay levels far below their earnings at Hawthorne—down to ten and even five dollars a week. In the central cities, grown men could be seen on sidewalks, selling apples for five cents each. Large numbers of the unemployed, as well as those working at wretched pay rates, faced problems of basic survival. Unable to rent a place to live, they were forced to double up with relatives or to find primitive shelter in the slums that sprang up. Unable to feed their families, they were driven to line up at soup kitchens. To no one's surprise, many of the victims became embittered toward the system and toward leaders of a system that tolerated such hardships and humiliation.

For long-service employees, the layoffs were agonizing in the extreme. Over the years many had saved enough to make the down payment on a house. To meet the mortgage payments, they depended absolutely on their income from Hawthorne. Having made the American Dream come true, their long service at Hawthorne was their shield against disaster. Upon being laid off, that shield vanished. They were then unable to meet the mortgage payments and lost their homes when the banks foreclosed. All else was lost—their faith in the American Dream, their belief in the economic system, their confidence in the national leaders, and their very hopes for themselves and their children.

Cuts in Pay

Shortening work hours and eliminating overtime had an immediate impact on Hawthorne's hourly-rated employees; their pay dropped at once. Those paid by the week or month were not immediately affected, but their time would come soon.

I had received a salary increase in January 1930; my salary rose from $320 to $380 per month. The succeeding salary changes were cuts. In July 1932, my pay was cut from $380 to $330. About the same time, an entire layer of supervision was eliminated. The title of assistant superintendent disappeared; those holding that title were designated as division chiefs. The downgrading of titles then continued:

division chiefs became department chiefs; department chiefs became section chiefs or nonsupervisors. This news was received in grim silence. In August 1933, my pay was cut further, from $330 to $285. For me that was the final cut. It brought me below the magic figure of $300 that provided entry to the monthly payroll, but I remained on the monthly roll.

Deflation

An astonishing feature of the Depression was deflation—a decline in prices. Occupancy rates for apartments plunged, driving rents down to record levels. Child's, a popular restaurant, offered "All you can eat for twenty-five cents." A full-time domestic helper commanded about six dollars a week, or about fifteen cents an hour. At the bottom of the Depression, one could buy a man's suit for fifteen dollars.

With such declines in prices, my family was not hurt by my cuts in pay. If anything, our standard of living went up. By remaining employed at a good salary, I could easily keep the wolf from the door, provide comfortable housing, finance my education at law school, provide Sadie with a full-time helper, rent a cottage on Lake Michigan for the summer, and so on. All that comfort took place amid years of anxiety; throughout the entire Depression, I remained fearful of being laid off.

Groping for Security

For me, the stock market crash was a wake-up call. Well before 1929, I had been concerned about my family's financial security. I made the simplistic assumption that they were secure as long as I was alive and well. In line with that assumption, I bought term insurance to protect them. I also saved money, mainly through the company's stock purchase plan.

Once the layoffs began, it became clear that my family could lose financial security even if I remained alive and well. The Depression could deepen to a point that would cause me to be laid off. I would then have trouble finding a job. If I did find a job, it would be at a salary far below what I was earning. Our savings could protect us for a year at most. What then? Faced with that threat, I became convinced that there was now a real risk that my family would be forced into poverty. I spent many sleepless nights brooding over that threat. Seeing no defense, I was terrified. The future was in the hands of forces over which I had no control.

As I pondered our plight, my thinking raised the broader question: *How can I reach a state in which I am in control over these outside forces?* That led me to look at the road traveled by my classmate and friend Archie McCrady. He was older and more mature than anyone in our class. Following graduation, McCrady studied law, was admitted to the bar, and then became employed as a patent lawyer—first in a patent law firm, then at Western Electric, and finally at Bendix Corporation. Meanwhile he authored a book, *Patent Office Practice,* that became the leading reference work on the procedural law in the field.

I was impressed by McCrady's approach. In my view, he had reached a state of being in control. He did so by earning a license to practice in a profession that had a monopoly on an essential service. Then, through research and writing, he made himself so useful to society that he virtually carried his security around with him. I was interested in carrying my security around with me, but my immediate need was to broaden my options in the event of being laid off. By mid-1931, I had taken the first step—I enrolled in Loyola University's law school, located in downtown Chicago.

Law School

Acquiring a law degree involved attending classes three evenings a week for four years, plus homework. I realized that those evenings away from home would create problems for my family; they would not understand why they were being deprived of my time. Here I made the mistake of not explaining to Sadie the threats we were facing. I had always shared good news with her, but I reasoned that I had a responsibility to shield her from worry. So Sadie did not understand the reasons behind some of my actions, and this led to unnecessary divisiveness.

I attended law school without interruption, completing my courses in 1935. I received my degree on February 5, 1936. Then I passed the bar examination and was admitted to practice on June 11, 1936. Meanwhile, recovery from the Great Depression was underway. The worst was over, and I had not been laid off. Armed with my license, I now had two options—embark on the practice of law or remain at Hawthorne.

It was an easy choice. To practice law involved a change of careers, including a return to the bottom of the ladder. In contrast, remaining at Hawthorne meant a comfortable perch several rungs above the foot of the ladder and required no change of careers. I had not studied law to change careers; my purpose was to add to my family's security if ever I were to be laid off. So in 1936, I opted to remain at Hawthorne. Nevertheless, the byproducts of studying law were most rewarding to me and profoundly affected my future outlook.

Law school gave me my first exposure to the humanities, an area at which I had scoffed while attending engineering school. Now I was greatly impressed by the concept of resolving disputes through a process of law rather than through physical combat—the law of fang and claw. I became aware that adoption of the concept of law has contributed greatly to setting the human race apart from the brutishness of other species.

I learned that to practice law, one must undertake certain demanding tasks: identify with precision the issues presented by a case; study prior cases to discover the precedents; establish the pertinent facts; and find cause-effect relationships. All this requires analytical skills fully as demanding as those required in science and technology. I learned also that practicing law demands mastery of the language—choosing appropriate words and phrases and clearly defining terms to avoid the confusion that arises from words' multiple meanings. And I found that practicing law demands the ultimate precision in writing, including punctuation. As a result of my studies, I improved my own precision of expression, both orally and in writing.

To this day I retain some links to the subject of law. My grandson Peter Juran is a practicing lawyer in Winston-Salem, North Carolina.

Now and then I express my feelings in legalistic language. Once I sent the following birthday greeting to my granddaughter, Melanie Ruth Juran:

> **Melanie the Law-Abiding**
> She speaks but the truth,
> my Melanie Ruth.
> Seldom have I seen her
> commit a misdemeanor.
>
> There are no reports
> of commission of torts,
> And as for a felony,
> never my Melanie.

A tangible consequence of my four years at law school was a Juris Doctor degree—Doctor of Jurisprudence. I did not hint to anyone at Hawthorne that I would welcome being called Dr. Juran; neither did I publicize my new acquisition. (To my engineering colleagues, a doctorate in law is the lowest form of doctorate.)   Not until I joined academia in 1945 did I become Dr. Juran.

The 1932 Elections

The autumn of 1932 witnessed the first campaign for the presidency since the beginning of the Depression. The Republican party candidate was Herbert Hoover, seeking a second term. The Democratic party candidate was Franklin Roosevelt, a former governor of New York state. He effectively used a new medium—radio—to get his message across.

Most companies were strongly opposed to Roosevelt, whose speeches blamed industrial leaders for having brought on the Depression by their greed. Roosevelt offered the country a "New Deal." At Hawthorne, the pay envelopes occasionally included literature stating the company's views on the campaign and strongly implying that Hoover's reelection would be in the best interests of employees. I was persuaded, and I did vote for Hoover. Roosevelt won in a landslide, 472 electoral votes to Hoover's 59. The Republicans were stunned.

Clouds over Europe

Until the Depression, I paid little attention to world events. Factual information was hard to come by. Radio was still nascent, and I did not read *The New York Times* or the magazines that carried such news. As a result, I was not well aware that the clouds gathering over Europe would soon pose a mortal threat to me and my family. The threat came from nationalist and fascist parties that were springing up in European countries. To varying degrees, all were anti-Semitic. By far the greatest threat came from Germany because of the rise of Adolf Hitler and his National Socialist (Nazi) party.

Until 1933 I was largely indifferent to Germany's problems, but after the 1933 elections, I was no longer indifferent. A savagely militant regime was now in control of a powerful country. This same regime was openly my enemy and a threat to my family. As yet the threat seemed remote, but it could not be ignored. I developed a seething hatred of the Nazis and their leader—a leader whose appeal to his followers included the reptilian claim, "I've got someone for you to hate!"

14
Reaching the Pinnacle of Corporate Success

Franklin Roosevelt took office on Saturday, March 4th, 1933. His inaugural speech was broadcast by radio, and the nation hung on every word. His sentence "The only thing we have to fear is fear itself" became lodged in every memory, but the proof was yet to come.

The New Deal

Not only were the elections of 1932 a landslide for Roosevelt; they also swept a horde of Democrats into Congress, enough of them to have a clear majority in both houses. The new legislators supported Roosevelt solidly; they enacted his proposals into law. Those proposals were strongly opposed by the Republicans, who included most industrial leaders. It was an exercise in futility; Roosevelt had the votes.

I parted with the Republicans on some issues, notably on federal insurance of bank deposits and social security. Here I thought the

Republicans' position flew in the face of common sense. I'd lost money during a bank failure, but it was a loss I could tolerate. I knew some people, however, who had lost virtually all of their life savings; their loss was devastating. It was the same with social security. I had bought life insurance to provide a safety net for the family, but I knew that most families were not adequately protected.

Kasley Passes On and Hazard Returns

In the spring of 1933, my boss, Jack Kasley, committed suicide. It was a shocking, grisly affair. According to plausible rumors, he had invested deeply in the stock market on margin and had been caught in the crash of October 1929. He also was heavily in debt. His burdens finally overcame him; he went into the woods and cut his throat, leaving his family destitute.

Soon the job of Superintendent of Inspection was filled by Allan B. Hazard. His career had begun in the Inspection Branch, where he initiated the system of increasing inspector productivity through pay incentives. He had then gone on to head the Manufacturing Development Branch. Now he returned to his origins, this time as the big boss. I had already met Hazard during the late 1920s. At that time he had strongly supported the innovations that Melsheimer and I had proposed to measure inspector accuracy and to revise the inspector pay system. Now I reported to him as his staff assistant.

My new boss's approach differed remarkably from that of the fun-loving Kasley, who was content to deal with problems as they arose. Kasley was no innovator. While he was intensely loyal to his function, he was sensitive to political realities and was quite willing to make deals with opponents.

In contrast, Hazard's loyalty was to the company, and his allegiance to all else was a distant second. He was a bold innovator. He sought out improvement goals and then pursued them relentlessly. His urge for cost-cutting became legendary. I found it easy to work with Hazard. He knew how to use staff departments, and we soon became an effective team.

Signs of Recovery

By the end of 1933, solid evidence of economic recovery had begun to emerge. Growth in orders from the telephone companies could no longer be met by working short hours; the shops returned to a forty-hour week. (There was no return to Saturday half-day work; that was a permanent casualty of the Great Depression.)

Next came the gradual recall of people who had been laid off. Those who had survived the Depression welcomed the returnees warmly, but the returnees' elation was subdued. Most had endured a grim, sobering life during their absence; many were reluctant to talk about it. During that absence, their shining hope had been to return to their jobs under Hawthorne's protective shield. Each time they moved, they kept Hawthorne informed of their new whereabouts. They were relieved to be back and to put the nightmare behind them.

Nearly conclusive evidence of recovery was the resumption of pay raises. In July 1934, my salary rose from $285 to $317 per month. I welcomed both the increase and the evidence, but I remained apprehensive enough to continue with my law courses. It took another year or two before the fear of being laid off had totally disappeared.

Hazard's Influence at Hawthorne

Hazard was an effective manager—calm, methodical, resourceful, and decisive. His long experience had taught him to focus his time on a few vital problems. He delegated recurring matters to subordinates by approving the procedures to be used. Thereafter, he exercised control through reviewing the reports and audits.

Hazard was also innovative, and his chief passion was cost reduction. On his arrival he lost no time making it a high priority for the entire Inspection Branch. His subordinates promptly fell into line and soon found ways to reduce costs by expanding the use of productivity goals, extending the use of sampling, and replacing manual testing with automated testing.

A broad measure of Hazard's drive on costs was the stunning reduction in the number of inspectors needed at Hawthorne. At the peak in 1929, the Inspection Branch had about 5,200 employees. By 1936, when production at Hawthorne had rebounded to nearly the 1929 levels, the Inspection Branch had only about 2,000 employees. There were, of course, other causes beyond those initiated by Hazard, but his influence was profound.

The Coming of Labor Unions

The New Deal labor legislation, notably the Wagner Labor Relations Act (1935), removed the existing obstacles for organizing industrial labor unions. Hawthorne's workers did organize, so all Inspection Branch supervisors and managers faced the new problem of how to deal with a union. I shared their ignorance. My sole experience with unions had been as an observer. In the summer of 1922, when I worked in a railroad roundhouse, I discovered that a labor union could become a tyranny over its members, fully as oppressive as some employers.

I was ambivalent about the need for a union. Western Electric was an enlightened employer, and I was surprised when the employees voted to have a union. Then, as grievances were filed, I learned that it was perfectly possible for employees to revere "Ma Bell" as a good employer and still feel that the grievance machinery left too much to the discretion of fallible human supervisors. Voting for a union provided a way of bypassing such supervisors.

Hazard was ideally suited to deal with a union. He was not awed by the newness of the problem. He had unswerving loyalty to the company but also had a fierce sense of fair play that earned the respect of the union leaders.

Hazard drew me into his meetings with the union. I drafted his presentations as well as his summaries of what took place. In those meetings I was impressed with some union leaders' abilities to present and defend their proposals to management. They exhibited capabilities that the company was not aware of and certainly had not utilized.

In addition I became deeply involved with a problem that was becoming national in scope— the assignment of "labor grades." For every shop job, it was necessary to assign a grade to serve as a basis for choosing its pay scale. In many companies, the assignment of labor grades was left to the supervisors' judgment—there was no system that set out the criteria to be used and the weight to be given to each. The opportunities for favoritism and misjudgments were legion, resulting in many grievances. These grievances were directed not only at individual cases; they also were directed at the root cause—the absence of a rational system for assigning labor grades.

In the Inspection Branch we had such a system, but we concluded that it would be difficult to defend if it were challenged by the union. At Hazard's request I organized a series of meetings with the managers, the goal being to develop a revised system. They were eager to cooperate; each could point to deficiencies in the existing system. We ended up with a list of criteria and weights that then stood the test of time as well as the challenge from the union.

Product Shops and the End of the Inspection Branch

As the Depression receded into history, Hawthorne changed its organization and the associated physical layout of its production facilities in revolutionary ways.

Hawthorne's organization had long consisted of functional branches—accounting, industrial relations, operating (meaning production), inspection, and so on. The production shops and their physical layouts were also organized by function. One area housed all the foundry facilities; a second, the forging machines; a third, the stamping presses; and so on with milling machines, lathes, drilling machines, threading machines, and other types of equipment.

The aim of the revolution was to create "product shops" in which all the facilities needed to produce a given product line were concentrated in a single geographic area. These shops would become the responsibility of a single hierarchy of supervisors and managers.

To create the revolution, Hawthorne set up a management committee to examine the pros and cons of both forms of organization and report their findings to the top levels. The top levels included two brilliant engineers—W. F. Hosford, Vice President for Manufacture, and David Levinger, Engineer of Manufacture, both of whom were advocates for change.

The committee did an excellent job of analyzing the two organization forms, including the pros and cons of a change as such. It concluded that "there is a chance of realizing considerable profit by a change, which should be proved or disproved by a trial." The idea of a trial was then accepted, and a product shop was created to build "subscribers' sets." These sets were located on the desks (or walls) of subscribers and included a transmitter, receiver, dial, ringer, and associated circuitry.

The trial was stunningly successful. There were dramatic reductions in the time required to build a set. Under the functional organization, the time interval from die-casting the base until the completed set was shipped to finished goods store ran anywhere from two to three months; in the product shop, it ran from twenty-four to forty-eight hours. There were equally dramatic reductions in the size of process inventory, the amount of transport between departments, and in the accompanying paperwork. An important disadvantage the trial revealed was the shortage of broadly trained managers to meet the demands of the new organization.

Following the success of the trial, more product shops were organized. As each one was created, it took over many activities that previously had been carried out by the functional branches. One such activity was product inspection and testing. As a result, product shops absorbed most of the Inspection Branch. What was left remained centralized; it included the various measurement laboratories and the inspection of purchased materials, as well as such services as measurement of inspector accuracy, auditing of the quality performance of the product shops, and membership (with Bell Laboratories) on the Quality Survey Committees. These centralized functions were placed in a newly created organization unit, the Works Inspection Control Division. I was promoted to head that division.

Promoted Once More

This new promotion was most welcome. It put me into an elite level of managers; I was now one of about fifty people who ran the Hawthorne Works. The job's salary range could provide me with generous increases for years to come. The promotion also yielded some useful perks, notably a private office and parking space in the company garage.

My new boss was J. M. Stahr, the Works Comptroller. I knew him well. He was a leading chess player and, in addition, an ardent bridge player. We often had played on the same or opposing teams and had developed a good rapport. Stahr's entire career had been in the Accounting Branch; his mastery of that function was complete, and he also understood broadly the functions of other branches, but was out of his depth when it came to the technology. Thus, I discovered that I would be running my job with no direct supervision in terms of the technology. I had never before been in such a situation, and at first it troubled me. Then, after some pondering, I concluded that I could get a form of supervision from peers and subordinates—they would be challenging my proposals and conclusions.

I failed to realize that in my new job, I became more visible to the inner circle—my new peers plus their superiors. At those levels, my tactlessness and arrogance were more conspicuous and less easily tolerated. Ideally, some boss of mine should have told me about my failings in blunt language and could have coached me or warned me to change my ways. But the message that came through to me was that each promotion was proof that I was doing just fine. So I continued in my tactless, arrogant ways.

Headquarters Beckons

In the autumn of 1937, I received an overture from a former boss, Allan Hazard. Hazard was now at the New York corporate headquarters, where he was responsible for several corporate engineering functions. He offered me a job; the title was Manufacturing Engineer but the role was that of Corporate Industrial Engineer.

Hazard's offer involved no promotion; in terms of rank it was a lateral move. But in terms of prestige, it was a long step upward. Corporate headquarters was the center of power. Few at Hawthorne understood what went on there, but all knew that awesome decisions were made there. For someone to be transferred to New York called for a gala farewell party with congratulations to match.

I spent very little time debating whether to accept Hazard's offer. I did no analysis listing the pros and cons, and neither did I discuss it in depth with Sadie. It all seemed so obvious. No doubt I was dazzled by the prospect of an office at the center of power. In addition, the job was attractive on its own merits. I would be providing the plant managers with information and recommendations in an area of great importance. I would have a small staff located at each plant as well as in New York. Moreover, I would have a familiar, supportive boss. Hazard and I had from the beginning, established a team relationship based on mutual respect and trust.

Q

15

Career Crisis, New York

The core activities of my new job related to wage practices for factory employees. At Western Electric, the wages of any factory employee were determined by several criteria:

1. The labor grade of the job. This was arrived at by a process called "job evaluation."
2. The base rate (or rate range) for the labor grade. This was arrived at by market research—by visits to companies in the local area to discover the base rates they paid for comparable labor grades.
3. The choice of actual pay within the rate range. This was decided by supervisory judgment during annual rate reviews.

Beyond these base rates (also called "day rates"), many factory employees worked on piecework and thereby had an opportunity to increase their take-home pay, depending on their productivity.

Job Evaluation

Manufacturers had long faced the problem of job evaluation and had evolved loose systems that included a generous amount of supervisory judgment. These systems led to complaints from employees that their labor grades were unfairly low in relation to other jobs. With the coming of industrial unions, these complaints became more insistent. The unions not only challenged individual cases; they also challenged the validity of the job evaluation *system*. The need for a more systematic approach came to the attention of the trade associations. One of these, the National Electrical Manufacturers Association (NEMA), undertook the project of developing a system that it could recommend to its members.

I was quite familiar with these evaluation problems. During the late 1920s, I was intimately involved in redesigning the system of evaluation for the jobs of Hawthorne's inspectors.

When NEMA set out to develop its job evaluation system, it sought help from its members. The NEMA engineer, A. L. Kress, convened a team of industry managers, of whom I was one. I found it fascinating to exchange experiences with my counterparts in other companies. NEMA emerged with a simple, practical system that was widely adopted within its industry. The system was also chosen by the National Metal Trades Association for recommendation to its members.

Rate Ranges

One of my functions was to determine the pay scales in the market—how much our industrial neighbors paid their employees for various labor grades. To this end, I had engineers at each factory location visit companies in the local area and secure their pay scales for various job grades. We limited our visits to companies that followed enlightened employee-relations policies. We were unwilling to have our surveys open to challenge on the grounds that we had included data from sweatshops. (In return for their cooperation, the companies were given copies of our summaries.)

Our senior managers wanted a single number to tell them how our pay rates compared with the market. Summarizing the data to produce such a composite was tricky; there were many ways to summarize, and the resulting totals could differ widely.

Piecework

Throughout the 1930s, use of piecework incentives remained an article of faith among most American plant managers. The prevailing belief was that in the absence of piecework, worker productivity would fall considerably.

Nevertheless, maintaining a piecework system had its price. It took a multitude of rate setters to establish the piece rates and to maintain them in the face of changes in processes. (It also took a multitude of clerks to compute the piecework earnings.) In addition, the resulting piecework rates were notoriously variable. Some rates were "fat"; workers could attain good earnings with modest effort. Other rates were "lean"; they gave rise to worker complaints. Supervisors learned which rates were fat and used this knowledge when assigning work. With the coming of unions, these grievances multiplied; even the very concept of piecework came under attack.

The Decline of Piecework

During the 1930s, Hawthorne's managers endured the costs and irritations of maintaining the piecework system because they believed that the gain in productivity outweighed the negatives. That belief persisted even when the coming of labor unions intensified the irritations. However, new forces emerged to challenge the piecework system.

The Conveyer. Henry Ford's use of conveyors to assemble automobiles was an alternative to piecework. The conveyor speed, not a piece rate, was decisive in achieving productivity. Ford's flat rate of five dollars a day was simplicity itself.

Automation. Where automation was cost-effective, productivity was engineered into the process.

Measured Daywork. Some companies abolished piecework by use of measured daywork. They used time studies to determine the work pace for a fair day's work, and this became the quota for workers. They set hourly pay rates for meeting the quota; it was then up to the supervisors, through training and coaching, to help the workers meet the quota. Workers who were unable or unwilling to meet the quota were transferred to other jobs or were terminated.

Growing Affluence. During World War II, labor shortages drove workers' earnings to higher levels. Many workers moved out of poverty and into the middle class. With growing affluence, those workers were less willing to work so hard; they could feed the family without driving themselves to exhaustion. For a growing number of workers, piecework was a declining stimulus.

The transition away from piecework was difficult in cases in which the earnings had been high. Workers and their unions took the position that high earnings (from fat piece rates) had become contractual entitlements—that workers were entitled to those earnings no matter what. They even contended that the rates were permanently attached to the processes even if the incumbent workers were no longer performing the work. Companies had to resort to various ways to get rid of fat rates: revising the processes; going to arbitration; and even "buying up" the fat rates—paying the incumbent workers for the right to abolish the fat rates.

General Motors and the Work of Vilfredo Pareto

My visits to other companies went beyond the narrow mission of securing data on their pay rates. I also made some visits in order to exchange experiences on wage practices in general. The most memorable of these was my visit in 1941 to General Motors headquarters.

At the time, General Motors (GM) was one of the largest corporations on earth. Its president, Alfred P. Sloan, Jr., had divided GM into autonomous divisions while retaining a corporate staff for coordination and control. My hosts were members of this corporate staff. As a manager from the giant AT&T, they accepted me as an equal, made me welcome, and extended many courtesies to me.

As part of that visit, I was shown research they had conducted relative to the work of Vilfredo Pareto, an Italian engineer and economist. Pareto had studied the distribution of wealth; he had found that a relative few families had acquired most of the wealth, while the many remaining families had very little. (No surprise there.) Pareto went a step further, fitting a logarithmic curve to the data. The GM researcher then found that the distribution of GM's salaries also followed a logarithmic distribution. The research was interesting, but I doubted that our Western Electric managers would make any application of the findings.

It was my first exposure to Pareto's work, and I filed his name away in my memory. Later, within a decade, I published an important discovery: the phenomenon of "vital few and trivial many" extended far beyond the distribution of human wealth; it was present everywhere. A relative few people committed most of the crimes, caused most of the accidents, and so on. I gave the name "Pareto Principle" to that discovery. In due course, the Pareto Principle became a widely used management tool—a *universal*. In addition, the name "Pareto Principle" became a part of the management vocabulary (Juran 1975).

Calm Waters

By 1939 I was comfortably settled in at headquarters. I understood my role and had become proficient at my work. I began to explore new concepts and new methods. I was enjoying and expanding my outside contacts. In addition, I had a most favorable relationship with my superiors.

My immediate boss was Allan Hazard. Both at Hawthorne and now in New York, we enjoyed an ideal rapport—mutual respect and trust. Although I reported to Hazard, he was actually two steps above me in rank. His title was Assistant Engineer of Manufacture, and he presided over several functions, including wage practices. The post of Engineer of Wage Practices was vacant, however; in that sense, Hazard was both Engineer of Wage Practices and Assistant Engineer of Manufacture.

Hazard's boss was David Levinger, the Engineer of Manufacture. I had been exposed to Levinger on several occasions, notably in connection with his paper for the CIOS Congress. We had arrived at a warm relationship, both personally and on a business level.

For a young manager, I was at an enviable convergence of benign job conditions. I was immersed in an exciting activity, and it occupied the time of high-level managers. My office was in the citadel of power—the AT&T building at 195 Broadway. I was well paid. I enjoyed the respect and support of friendly bosses. My prospects for the future seemed limitless. It was an era of good feeling.

The Gathering Storm

That agreeable state of affairs was soon jolted. It began when Hazard was promoted to General Sales Engineer, which removed him from the Manufacturing Department. In the process, I lost the influence of a strong supporter. For a brief time I reported directly to Levinger. Beyond our activity in the area of wage practices, he used me to help him in other ways—drafting and reviewing his speeches, communicating with his assistants in the plants, and so on. It was an unstable arrangement. There were now two vacancies above me. I knew that the company would soon fill those gaps, and I was more than curious about what would happen.

The next jolt came when Levinger was promoted to be Works Manager at Hawthorne. His successor as Engineer of Manufacture was Stanley Bracken, who had been Levinger's assistant at Hawthorne while also serving as president of Teletype Corporation, a Western Electric subsidiary.

My contact with Bracken at Hawthorne had been limited; now I was directly exposed to him. I soon came to admire him as a manager. Of compact build, he was equally solid in his approach to the job. He listened, asked incisive questions, thought out loud, and then reached decisions that were notable for their common sense.

Despite my respect for Bracken as a manager, I felt no warmth in the relationship. That didn't trouble me. It was similar to the relationship I had with earlier bosses such as Max Swan and S. M. "Smo" Osborne, both of whom I also respected for the dispatch with which they managed. Moreover, in my observation, Bracken's approach to others was the same as it was to me. No doubt I would have liked a warm relationship such as had developed with some of my bosses—Melsheimer, Stahr, Hazard, and Levinger. With them I was just lucky.

Nevertheless, there was another aspect of Bracken's approach that might have been enormously helpful to me had I been a subordinate of his much earlier in my career. Bracken did not hold back his views on subordinates' strengths and weaknesses; he was blunt yet tactful. Had he been my boss earlier, he might well have put it to me plainly: "You are offending a lot of people, and you had better put a stop to it." I might have heeded such a wake-up call (or I might not have).

The Era of Supreme Stupidity

The storm broke in about mid-1939, when W. K. (Kelly) Wiggins was appointed Engineer of Wage Practices. The opening above me had now been filled, but not by me.

Now began a two-year span during which I practiced stupidity at its worst. I felt I had been betrayed. For the first time in my fifteen years with the company, an opening above me had been filled by someone other than me. I seem to have felt that promotion to an opening above me had become an entitlement. I resented being passed over, and I resented Wiggins for having been moved in. Worse yet, I took no pains to conceal my resentment. Not only did I fail to make Wiggins welcome; I gave unmistakable hints that he was unwelcome (again, revenge on the innocents).

Despite my inexcusable conduct, I did my job and did it well. An indicator of the state of affairs was the occasion when Wiggins commented to me, "Whether you like it or not, I appreciate how you handled that assignment."

Wiggins was aware of my black moods and no doubt shared that knowledge with others, including Bracken. In addition, Wiggins took countermeasures. He deliberately excluded me from some important meetings; instead he took along a subordinate of mine, W. C. Snell. I then had to learn from Snell what took place at such meetings. I was humiliated, but, of course, I had asked for it.

Stupidity: Why?

Today I marvel that I could have been so stupid. The basic employer/employee relationship is a contract. The employer agrees to provide employment, pay, benefits, and so on. In return, the employee agrees to obey the assigned boss's orders, perform the assigned duties, and work with assigned coworkers. The employer retains autocratic power; it is the employer, not the employee, who chooses the boss, the work assignment, and the coworkers. I knew very well that such were the rules of the game, but I acted stupidly all the same.

To my knowledge, I remained rational in other respects; my being irrational was highly selective. My swift series of promotions had become the basis of a new goal—to rise in the company hierarchy. That goal in turn stimulated an urge to fill the next opening for promotion, which then intensified and finally transformed itself into an assumed property right that I regarded as inviolate. When it was violated, I mutinied. All this took place in my mind without regard for the realities. (The dictionary has a word for such selectively irrational behavior: "obsession.")

Bypassed, Again

In about mid-1941, the situation changed abruptly. Wiggins was promoted to become Assistant Works Manager at Hawthorne. He was replaced by A. O. Avery, an amiable long-service manager who was nearing retirement. For the second time, an opening above me was filled by someone else.

This new development left me chastened and numb. It soon dawned on me that irreversible damage had been done to my career. The door to further advancement had probably slammed shut; very likely I would spend the rest of my days stuck at the same level while younger men moved upward and passed me. Such a fate now seemed tragic yet unavoidable.

Under such a scenario, the saving feature was financial security. My salary had already reached a level that was providing comfortably for my family. (As of January 1942, my salary had risen to $675 per month, or $8,100 per year—quite a comfortable rate.) At retirement age, my pension plus the new Social Security pension could provide an adequate retirement income. Yet I saw a life of bitter resentment ahead, with inevitable negative fallout on my family.

Even worse scenarios were also possible. My conduct had roiled superior forces, and these now swirled around me, possibly poised to strike. I had lost control. As 1941 drew to a close, I had much to think about, none of it positive.

Blame

Curiously, I didn't blame myself. I blamed anti-Semitism, envy by some of my peers, talebearers, and still other enemies under the beds. No doubt some of these species were present to some degree, but collectively their influence was minor.

In later years I made visits that shed considerable light on the events of 1941. Much of this feedback came to me from Hazard, who had retired from Western Electric and was living in Princeton, Illinois. According to Hazard, Levinger had been a strong supporter of mine. Had he remained Engineer of Manufacture or gone on to become Vice President of Manufacture, things would have been different.

Bracken never warmed up to me. "Bracken didn't like you" was how Hazard put it. (Hazard didn't know why.) Also, Bracken had criticized Hazard for bringing me to headquarters. Hazard felt I had been wise to leave when I did. He was convinced that Bracken would have held me down indefinitely.

More feedback came to me from W. C. Snell, who had been one of my subordinate department heads in New York. Snell recalled that Wiggins had excluded me from important meetings, but Wiggins never told him why. Snell also gave me his views concerning the image I presented in those days.

I was regarded as a brilliant thinker, but uncompromising. My unwillingness to compromise extended not only to my peers but even to people who outranked me, stopping only before those who were very high in the organization. There was a general feeling that I had not grasped the facts of life as far as compromise was concerned.

Race prejudice was not a factor. My behavioral characteristics were distinctive enough to cause people to form definite judgments about me quite aside from any question of race.

Today the trail of blame for my predicament at company head-quarters seems to lead to a convergence of two causes:

1. I had offended many peers with my sharp tongue and arrogance. The cumulative backlash reduced my chances for promotion, although I may not have gotten it in any case.
2. I had developed an unrealistic sense of entitlement toward promotion. I have thought about the origin of this feeling, but that speculation is in the realm of theory. I doubt that I will ever find a full factual explanation for that unrealistic belief.

Q

16

The Beginnings of My Writing Career

My transfer to company headquarters introduced me to two new worlds. One was the upper hierarchy of Western Electric; the other was a world outside the company that I entered by becoming active in professional societies.

Professional Societies

Soon after my arrival in New York, I discovered that numerous professional societies were headquartered there and that the following were active in the field of management:

- The Society for the Advancement of Management (SAM)—Its New York Chapter held monthly meetings on various aspects of what today we call "industrial engineering," including wage practices.
- The American Society of Mechanical Engineers (ASME)—I joined ASME because it had a management division.
- American Management Association. (AMA)—It focused exclu-

sively on the subject of management. It held large annual conferences on such subjects as general management, marketing, manufacturing, personnel, finance, and so on.

- The National Industrial Conference Board. (NICB)—It published useful economic statistics. In addition, it conducted excellent research on how companies manage with respect to selected important problems.

I found most society meetings to be informative. While companies tended to be secretive about their technology, they were quite open about their methods of managing. From some speakers I learned of innovations that seemed applicable at Western Electric.

My activities with the societies also brought me into contact with many practitioners in the field of management: industrial managers, labor union officials, university professors, industrial consultants, public officials, and others. In SAM I organized meetings, some on topics outside of my direct experience; I was also charged with finding speakers. When I was president of the New York chapter, I discovered that I had easy access to many local managers. I received exposure and publicity from the meeting announcements and press notices as well as from presiding at meetings. All these contacts and exposures greatly broadened my horizon while incidentally feeding my ego.

I relished writing papers for presentation and publication. I had done a bit of this while at Hawthorne; the audiences were local managers and supervisors. The first presentation before an outside audience was at a session of the ASME conference held in Cincinnati, June 19 to 21, 1935. The subject for the session was quality control, and my paper was titled "Inspectors' Errors in Quality Control." It was published in *Mechanical Engineering*, October 1935. That session was attended by only about fifty persons, an indication of the subject matter's limited attraction in those days.

Time and Motion Study Cross Examines Itself

This was a seminal paper presented on February 15, 1940, at a meeting of the New York Chapter of SAM. It never secured Western

Electric's clearance for publication. The paper dealt with the precision of "rating" time studies then used by industrial engineers. It is easy for an engineer to measure the *actual* productivity of a worker—the number of pieces produced per unit of time. The engineer is then faced with setting a work standard despite the fact that during the measurement, the worker's pace might have been fast or slow. What the engineer does is to "rate"—to make a subjective judgment of the difference between the worker's actual pace and the engineer's judgment of what is the "standard" pace.

The findings described in the paper were disturbing to the industrial engineering managers of that era; the prevailing variability was much higher than the industrial engineers' claims. There were other disturbing findings. The paper recommended ways to improve the rating process, it suggested some additional lines of needed research, and it suggested that a society committee should be created to get the needed research done.

SAM did create a committee to research the subject, and I was appointed chairman. The committee held its first meeting in December 1940 and published its first report in the July–September 1941 issue of *Advanced Management*, the journal of SAM.

Within months the United States was plunged into World War II, and the committee went dormant for the duration. Following the war, it created a series of films as an aid for training engineers to rate time studies in order to conform to the standards of a "fair day's work." The committee solicited grants from industrial companies to finance the research, and it received a total of $32,500—a goodly sum for those days. More than enough of the films were sold to enable the committee to recover the amount that had been received from the companies.

Service on a Committee

My work with the Committee on Rating of Time Studies was my first experience as a member of a self-directing committee of a professional society. It turned out to be rewarding. Of the nine members, seven were active participants—a high ratio for such committees. Our mission, although unknown to society in general, was important to the economy, and we took our responsibility seriously.

As chairman I had no command authority; all progress depended on securing consensus through persuasion. Despite my problems at my company, I maintained an excellent rapport with the committee members. The absence of command relationships very likely contributed to the harmony that prevailed.

One bonus from my committee activity was the enduring relationships it fostered. Some ripened into enduring friendships, whereas others led to joint activities in the future. For example, Professor David Porter of New York University (NYU) was a member of the committee. My relationship with him was influential in my later joining NYU as chairman of its Department of Industrial Engineering. Keith Louden's committee membership not only led to our lifelong friendship; it also resulted in our working together within the American Management Association.

Book Reviews for the *New York Times*

In 1943, Waldemar Kaempffert, science editor of the *New York Times*, asked if I would be willing to review technical books for the *New York Times Book Review*. (George Stetson, editor of *Mechanical Engineering*, had given him my name.) I was decidedly willing, and so I began an association of about eight years. During that time I received more then a thousand books from the editors of the *Times Book Review* section. The subject matter was chiefly technology but also included books on industry, management, and other topics.

Scanning those books and reading some was decidedly enlightening. Equally enlightening were my visits with Dr. Kaempffert (in German, the name means "warhorse.") He was well versed in a broad spectrum of technological disciplines and had a knack for communicating in lay language.

During my eight years of reviewing for the *New York Times*, about 100 of my reviews were published. Incidentally, I discovered that a well-done book review demands much time and effort, plus a high level of literary craftsmanship. As a result of this adventure, I was later able to present the Engineering Societies Library with over a thousand books on science and engineering. They were elated.

Management Consulting

At society meetings, I met management consultants. Some were officers in the societies; some were speakers on the programs; some wrote articles for the journals. I knew that they used such activities to advertise their capabilities, but I was nevertheless intrigued by their lifestyle, which seemed to offer them extensive freedom.

Actually, I had done some consulting during my years at company headquarters, although I didn't recognize that I was playing the role of consultant. Factory quality managers occasionally asked me to share my experience with them. Since I had officially been transferred out of the quality function, my role became that of consultant rather than that of manager. Mr. A. L. Kress of NEMA invited me to join an informal committee of industry experts to design NEMA's job evaluation plan. On that committee, I was a consultant to NEMA. The Southern New England Telephone Company undertook a project to design a job evaluation plan for certain personnel categories. They asked me to meet several times with their committee, and I did so as a consultant.

During such consulting stints, I was not in a command position, nor did I have a voice in the decision making. I was an outsider; my role was limited to sharing my expertise and making recommendations. I could hope that those recommendations would be adopted, but I could not order my clients to do so. I was then limited to using the tools of persuasion and the authority of knowledge rather than the authority of command.

As it turned out, *I instinctively adopted tact* as one of the ways for getting my recommendations accepted. At the time I was not at all aware that consulting required what no human superior had ever demanded of me: to get rid of my tactlessness and arrogance. Neither was I aware that during those consulting stints, I was instinctively mending my ways. *The consulting relationship was more effective in changing my behavior than any personal boss had ever been.*

Four Years of Change for the Worse

When we came to corporate headquarters late in 1937, our world was peaceful and benign. My prospects at the company were at their most promising. The family was safe and thriving. The dark clouds seemed few, though some were present: the distant, menacing Nazi regime in Europe; the German-American Bunds, training for the day when they might become the Nazis' fifth column here; anti-Semites, such as the radio priest Father Charles Coughlin, spewing out their venom.

Four years later, by December 1941, all had changed for the worse. My career at the company lay in ruins. Our domestic peace was threatened by Bob's increasingly strange behavior. The world was at war. Germany had conquered central Europe and now was deep into Russia. Great Britain stood alone, enduring bombings and the threat of invasion. Japan had conquered China and was poised to attack Southeast Asia, the Philippines, and Indonesia.

Clearly, during those four years the family had suffered severe setbacks, some the result of my own folly. Some of our hopes had vanished; others were under threat. Our very existence was increasingly threatened and could no longer be taken for granted. We had realized the American Dream, but continuation of that dream now absolutely depended on the national security of the United States.

That national security was under threat, and I felt the need to do something about it. Aside from the danger to my family, I felt that I owed a debt to the land of opportunity. I could respond by joining the armed forces, but that course posed a different threat to the family. I seriously doubted Sadie's ability to manage the family in my absence, quite aside from the severe financial problems she would face.

Such were the thoughts that swirled in my mind until the circumstances of December 1941 took me in a new direction.

Q

17

World War II, Washington, D.C., and the Lend–Lease Office: Using Statistics to Wage War

On December 7, 1941, Japanese armed forces bombed the American naval base at Pearl Harbor, Hawaii. Many Americans died, and there was enormous damage to the American fleet. Soon the United States was at war with Japan and Germany.

On December 20, 1941, Western Electric president C. G. Stoll received the following telegram:

Very anxious to secure services of J. M. Juran ... on loan basis for six weeks to make very important analysis of Statistics

Division of Lend-Lease Administration and assist in reorganizing it. Government will pay salary ... up to and not exceeding rate of $8,000 per year, which is civil service limit. Desire immediately ... and will deeply appreciate your cooperation. Please advise.

E. R. Stettinius, Jr.
Lend-Lease Administrator

The telegram was the work of Charles L. Terrel, who had once been a subordinate of mine at Hawthorne. Terrel was now employed by the U. S. Treasury Department but was on loan to Lend-Lease.

The overture could not have come at a better time. Here was a chance to join the war effort, even if for only a short time. I would also have an opportunity to be away from the company for a few weeks, long enough to collect my wits after the disappointments I had experienced.

Sadie was concerned about being left alone to manage the family while I was gone. The fact that it was only for six weeks carried the day. I had no trouble securing a leave of absence from the company, and I commenced work at the Lend-Lease Administration on Christmas Day, 1941.

Status of the War

By the end of 1941, the war in Europe had unfolded enough to make me most apprehensive about the outcome. The shooting war began with the German invasion of Poland in September 1939. By December 1941, the Germans had conquered France, the Benelux countries, and most of central Europe. In addition, they occupied Norway and Denmark and were deep into Russia. Britain endured savage bombings while bracing itself for the expected invasion.

I was thoroughly frightened by the Germans' unbroken success record. I assumed that the Russians were doomed to defeat and that the British would be next, leaving the Germans as masters of Europe. Once Europe was under Nazi control, and given the unlimited Nazi appetite for conquest, the United States would then assuredly become their top-priority target. Given also the Nazis' ferocious anti-Semitism, my family would be in mortal peril.

The events at the company were eclipsed by the new, ominous threats we were facing. I became convinced that my family's survival was at stake. The long dormant fears of pogroms sprang to life and began to haunt my sleep as well as my waking hours.

Lend-Lease—The Background

From 1939 to1941, as the war in Europe raged, America debated its policy toward that war. President Roosevelt favored intervention by the United States to save Britain and rescue Europe. In this he was bitterly opposed by the isolationists. They insisted that Europe's quarrels did not concern the United States. They were willing to sell arms to the Allies, provided the Allies paid "cash on the barrelhead."

During 1939, Roosevelt and his advisers looked for ways to help the Allies, whether through legislation or presidential order. In November 1939 the U. S. embargo on export of arms to belligerents was repealed, subject to "cash and carry." This enabled the Allies to buy war matériel for cash, but their cash reserves soon ran low. In addition, the convoys transporting that matériel were being torpedoed by the German U-boats and bombed by the German air force. It became essential to find ways to protect those convoys and to bypass the need for cash purchases.

In September 1940 came the "destroyers for bases" deal, a noncash transfer of fifty old "mothballed" navy destroyers to the British in exchange for a ninety-nine-year lease of an arc of bases stretching from Newfoundland and Bermuda through the Caribbean and on to British Guiana. Then, in December 1940, the president unveiled the "garden hose" analogy—lending a garden hose to a neighbor whose house was on fire. It was the first hint to the public of the lend-lease concept.

In January 1941, a lend-lease bill was introduced in the U. S. Senate and the House of Representatives. In essence, it authorized the U. S. government to make (or procure) and lend (or lease) "defense articles" to any country "whose defense the President deems vital to the defense of the United States." In March 1941, after much intense debate, Congress approved the bill, the president signed it, and Congress enacted the first lend-lease appropriation—seven billion dollars.

Meanwhile the Allied countries established purchasing agencies to acquire goods and services (especially war matériel) from the United States, first for cash and later through lend-lease funding. Once the first lend-lease appropriation was approved, these agencies filed a flood of requisitions to be filled out of lend-lease funds. Those requisitions then had to be cleared by Harry Hopkins, whom the president had designated to oversee the lend-lease activity. At the time, Hopkins lived in the White House and used his bedroom as an office. He was overwhelmed by those requisitions, and a bottleneck developed. It could take weeks, even months, for requisitions to clear Hopkins' bedroom.

Steps were then taken to break the bottleneck. On August 28, 1941, Edward R. Stettinius, Jr., was appointed to run the lend-lease program. Two months later, a formal agency, the Office of Lend-Lease Administration, was created in the executive branch. That same Lend-Lease Administration became my destination in Washington.

I arrived in Washington on my thirty-seventh birthday, December 24, 1941. Terrel was most helpful; he let me share the suite of rooms he was renting at "The Little Tea House" in nearby Arlington, Virginia.

On the next day—Christmas day—I accompanied Terrel to the Lend-Lease office, an unfinished apartment building that had been requisitioned for government use. I was briefed on the Lend-Lease mission and its processes. I learned that Lend-Lease received requisitions from the various nations, decided which to approve, and allocated the funds needed to get the requisitions filled. Lend-Lease took no active part in placing contracts to acquire goods and secure services such as transportation, for example. Those functions were carried out by regular agencies and departments (such as the Army, Navy, Treasury, Agriculture, and so on), which were experienced in buying goods and services. This organization plan enabled Lend-Lease to operate with a small staff but demanded close cooperation with other agencies.

Executive Reports

I immediately dug into the workings of the Statistical Section. I found that during the creation of Lend-Lease, two systems of reporting needed to be designed. One was to track what happened to the money that Lend-Lease allocated to the various agencies. That system was designed by experts from the Treasury Department and the Bureau of the Budget, who made it compatible with the systems prevailing in the government generally.

The second system of reporting related to the goods and services bought with Lend-Lease money. In this case, there was no design at the outset by experts; instead, Lend-Lease was left to work it out on its own. None of the top executives in Lend-Lease had expertise in designing reporting systems, so by default the designing was done by the lower-level supervisors. To them, the goal was to provide the information needed for the quarterly reports to Congress. (The Lend-Lease Act required the president to make quarterly reports to Congress on the progress of the program.)

The reports mandated in the Lend-Lease Act, while necessary, were not sufficient; it was also necessary to provide executive reports— reports that could help the Lend-Lease executives run the agency on a week-to-week basis. This latter need had already been identified by Stettinius, and he asked Thomas B. McCabe, his deputy, to arrange for preparation of weekly reports on the export of significant products, along with up-to-date figures on the status of funds. This work had not yet begun at the time I arrived on the scene.

On January 14, 1942, I presented a proposal to McCabe. I identified two needs, as follows:

1. **A depository of information for long-range usage.** This relates to information ... that will determine who owes whom how much. Because such a determination will probably be made years from now, the current urgency is almost nil, and the current problem is primarily a matter of completeness and identification of papers so that the story can be unraveled at a future date.

2. **A source of current information for present action and control.** In the case of this problem, the long-range usage is com-

The Lend-Lease senior staff, about 1942

paratively limited, whereas the immediate usage is of the greatest importance and requires setting up for very prompt reporting of what is happening.

In addition I spelled out the details of those current needs and how I proposed to deal with them. McCabe responded positively to my "very intelligent memorandum."

I then made short work of designing and installing the system of executive reports. The result was satisfactory to McCabe. I also reached agreement with the various government agencies for receiving the information needed to serve as a database for the executive reports. I drafted formal letters to the heads of the agencies involved, describing the proposed changes and asking for their approval. McCabe signed the letters, and the agency heads replied with their approvals.

In for the Duration

On March 21, 1942, Lend-Lease appointed me Assistant Administrator in charge of the Reports and Records Division. As far as I was concerned, I was now in the war for the duration, and that is what actually happened. I had been placed on the government payroll effective January 15, 1942. Each year, Lend-Lease asked Western Electric to extend my leave of absence, and each year the company did so.

Government Inefficiency

During the creation of the executive reports, I also dug into the entire system of data collection and analysis—a system that threaded its way through numerous areas of Lend-Lease as well as other agencies. I was dismayed by the extensive duplication and the useless work that I found in the system. In my role of Assistant Administrator, I presided over the entire Reports and Records Division, so I wielded much authority over the procedures. The Division included several procedures analysts; I asked them to study the existing procedures and recommend changes. They came up with numerous proposals, and I approved most of them. By mid-April 1942, the new executive reports were already emerging. As a result, personnel in the Statistics Section shrunk from 65 to 35 employees.

The personnel reductions created some apprehensions in the Statistics Section. I examined the figures and found that no one had become unemployed. A massive manpower shortage was building up in Washington, and it was easy to transfer people into other government agencies. No one had suffered a loss in grade, while about a fourth had found higher-grade jobs.

I received expressions of confidence from the employees and upper levels. A memo from McCabe included the observation, "I think you are doing an excellent job and want you to know that I appreciate it."

Oscar Cox, the Lend-Lease General Counsel, went out of his way to write to McCabe as follows:

> If you have not already done so, you ought to read Juran's memorandum of April 15th to Philip Young (McCabe's assistant). The approach used and the results obtained in reorganizing the Statistics Section ought to be a model for the

Government. And the memorandum is one of the best gotten up and most lucid jobs I have seen in many a day.

Beyond such comments from the very top officials of Lend-Lease, there was one from the Bureau of the Budget, the government's management watchdog. The Budget Bureau was conducting surveys of management practices in the various war agencies, including Lend-Lease. They made their report to McCabe, who then reported their findings at one of the Lend-Lease senior staff meetings (at which I was a regular attendee). One of McCabe's comments was, "They feel Joe Juran is doing one of the best jobs in Washington."

All in all, I had reason to conclude that I was on the right track, that I was helping the war effort. In addition, I felt that I was being accepted into a world that I had never known until a few short months before. So it seemed.

My appointment to Assistant Administrator enlarged and changed my responsibilities dramatically. At the work level, I now supervised additional sections: Requisitions, Accounts, and Control. Together with the Statistics Section, these sections added up to about a third of the Lend-Lease employee body, and they interacted closely with outside agencies as well as with other areas of Lend-Lease. The new job also catapulted me into the upper reaches of Lend-Lease, where I participated in high-level decisions.

The Budgetary Process

One of my chief new assignments was to preside over the preparation of the Lend-Lease budget. Securing an appropriation requires preparation of a budget request, followed by hearings before the cognizant committees of Congress.

The Lend-Lease budget requests came to many billions of dollars annually. There were about thirty Lend-Lease nations; their requests extended over numerous appropriation categories: ordnance, aircraft, tanks, other vehicles, production facilities, agricultural commodities, repair of ships, and so on. In turn, these involved hundreds of subcategories—product and service codes.

To coordinate preparation of the budget request, there existed an informal committee of members from each major organizational unit of Lend-Lease; I served as chairman. The overall preparation process took about three calendar months, and the final weeks were hectic, demanding long hours from many participants, including some of the senior managers.

The resulting budget request was then reviewed by Oscar Cox and by Stettinius. Next came hearings with the Bureau of the Budget to secure their approval, after which a letter was prepared for the President, recommending submission to the congress. Finally came the Congressional hearings.

Congressional Budget Hearings

During the life of Lend-Lease, the Democrats held majorities in both houses of Congress. These majorities had been overwhelming during the presidential elections of 1932 and 1936. By 1940 they had narrowed, enabling the Republicans to become more aggressive with their questions and challenges, as well as with proposals for restrictive amendments.

Stettinius took the Congressional hearings seriously despite the time they ate up. Hearings typically took anywhere from a few days to more than two weeks, since the Congressional committees called in the buying agency heads as well as the Lend-Lease officials. Stettinius went even further; he attended the final floor debates, sitting in the gallery, where his white hair and dark eyebrows readily identified him.

At scheduled hearings, Stettinius always took several aides with him; these invariably included Cox and me. He went to great lengths to arm himself and had us prepare for him a well-organized book that could give him prompt access to information he might need during the hearings. He set up briefing sessions during which several of us would raise questions that might arise during the hearings. We even supplied Clarence Cannon (chairman of the Appropriations Committee) with a few prepared questions on controversial matters, in order to put those questions into friendly hands.

The Paperwork Gridlock

Early in 1942, we ran into two serious problems in getting Lend-Lease exports to their destinations in Great Britain and Russia. We were losing ships (plus their crews and cargo) to German U-boats at a shocking rate. Solution of this problem required military action. We also had an extensive paperwork gridlock. Goods could not be shipped out because of paperwork snags, such as goods arriving at port without essential documents, errors in the documents, and so on.

The latter problem was severe enough to be mentioned at one of the president's cabinet meetings. Mr. Roosevelt asked Morgenthau, the Secretary of the Treasury, and McCabe, the Acting Lend-Lease Administrator, to look into it and see what they could do. Their conclusion was to assign the problem to an interagency committee. McCabe then asked me to organize and chair such a committee. I contacted the relevant agencies and ended up with a committee consisting of representatives from ten agencies. It became known as the Committee on Lend-Lease Export Procedures.

The committee met regularly for the next few months. At each meeting, we reviewed the progress made since the previous meeting, decided what to do next, and assigned responsibility for getting the action items done. We brought in nonmembers as needed, including officials from the British and Russian governments.

It was fascinating to see how the committee rose to the occasion. Each member knew very well what went on in his agency, but no one understood the overall picture—the entire flow of documents from the time a shipment left the factory until it arrived at its destination abroad. We had to find a way to enable each member to understand the complete picture. To this end, I came up with the diagram shown in Figure 17-1.

In the diagram, each horizontal row shows one of the eighteen principal documents then in use. They include the shipping report, receiving report, packing list, invoice, bill of lading, and so on. Each vertical column shows one of the forty-one items of information carried by the documents. These items include the Lend-Lease requisition number, description of goods, gross weight, cubic volume, and so on.

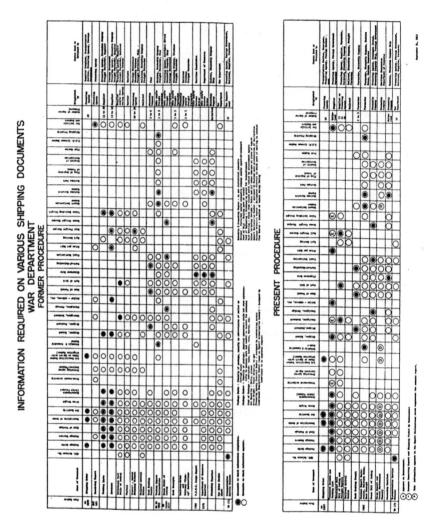

Figure 17-1. Documents relative to Lend-Lease exports

Some of the intersections of rows and columns contain coded circles; each circle means that the designated item of information appears on that document. A black circle means that the item of information originated on that document. A hollow circle means that the item of information was copied from another document.

The diagram made clear that some documents were virtually identical with others; a huge amount of copying was going on—an obvious source of errors.

The committee recommended reducing the number of documents from eighteen to nine. This was to be done by combining certain documents that were almost identical, using extra copies of basic documents to become equivalent to new documents through endorsement of additional information items, and designing some documents so that they registered with each other and therefore could be duplicated in one setup of a machine.

The recommendations were put into effect by the War Department, which in those days included the Air Force. The other buying agencies adopted the recommendations only partially. The committee's final report (October 1942) concluded that the net result had been the following:

- Reduction in the number of times that something had to be typed;
- Greater accuracy because papers duplicated in one setup are bound to be alike whereas recopying breeds mistakes;
- Greater ease of association of papers, because there are less papers to associate;
- Less delay because papers do not need to halt to be recopied;
- A very sizeable reduction in man-hours of effort required generally.

Stettinius sent copies of the committee report to the heads of many agencies—those who had been represented on the committee as well as others who were affected by the findings. We were surprised and gratified by their responses. A few sent routine thank-you letters, but most went beyond this; they expressed appreciation for the job done and offered an update on the actions they were taking (or not taking) and why.

I was impressed by the extent to which the buying agencies adopted the committee's proposals. There certainly was cultural resistance; any employee whose job grade depends in part on preparing or approving some document will fiercely resist a proposal to eliminate that document. In addition, the buying agencies were highly independent; each had an autonomy derived from the U. S. Constitution

or through presidential fiat. Nevertheless, cultural resistance gave way
to the force of patriotism; the agencies were reluctant to resist proposals aimed at helping the war effort.

Other Special Assignments

Beyond chairing the paperwork gridlock committee, I received other
special assignments. These included the following:

Cargoes, Inc. This government corporation was organized as a subsidiary of Lend-Lease. Its chief mission was to build a ship (to be called
"Seamobile") to test out the concept of relieving the shortage of large
marine engines by using multiple small engines, for which there was
underemployed manufacturing capability. That concept, advocated by
a commander in the Navy, had been resisted by the Bureau of Ships.
The dispute was leaked to the press, who blew it up to absurd proportions. It came to the attention of President Roosevelt, who then
bypassed the Navy by assigning the job to Lend-Lease.

I was appointed secretary-treasurer of Cargoes and a member of
its board of directors. With the president following its progress,
Seamobile was built in short order. It did not meet the hopes of the
advocates. The small engines still needed scarce materials and competed directly with large engines for essential components.

Cargoes also explored the concept of using helicopters to help
protect cargo ships against attack from submarines. One helicopter was
built and turned over to the Coast Guard, but it never saw service.
Meanwhile, the escort program for convoys became operational and
quite effective.

Interdepartmental Valuation Committee. In September 1942, the
heads of seven government agencies created an Interdepartmental
Valuation Committee for the purpose of "considering problems of valuation and revaluation of goods, information and services given or
received under the Lend-Lease Act." I was appointed chairman. The
committee met four times and published its final report on October 29,
1942. In retrospect, the committee did an excellent job of analyzing the
problems of valuation. Its recommendations have stood the test of time.

The Dutch Liquidation Project. I also became involved with what came to be known as "The Dutch Liquidation Project." Before the Dutch were drawn into World War II, they had placed contracts in the United States for manufacture of military goods—tanks, ammunition, and so on. After Holland was overrun, along with the Dutch East Indies, the Dutch wanted to liquidate the contracts and asked the U.S. government to help out. The job was assigned to Lend-Lease, and I was appointed to be the Lend-Lease liaison man. There were many contracts, so it became a drawn-out affair, including a gritty arbitration that exposed me to the seamy side of dealings with arms merchants.

Managing the Reports and Records Division

By March of 1942, the end was in sight for setting up the executive reports, so I began to tackle the job of managing the Reports and Records Division. The work on executive reports had already made me familiar with the Statistics Section—enough so to enable me to improve its operations as a result. Now I could examine the three other sections: Accounts, Budget, and Control.

I concentrated on the Control Section. It had been created during the early days of Lend-Lease, when confusion reigned. For every requisition, it maintained a log of its progress through the procedural steps. The logs then provided a central source of information about the status of each requisition. During the era when confusion reigned, this information was an aid to the Lend-Lease personnel.

During April 1942, a review of the operations of the Control Section found that requisitions now cleared the procedural steps within twenty-four hours instead of the weeks formerly required. The review also found that, with minor exceptions, what the Control Section did was duplicated in the Statistics Section. The procedures analysts recommended abolishing the Control Section, subject to transferring to the Statistics Section any essential unduplicated work. I reviewed the analysis closely and agreed with the recommendations.

Mrs. Castle, the head of the Control Section, did not agree, and she put up vigorous resistance when I told her of my plan to eliminate the duplication by abolishing her section. My explanation of the merits did not convince her, but I was simply unwilling to let the duplications go on. Finally, I decided to eliminate the section despite her protests.

As matters turned out, Mrs. Castle had the last word. She went over my head to Philip Young, the recently appointed Deputy Administrator. He then asked two Lend-Lease officials to "... make a survey and report on existing statistical and accounting reports, records, procedures, etc. giving reasons for their existence..." He also asked me to continue the Control Section until the study was completed.

In due course, the "survey" was completed and a report was issued (by only one of the appointees). I found it easy to demolish the report; it was loaded with factual mistakes and erroneous conclusions. There followed a dead silence, during which I thought I had seen the end of being investigated. I was mistaken; the worst was yet to come. Young asked Harry M. Kurth, a career government manager borrowed from the U.S. Treasury Department, to "determine the adequacy and accuracy of the fiscal and statistical records of the Lend-Lease Administration."

The Kurth Survey

Kurth was a career public servant who had been immersed in the government's fiscal system for years. He took the time to do a thorough job—his report was issued five months after he was appointed. He dug into the history of Lend-Lease in order to uncover the trend of events. He conducted numerous interviews in depth with agency managers as well as within Lend-Lease.

With respect to fiscal matters, Kurth concluded that there were numerous inaccuracies and that many of these were traceable to lack of standardized practice among the buying agencies. He recommended that Lend-Lease prescribe the procedures to be followed by the agencies, and then it should formalize the procedures into manuals of practice. Even though he was aware of the difficulties involved, he felt that they should be tackled nonetheless. He reported that the agencies were "anxious and willing to follow Lend-Lease's lead."

I was impressed by this part of Kurth's informative report, especially because some of his factual findings were new to me. It turned out that our goals were the same; both of us wanted accurate accounting. We differed, however, on where to strike the balance between the degree of accuracy needed and the effort required to attain it. Like Kurth, I had found agency *accountants* to be "anxious and willing," but it was otherwise with agency *operating managers,* especially those in the Army and Navy. In the latter agencies, there arose practical situations that demanded "action now," resulting in a spirit of "can do" that ran roughshod over the government accounting manuals.

There were limitations on accuracy. Goods bought with Lend-Lease funds did not necessarily get shipped to Lend-Lease countries; "Material Assignment Boards" decided where finished goods should go in order to be of maximum aid to the war effort. Some limitations were because of unforeseen developments: ship sinkings, aircraft "fly-aways," and retransfers. Others were due to price estimates that differed from the subsequent contract figures. Still others were caused by statistical quirks.

On one occasion, I saw that exports for an entire category of goods exceeded the amount produced. Without a miraculous pitcher, this seemed impossible. The reason turned out to be a delay in processing the production data; the goods had moved faster than the agency's data processing.

Generally the accuracy of the accounts was adequate for decision-making purposes but not enough to keep the books balanced. All in all, I thought that Kurth was applying peacetime thinking to the turbulent conditions prevailing during wartime. However, he was aware of the problems to be faced in achieving complete accuracy.

Kurth's conclusions on statistical operations were far more damaging. He reported that the Lend-Lease officials were "dissatisfied and frustrated" because they were not being supplied with adequate reports. My division had shown little initiative in anticipating the needs of the Lend-Lease officials; my division had given high priority to reducing duplication while giving low priority to determining and meeting its customers' needs.

These were fair and important conclusions, but I was taken aback. My chief reaction was, "That should have been obvious."

I saw no point to airing my differences with Kurth. Instead, I promptly advised Stettinius that I agreed with Kurth's report, including his plan of reorganization to make his recommendations effective. Then the ax fell. I was relieved of the job of supervising the Reports and Records Division. I retained the title of Assistant Administrator and the job of preparing the Lend-Lease appropriation requests. I also retained the job of Secretary-Treasurer of Cargoes, Inc., plus some other duties.

Lessons Learned

I was shaken by that dizzying series of events, but in contrast to what had happened at Western Electric, I didn't look for someone to blame. Neither was I embittered; Kurth's report convinced me that my downfall was my own doing. What was not clear to me was just how it had happened. What had I done, or failed to do, to bring it about?

Fifty-five years later, while writing these memoirs, I looked back, trying to understand the reasons behind those events. I concluded the following:

- My work had earned praise from senior executives—McCabe and Cox—men whom I respected.
- I did not go out and listen to my broader array of customers, so I was unaware of the prevailing "dissatisfaction and frustration." I may even have known about some of it but elected to ignore it.
- I lacked expertise in government fiscal policies and procedures. (I probably assumed that I could handle all problems through logical reasoning.) I should have brought in someone like Kurth to conduct a survey and offer recommendations!
- I failed to develop a firm rapport with Phil Young once he was named Deputy Administrator.
- I failed to grasp *the crucial difference in emphasis when moving from an industrial culture to a government culture.* In our industrial culture, cost reduction is one of the higher priorities and is reflect-

ed in the managers' reward system. When I joined Lend-Lease, that industrial emphasis was part of my baggage. I did a creditable job of reducing government costs, but while doing so I underemphasized the needs of my customers. Kurth's report glossed over the former but emphasized the latter. Under the prevailing culture, Kurth was dead right.

I also reached another conclusion soon after that setback. I had looked for commonalities between what took place at Western Electric and at Lend-Lease. Each of their parent organizations—AT&T and the U.S. government—was a huge bureaucracy. As a manager in each, I should have worked in harmony with other managers, but my formative years had shaped me into a loner. My conclusion was that I didn't belong in a large organization—that I simply was too individualistic. (The idea of transforming myself into a team player didn't occur to me.)

Regrouping

As I collected my wits, I realized I had gone through a sobering experience. Despite my unchanged title, the people in Lend-Lease and in the other agencies soon learned that I had lost status and thereby, influence. Nothing was said; Washington was unemotional about such matters. It wasted no time on losers; it focused its attention on rising stars.

I was fed up with being investigated, but I was not fed up with contributing to the war effort. That flame never lost its intensity. Uppermost on my mind was the fact that in 1943, the war was going badly. We were all in peril—the country, our way of life, my family. I wanted to remain where I could best help to win the war, and I knew well that Lend-Lease was vital to our allies and ourselves. So, despite concluding that I didn't belong in a large organization, I elected to remain in the government for the duration.

Foreign Economic Administration

In September 1943, Stettinius was appointed to the post of Undersecretary of State—the number-two post in the State

Department. Within days, Lend-Lease was folded into the newly created Foreign Economic Administration (FEA). The components of FEA were all war-related; in addition, all were relevant to economic matters. Beyond Lend-Lease they included the Office of Economic Warfare plus units plucked out of several other government agencies.

Leo T. Crowley, a former public utility executive, was appointed Administrator of FEA, and Oscar Cox became one of his Deputy Administrators. I was appointed Special Assistant to Crowley and retained all of my previous duties (coordinating preparation of the Lend-Lease appropriation requests; secretary-treasurer of Cargoes; Inc.; the Dutch Liquidation Project). In addition I was given the job of "ascertaining and determining the necessity for the personnel employed by all of the procuring and service agencies which are financed from Lend-Lease and FEA appropriations."

I took easily to Crowley. He was an experienced manager, capable and decisive. He had never gone through an appropriation request cycle, and he had an amused contempt for the mass of figures I brought to him. "Joe, that's just a lot of statistical trash," he said. "We've got the votes." We did have the votes, but that was of no help to him when he was testifying before the House Appropriations Committee. He lacked answers to many of the questions and appreciated my intervening to help out.

Beyond our working together on the appropriation requests, I had little occasion to see Crowley. Instead, he asked me to work through his other deputy, Henry W. Riley. Riley was a pleasant, courteous southerner but he had loose hands on the reins. As a result, my time in FEA was virtually without supervision.

I took seriously my new duties of "ascertaining and determining the necessity for the personnel." I reviewed the managerial processes of FEA and the buying agencies and made field visits to seven contractors to look at agency procedures for expediting and inspection. Such reviews yielded little in the way of specifics; I lacked the staff to go into the sort of detail needed to produce the improvements similar to those made at Lend-Lease during early 1942. In the FEA, my recommendations went mostly unheeded.

I also teamed up with several managers in the FEA to create the Management Round Table (MRT). Together we identified fifty-two potential improvement projects and then prioritized them, after which the MRT followed and stimulated progress. The concept of an MRT turned out to be useful. Membership and attendance were voluntary and informal. The MRT provided a forum in which the interested managers could get to know each other and discuss issues without becoming overheated.

Exodus

The departure of Stettinius from Lend-Lease plus the creation of the FEA were examples of many changes that took place during World War II, but their effect on the senior managers of Lend-Lease was profound. A gradual exodus set in and then speeded up as the war neared its end. Some managers had no interest in a government career; they looked forward to returning to their former fields. Government careerists planned to stay on, but they saw little future in the war agencies; their future would lie with peacetime agencies. Still another reason for the exodus was the change in the leadership. Stettinius's personality had attracted an uncommon loyalty that supported a teamwork approach. To some, the remoteness of Crowley and Riley left teamwork to be initiated by the lower levels.

External Activities

Being relieved of the job of managing the Reports and Records Division brought me one welcome byproduct—a reduced workload. My overtime hours shrank dramatically, leaving me more time to spend with the family and to pursue activities outside of my official duties. My energy level remained high, and soon I became active in other fields, especially those involved with improving management in government.

To me, the need for improvement seemed obvious and important. Labor shortages had emerged. During the war, there were social upheavals to meet those shortages; huge numbers of jobs opened up for women and minorities. My views also may have been somewhat self-serving. Long experience in an industrial culture had taught me to hate waste, and I had developed skills for dealing with it.

Better Management in Wartime Government

SAM had a chapter in Washington. I became active in that chapter and was made welcome. During one of our planning meetings, we agreed it would be appropriate to hold a conference called "Better Management in Wartime Government." They asked me to be general chairman, and I agreed.

The conference was a two-day affair and was held in August 1942. It required recruitment of numerous speakers, which turned out to be surprisingly easy; the town teemed with agency heads and other luminaries, many of whom were willing to serve as speakers or panelists. The SAM volunteers did a masterful job of recruiting speakers, as well as solving the numerous logistical problems.

The conference was well attended (there were about 250 registrants) and was well received by participants and by the press. As a result, SAM organized a follow-up conference, which was then held in April 1943.

Despite the seeming success of such conferences, they provided no lasting stimulus for improvement. This had also been the case for the various blue ribbon commissions created periodically to come up with recommendations for improving management in government. The commission members were capable, and their proposals had merit, yet there were few enduring effects. The cultural resistance was massive while the proposed machinery for execution was inadequate.

In the export-paperwork gridlock case, we found that during wartime, cultural resistance gave way to the force of patriotism; no agency wanted to block proposals aimed at helping the war effort. To improve government in peacetime requires finding the peacetime equivalent of patriotism. As yet, no such solution has emerged.

An Initiative to Raise Government Salaries

Before joining the government, my views of civil servants were similar to those widely held by industrial managers—civil servants are an indolent lot; they are unable to qualify for jobs in industry, so they resort to feeding at the public trough. Once in the government, I soon acquired a more enlightened view of its roles. I discovered that civil servants were quite as capable as their industrial counterparts. I learned that in the top-level grades, civil servants held responsibilities paralleling those of senior executives in industry.

I also learned about the salary scales in government. For lower-level grades, government salaries were competitive with those in industry; at upper levels, however, government salaries were much lower than those in industry. That difference worried me. I felt that the United States, in its new role as an emerging economic superpower, should be managed by people of the highest capability, and that this would not happen under existing salary scales. During the war the government did recruit capable industrialists, but that was possible because of patriotic fervor. I feared that once the war was over, industrialists who had joined for the duration would return to industry, and some or many capable career civil servants would be tempted to transfer to industry.

By early 1944, I concluded that government salaries for the top-level jobs should be raised to narrow the gap. I then undertook a one-man initiative to get this done. I began by contacting influential people in key agencies, such as the Bureau of the Budget and the Civil Service Commission, as well as my friends in Lend-Lease. All agreed on the need to raise government salaries for the top jobs. They also agreed that the chief obstacle would be getting Congress to pass the necessary legislation. They pointed out that Congress would be unwilling to raise executives' salaries beyond the $10,000 then prevailing for Congressmen. Hence, any revision would have to include raising Congressional salaries as well. Those comments led me to discussions with Representative Robert Ramspeck, Chairman of the House Civil Service Committee.

Ramspeck pointed out that during the 1930s and 1940s, a Congressman's workload had grown from a part-time job to an overtime job, with the need for two residences and with new problems of keeping a business going at home. Moreover, Congressional salaries had remained static for a long time. (It was now 1944; the last change had been in 1917, when Congressional salaries were raised from $7,500 to $10,000.) Many Congressmen were afraid to raise their own salaries; $10,000 looked like a generous salary to most of their constituents. There was fear of repetition of a public outcry of "Bundles for Congress," which had killed an earlier effort to raise Congressional salaries.

From all such discussions, there emerged a set of criteria to be met by a successful initiative: the perceived initiative would have to come from outside the government to avoid the appearance of self-seeking; the specific recommendations would have to come from a committee of prestigious, impartial people, none of whom would currently be government employees; and the proposed increases would have to apply to all three branches of government—executive, legislative, and judicial.

I dutifully drafted proposals that met the criteria and circulated them. In due course, those proposals were accepted by each of the key organizations: Bureau of the Budget, Civil Service Commission, House Civil Service Committee, and Senate Civil Service Committee. It remained to get the proposal cleared by the White House, and there I ran into an impasse. I had previously discussed the matter with one of the president's "anonymous six" assistants, and he seemed sympathetic. Later, when I tried to follow up, he failed to return my calls—I was brushed off.

Matters did not end there, however. Some influential industrialists had taken an interest in the initiative, and they kept it alive. One was William V. Griffin, an assistant to Stettinius and an important industrialist—he served on the boards of some prestigious companies, including Time, Inc. On June 26, 1945, Griffin wrote to Eric A. Johnston, president of the U. S. Chamber of Commerce, urging him to propose "that the President set up a committee to make a survey of the Government pay rates and that the committee consist of the following . . . ." (Griffin's list was taken verbatim from one of my drafts.)

By the end of 1945, I was out of the government and busy with other matters, so I no longer pursued the government salary initiative.

Then, in December 1948, I noticed in the press that Senator Flanders of Vermont, a member of the Civil Service Committee, was active on the same initiative. I wrote to him, summarizing my adventures in the subject and concluding, "Looking back, I would say that considering my amateur standing, I went quite a ways before I was stuck."

Senator Flanders replied with gratifying news:

> That is a most interesting experience which you have detailed in your letter of.... You will be glad to know that the under-taking now has full White House support and the President has already begun to put pressure on the leaders of the Senate and, I presume, of the House also. It will probably be best at this state to go on with the straight salary proposed rather than following your earlier and well thought-out project.

Managing for Quality

Throughout the war I maintained contact with the field of managing for quality but only as an observer. I thought it quite possible that at the end of the war, on my return to Western Electric, I would be assigned to a quality-related job.

As it happened, the War Production Board (WPB) set up a special department to help improve the quality of war production. I welcomed that initiative; I was aware that we were having some serious quality problems on the war front. Early in the war, Japanese Zeroes outperformed our fighter planes; our naval torpedoes were ineffective in a shocking percentage of firings.

The WPB assigned two professors of statistics to head the new department. The professors decided to carry out their mission by training government contractors in how to use the tools of Statistical Quality Control (SQC)—the same tools that had been developed fifteen years earlier by the Bell Labs-Western Electric initiative in which I had participated as a young engineer.

The WPB training courses were created with the aid of experts such as Professor Eugene L. Grant of Stanford University and Dr. W. Edwards Deming of the Bureau of the Census. The courses ran for eight days and were offered, tuition free, to government contractors. They were held in many locations and were well attended. The focus was, first, on improving inspection by use of scientific sampling, and, second, improving process control by detecting significant process changes through use of the Shewhart control chart.

The WPB courses had little effect on the course of the war, but there were some influential and enduring outcomes: the emergence of a new job category—quality control engineer; the emergence of quality control departments and quality control managers to preside over quality control engineering and also over inspection departments; and the creation of local quality control societies, which then merged in 1946 to create the American Society for Quality Control (ASQC), later renamed the American Society for Quality (ASQ).

In Retrospect

As mentioned before, once I was relieved of managing the Reports and Records Division, I could meet my job responsibilities within standard hours (except during the hectic weeks of budget preparation). The remaining time was then available for the family and for external activities. (Sadly, the latter was too often done at the expense of the former.)

Activities outside my job duties enlarged my status outside the government. My willingness to serve on committees and to prepare papers generated invitations from professional societies. I was also in demand because I had experience both in industry and government. My status on the outside grew, as it had begun to even while I was still at Western Electric.

The most subtle effect of those external activities was the deep satisfaction I derived from contributing to *pro bono* activities. Serving professional societies was inherently a *service to society* and was done voluntarily, without any financial reward. Over the decades, the concept of service to society has risen on my priorities list until, by the 1980s, it was among the very highest of my goals.

My four years as a government official were also an intense learning and broadening experience. From my narrow outlook as a middle manager in a manufacturing company, I was catapulted into the world arena while a savage war was raging, with the lives of tens of millions at stake. I was exposed to men from widely different backgrounds and with widely different viewpoints. I had access to highly classified information. I participated in decisions involving matters of substantial importance. Anyone exposed to such a spectrum of experience was bound to emerge with a greatly enlarged outlook on world events.

Despite my failings, I contributed usefully to the Lend-Lease mission and to its reputation as a well-run government agency. In addition, my external activities were appreciated by the advocates for excellence in managing the government. I emerged from Washington as a more worldly person. That increased breadth, acquired in a few short years, would serve me well for decades to come.

Bibliography

Working, Holbrook, "Statistical Quality Control in War Production." *Journal of the American Statistical Association,* 1945, pp. 425–447.

Q

Part Three

Teaching Quality to America and the World

18

After the War: Starting a New Career at Age 40

By the end of 1943, civilians had done their job of putting the country on a war footing. Industry was now solidly yoked to the war machine. Huge areas of production capacity had been shifted from civilian goods to armaments and other military needs. The resulting torrent was rushing to the combat zones and the staging areas in Britain. Our civilians were enduring shortages but were also building up a massive backlog of purchasing power. The civilian economy was in a holding pattern; now it was up to the soldiers to fight it out.

Fight it out they did. The year 1944 brought a succession of joyful events—joyful despite the fact that each was drenched in blood and choked with suffering. On the eastern front, the siege of Leningrad was lifted while Russian armies continued their march westward, liberating more and more of their country. In the Pacific, American naval and ground forces made giant strides, recapturing island groups as they advanced toward Japan.

The long-awaited D-Day invasion of Normandy took place on June 6, 1944. We held our breath as a beachhead was secured. From there, the Allied armies burst out across Europe amid intense resistance. Country after country was liberated even as London endured the new V-2 bombs. The Allied advance also uncovered the Nazi extermination camps—the undeniable evidence of the Holocaust. (The first photos of those grisly sights went far beyond the terrifying nightmares of my childhood in Gura Humora.) By the summer of 1944, the outcome of the war in Europe was hardly in doubt, and it became time for me to face the question, "After the war, what next?"

I was now forty years old, and for the first time in my life I planned my next move with thoroughness. I listed my needs, capabilities, and limitations (as I perceived them). I listed my options and the pros and cons of each. I then designed an action plan to test out the realities of each option.

Needs, Capabilities, Limitations

Supporting the family, while indispensable, was only one of a number of needs to be met. I also needed to provide security for them in the event I died or became disabled. My new activity had to be challenging and allow me to use one of my chief assets—my analytical capability. My work atmosphere should not expose me to undue irritations, such as the problems inherent in large bureaucracies. There should be opportunities for creativity through research, consulting, and writing. At Western Electric and during the war years, I had acquired a degree of public standing. The new activity should be able to make use of this.

I knew that despite my qualifications, I had twice come to a barricade that blocked future progress. Here my analysis was suspect. I lacked the objectivity needed to realize that I was part of the problem; my list of theories did not include my own conduct. Lacking this objectivity, my conclusion was rudimentary: "I am just too individualistic to fit into large organizations."

Options

As part of my planning for the future, I wrote out a list of my options, along with the pros and cons of each. Going through that exercise gave me perspective and helped me to evaluate the merits of the various options.

Returning to Western Electric was a return to a safe haven. I would remain a middle manager and would be able to provide comfortably for my family. I'd also be able to retire with a decent pension. However, I would be denied any further rise in the hierarchy. For me, that would mean a lack of job satisfaction. It would gnaw at me for the remainder of my career and beyond and would inevitably invade my home atmosphere.

I spent very little time on the option of remaining in the federal government. There I would be employed by a big bureaucracy but without the predictability provided by Western Electric. Once the war was over, wartime agencies were doomed to disappear. I would then have to scramble to remain at my grade. I had no well-placed political sponsor and no standing as a career public servant.

The most imaginative option was to become a "freelancer"—one who operates alone, without ties to any organized entity. My concept was to devote the rest of my life to the field of management—a field in which I already had good credentials. I would philosophize, research, write, lecture, consult—the works—all in the field of management. I thought it was a brilliant concept, aglow with visions of an exciting and rewarding life. It would follow the memorable lines of Robert Frost:

Two roads diverged in a wood, and I,
I took the one less traveled by.

The realities did not support those visions. Society did not recognize such a collection of activities to be a job for which it would pay enough to meet a family's needs. To be sure, once I earned a status of mastery in the field, I could have ample income from consulting fees, lecture fees, book royalties, and so on. It would take a few years at the least, however, to reach that state of perceived mastery. During that time, I would have to solve the problem of supporting my family.

By the end of 1944, my mind was made up—my goal was to be a freelancer in the field of management. While striving toward that goal, however, I would need to bridge a gap—to provide for my family. That need then became an interim goal that required its own planning.

Bridging the Gap

I needed a source of income that would also give me the flexibility to pursue all the activities of freelancing. I could philosophize and write at home; my Sadie was able and willing to provide the typing service. I also needed a conventional office for receiving visitors, telephone service, secretarial service, and the like.

There was more. Activities such as research and consulting can be voracious consumers of time. On some projects, they demand uninterrupted stretches of time. Clearly, there was a risk that bridging the income gap would emerge as a fatal obstacle toward my becoming a freelancer. Nevertheless, as I addressed the problem, several options came to mind, and I examined each of them.

I thought of taking employment in some organization that was doing research in management. An obvious example was the National Industrial Conference Board (NICB). (Its name is now The Conference Board.) One of its activities was conducting research into how companies managed when carrying out specific functions, such as relations with unions or inventory control. It would send a researcher to visit a few companies to learn how they carried out the function in question, what their results had been, and what the lessons learned might be for industry generally. Then it would publish the findings, deriving part of its income by selling the reports. I secured a date with the head of NICB to see whether there was any mutual interest. The interview went poorly; the man seemed to have his mind on other matters. That was unfortunate, since such a job would have enabled me to bridge the gap while doing research and writing about it.

Another option was to join a consulting company. Beyond conducting some consulting projects, I would learn how the consulting business is carried out. I explored the possibilities with three consulting companies. In each case I sent them copies of my first two books for their perusal prior to my interview.

I secured an interview with the head of Stevenson, Jordan, and Harrison, then one of the largest consulting companies. He liked my books, especially *Management of Inspection and Quality Control*. He also seemed to enjoy talking with me. But he told me bluntly that even at my existing salary level, I would not fit his business formula. He was really in the business of selling the services of his staff at a profit. At his "markup," my per diem rate fell outside of what he thought was the market range.

I also talked with some of the partners at Booz Allen Hamilton, especially Harold Smiddy. They were keenly interested in me and offered me a full-time job as Research Director with a starting salary of $15,000 a year. That could definitely "bridge the gap." We were close to a deal until I sat down with the partner who would become my immediate supervisor. He turned out to be a pompous, arrogant individual, enough so that I concluded then and there that I would be unable to put up with him. That was a pity, since, in other respects, it was a promising arrangement.

My third possibility of an alliance with a consulting company was with Wallace Clark. His was a small company with a high professional standing that was international in scope. Clark had been an associate of Henry L. Gantt, one of the very first pioneers in the field of industrial engineering. Clark's book, *The Gantt Chart*, was the leading work on scheduling of facilities.

Clark was definitely interested in an alliance. We agreed that after the war, I could take charge of some projects, on a per diem basis. He proposed a starting rate of $70 per day and I agreed to it. We had no written agreement; we trusted each other.

Yet another option was to form an alliance with some college department in the management field. I had met Professor David B. Porter of New York University's (NYU) College of Engineering while I was Corporate Industrial Engineer at Western Electric's headquarters. From Porter, I had learned a bit about life in an engineering college. I also learned that Dr. L. P. Alford, the head of NYU's Industrial Engineering department, would be retiring in a few years and that they were already looking for his replacement. I had also met Alford, and we likewise had talked about life in academia.

Those prewar contacts came to mind early in 1945 when I was facing the question of what to do after the war. By this time Alford was gone, and NYU had not as yet found a replacement. I contacted Porter, and he suggested that I meet with Thorndike Saville, the Dean of NYU's College of Engineering. I did meet with Saville in June 1945; our meetings quickly led to his offering me the post of Professor of Industrial Engineering and chairman of the department. By agreement, the appointment was to be for half-time during the 1945–1946 school year, and full-time thereafter. The full-time salary was to be $7,000. I was to assume my duties on September 1, 1945.

On the face of it, my deals with NYU and Wallace Clark would solve the problem of "bridging the gap." But would the realities meet the expectations? Clearly, there was a risk that they would not. Either or both of those deals might not work out. Even if they did, I might fail as a freelancer. What then?

My concerns were heightened by the reactions of a few friends to whom I confided that I might not return to Western Electric after the war. Without exception, they were stunned. To them it was unthinkable to walk away from the security of a good salary and a twenty-one-year equity in a generous pension plan. The offer from the Booz, Allen, and Hamilton consulting firm, with its handsome salary of $15,000 per year (which I had turned down), convinced me I had become much more marketable than I was aware. I concluded that if worst came to worst, I could reenter the job market and take care of the family through a conventional job.

Farewell to Government and Western Electric

I resigned from the government effective on August 15, 1945. Victory in Europe had been won, and the outcome in the Pacific was no longer in doubt. As it happened, the war in the Pacific ended one day before my resignation took effect; Japan's surrender came on August 14, 1945. I took deep satisfaction in having served the country "for the duration."

My letter of resignation from Western Electric went to W. F. Hosford, then Vice President of Manufacture, and was dated July 3, 1945. I agonized while writing that letter; it stirred deep emotions. I quote from it:

"You must understand that it is no trivial reason which has caused me to break a tenure of over twenty-one years with the Bell System. For most of that time there existed, between a big corporation and an immigrant boy, a relationship that, if it could be put into words, would be an eloquent testimonial to "The Land of Opportunity."

It is mainly because the road of opportunity has recently seemed for me to be approaching a barricade that I have concluded I should take another road. Why is there a barricade? It is all very complicated. Perhaps some day there will be fewer barricades and less wars. But the barricade did seem to be there, and that is why I have taken a new road.

All this in no way detracts from my unbounded admiration of the Bell System as a foremost example of enlightened Big Business. Neither does it detract from my very real fondness for the integrity and the capability of the men of the Bell System. The problem which confronted me has its roots in the dim past, long before there was any Bell System.

Launching a Canoe: a Revision of Goals

As it worked out, my detour into the government during World War II enabled me to look back at my experience at Western Electric with the benefit of detached reflection. My conclusion (for the wrong reason) was to leave the security of that sturdy ocean liner and instead launch a fragile canoe. It's small wonder that my friends were stunned.

That same conclusion required a revision of goals. Before 1941, my sequence of goals (some deliberately chosen, most instinctive) had consisted of the following:

- Help our immigrant family to survive.
- Secure a college education.
- Get a steady job at steady pay.
- Meet the needs of my growing family.
- Create a safe haven during the Great Depression.
- Climb the corporate ladder.
- Prepare my children for their future.
- Provide old-age security for Sadie and me.

World War II then injected a new goal that took top priority for the duration: help the country win World War II.

Then, as I pondered "what next," a totally new goal emerged: start over as a freelancer. That new goal destroyed the security I had acquired at Western Electric. If I succeeded as a freelancer, I would regain security and could carry my security around with me.

I was not yet aware that even if I met the totally new goal, still other goals would emerge and rise to the top of the priority list.

19

Academia

NYU's Engineering College was located at the University Heights campus in New York City's Bronx borough. The showplace building on the campus was the handsome, circular Gould library, designed by the famous architect Stanford White. In addition, the campus housed the Hall of Fame, where bronze busts of many famous Americans were arrayed in a serene setting. My department, Industrial Engineering, had its own little aging office building.

The Culture

I soon learned that the culture in academia was quite different from that prevailing in industry. The hierarchy in academia was professional in nature and consisted of four grades: professor, associate professor, assistant professor, and instructor. The top two grades had "tenure," a form of guaranteed lifelong employment. A tenured professor could not be terminated except for cause; others could be terminated by not renewing their appointment. Deans and assistant deans were faculty members whose duties at the moment were mainly administrative. Administrative duties were not tenured; if the men were relieved of such duties, they still retained their tenured professional status.

Salaries at NYU were, in my view, surprisingly low, although they applied only to the school year (about ten months). In contrast, pensions and other amenities were comparatively generous. Interestingly, teachers' pensions and insurance were portable! A professor transferring from one university to another carried these with him through an intermediary—TIAA-CREF, the Teachers Insurance and Annuity Association and the College Retirement Equities Fund. I thought this idea of portability merited adoption by industry.

The Faculty

The dean of the NYU Engineering College was Thorndike Saville. I respected his intelligence and professional dedication but not his personality. When I was engaged in recruiting additions to my staff, one of the candidates for a job of assistant professor was a personable young black engineer. I liked his credentials and promise, and I put him on the short list to be discussed with Saville. Once Saville learned that the man was black, that ended his candidacy. (In those days laws against discrimination had not yet been enacted.)

Very likely I gave Saville as many problems as he gave me. I became involved in external matters to a degree beyond that practiced by the other department heads. I behaved as though NYU was a way-station en route to something else (which was indeed the case). This behavior must have given discomfort to Saville—to him I was a prickly maverick. It would not surprise me if, at the end of our association, he concluded that he didn't like me.

I met frequently with the heads of other departments. They were generally a congenial lot, so the atmosphere was cordial. They were not in competition with each other for administrative posts, and each had a good deal of autonomy in professional matters. At the engineering college, as at most colleges, questions of policy, along with other matters of broad interest, were decided by vote of the assembled faculty.

Industrial Engineering (IE)

The IE department enjoyed the lowest status on the engineering campus. This low caste was based on the widespread assumption that the content of IE courses made the least demand on its students for depth in technology. Some of the other departments had open contempt for courses such as Time and Motion Study or Job Evaluation and Wage Incentives. The department was also widely regarded as a dumping ground for students who were incapable of making the grade in the high-caste "true" engineering departments.

The IE curriculum related chiefly to management of manufacturing companies. The choice of courses paralleled the functional activities of such companies. I taught courses chiefly in industrial management, quality control, and accounting. In this way the students could work on projects that simulated conditions they would meet on their jobs.

For the course in quality control, I used my book *Management of Inspection and Quality Control* as a text. The book made no provision for assigning projects to students, so I assigned projects they could carry out within their companies. A usual assignment was to evaluate the "process capability" (the inherent uniformity) of some manufacturing process used in the company.

A notable project was that by Anthony Oladko, a graduate student employed as a foreman by Johnson & Johnson, a giant manufacturer in the health-care field. Oladko's department made Band-aids, so he studied the process capability of the "calendering" machines in his department. His findings then led to quality improvements, substantial cost reductions, and a seminal published paper (Oladko 1949).[1]

In all courses, I gave the students a strong incentive to do a thorough job on their projects. I did so by giving the project reports one-third of the weight toward the course grade. Their response was gratifying. Some of their reports were masterpieces of analysis.

Relations with Students

My busyness included meeting with individual students, whether to resolve problems or for counseling purposes. Some of these meetings were memorable.

On one occasion I called in a neighborhood plumber to remedy a problem with my heating system. He did so, but then he refused payment. He explained that his son had been a student of mine who had visited me to secure counseling. "That visit changed his life." I was deeply moved, but I nevertheless insisted on paying the grateful father.

Probably the most memorable of such meetings was with Enrique Maso, a young Spanish engineer who wanted to enroll as a graduate student. When he came to see me, he was accompanied by an interpreter—his own English was as yet limited. My reaction was to defer enrolling him until his English was adequate. He was quite persuasive, however, so I enrolled him and gave him special treatment, such as oral examinations. In later years he became one of the leading industrialists in Spain, served as mayor of Barcelona, and distinguished himself in still other ways. Ours became an enduring friendship, and we found numerous occasions to visit, both in Europe and in the United States. He usually told others that when he was a student in America, I was like a father to him.

Executive Round Tables

Starting in 1946, I initiated a discussion seminar called the Executive Round Table. The aim was to bring managers from various industries together to discuss current problems in management. By the time I left NYU, twelve such seminars had been held, with the topics as follows:

1. Four were on the subject of quality control, with a focus on better quality at lower cost. I served as discussion leader;
2. Six were on "work simplification"—a broadening of the concept of productivity improvement. Professor David B. Porter served as discussion leader;
3. Three were on topics of special interest to upper managers. Peter Drucker and I served as discussion leaders.

The seminars were limited to fifteen participants and met one day a week for ten weeks. I also brought in, as guest leaders, experts in specific aspects of the subject matter.

The Executive Round Table did not survive my leaving NYU. The seminars demanded much of my time, and the economics were marginal. Moreover, Saville was skeptical of the entire concept; he was not convinced that it bore a close enough relationship to the subject of engineering.

Peter Drucker

I first encountered Peter Drucker through his early books: *The End of Economic Man*, *The Future of Industrial Man*, and *Concept of the Corporation*. I was much impressed by these and especially by Drucker's uncanny ability to identify and expound great truths that had been overlooked by the rest of us. The reader's reaction was, "That should have been obvious."

During the late 1940s, I became determined to meet him. He was then a professor at Bennington College in Vermont. I arranged to drop in on him while on the way to visit my son Don's summer camp. That visit was the beginning of a lifelong friendship based on mutual respect.

In the years that followed, Drucker emerged as one of the foremost thinkers in the management field. His books on the subject have been the most widely read; to this day he is in demand as a lecturer and consultant. He has no equal as an interpreter of the macroeconomy to senior managers.

Departure from NYU: Reflections

By the late 1940s, I had concluded that an engineering college was not the best base for a freelance consultant in the field of management. I gradually reduced my academic commitments; by 1951 there remained only a slender linkage as a part-time adjunct professor.

A major limitation within the school was the absence of a living laboratory. For the subject of management, such a laboratory exists only where living operations take place—factories, offices, warehouses, and so on. In contrast, my activities in the American Management Association (AMA) gave me easy access to many managers active in the field. Those managers provided me with management problems, some that they had solved and others that still defied solution. I preferred to spend my time amid those realities. My association with AMA brought me a long step closer to the goal of becoming a freelancer.

Note
Oladko, Anthony, "Developing a Calendergraph," *Rubber Age,* September 1949.

20

The Gillette Razor and Other Early Consulting Projects: 1945-1949

I began to do management consulting immediately upon leaving government service in August 1945. While still in government, I had formed an alliance with Wallace Clark, a management consultant I had met through the professional societies. I did my earliest consulting for Clark's clients.

Wallace Clark's Consulting Company

Clark was well qualified to do management consulting. After ten years with the Remington Typewriter Company, he became a staff engineer for H. L. Gantt, an early pioneer in "scientific management." Clark created his own company in 1920. His clients included government monopolies in Poland, Turkey, and Persia (now Iran). During World War II he was a consultant for the U.S. Army. His quiet ways and ethical conduct earned him an enviable reputation.

Clark's staff consisted of about a dozen engineers plus their clerical support. Clark's income came chiefly from selling the services of his engineers at three times the rate he paid them. His chief challenge was getting clients, whether by extending existing contracts or creating new ones. Clark's reputation brought him useful leads, some of which then yielded consulting contracts. Still, he also had to engage in marketing to create new leads. To this end, he prepared and sent out brochures explaining his services. He also resorted to sending engineers out to make "cold calls" on companies in the hope of arousing their interest.

The Alliance with Clark

My alliance with Clark gave me a valuable introduction to the management consulting business. During the life of the alliance, I provided consulting services to about ten of Clark's clients. I also did some marketing; I wrote brochures and made cold calls. (The yield from cold calls was shockingly low. Of thirty such calls I made, only five led to contracts.) Collectively, those activities gave me a good inkling of what a freelancer faces in securing clients and then doing the consulting work.

By early 1947, the alliance was under threat because of demands on my time. Beyond my duties at NYU, I was doing much writing, especially for my third book, *Quality Control Handbook*. I explained all this to Clark, and he was sympathetic; he remained willing to get whatever time I could spare him. He did, however, prepare a document covering his rights if I terminated the alliance, which I signed in April 1947.

Then came an unforeseen event—Clark passed away in July 1948, and his widow took over the management of the company. She had been active in the finances for years, but her expertise did not extend to operations. She soon became aware of her limitations and decided to sell the company. I completed the projects I had begun, but by early 1949, my alliance with the Clark Company had ended.

Learning about Consulting

Management consulting in the United States is largely a twentieth-century phenomenon. A leading pioneer was Frederick W. Taylor (1856–1915), founder of scientific management. His area of operation was the factory floor, and his chief analytical tool was time study. Taylor's early followers included Frank B. Gilbreth (1868–1924), who relied heavily on motion studies, and Henry L. Gantt (1861–1919), who focused on systems and on project management. (Gantt was Wallace Clark's mentor.)

The late 1940s witnessed an explosive growth in management consulting companies, as well as the emergence of several distinct organization forms for doing consulting work. One category was freelancers—lone specialists in some area of marketable expertise.

A second category comprised the small companies (like Wallace Clark's) that employed relatively few trained and experienced consultants who could serve clients with minimal supervision by the owner. A third category was large consulting companies. They also employed relatively few trained, experienced people—senior consultants and partners—but they employed a far greater number of juniors who did the labor-intensive work of data collection and analysis. Today some of these companies are huge, operate internationally, and employ thousands of people.

I gave much thought to these forms of consulting companies. My experience with bureaucracies had made me wary of involvement with large organizations. This wariness extended even to small organizations, but I regarded Wallace Clark's firm as an exception. My relationship with Clark was one of mutual respect and trust. For the long run, however, I did not want the status of either subordinate or boss; I wanted to be simply a *free*lancer.

In these memoirs I will describe only those consulting engagements that are of special interest: they produced stunning results for the clients, they demanded invention (or reinvention) of unique methods of analysis, or they required unique ways of dealing with cultural resistance.

The Gillette Company

Gillette was the world leader in shaving systems. It mass-produced razor blades and razors, the devices that held the blades in place and protected users from cuts (hence the name "safety razor"). Shaving with a safety razor was much safer than shaving with a large straight razor, and it was far more economical and convenient than getting shaved at a barbershop. Blades gradually became dull during use, however, forcing the users to discard them and buy new ones. These repeat sales were highly profitable; the blades were sold in huge numbers.

Razors were not profitable; they were deliberately sold at a price below cost. Gillette would gladly have given them away in order to secure the highly profitable blade business.

When I made a cold call on the South Boston factory, the manufacturing vice president, Howard Gambrill, conceded, "We have a quality problem." That was quite an understatement. Following my visit, Gillette entered into a consulting contract with Clark. The end results included extensive reductions in manufacturing costs of razors; revision of the company's "shave test," resulting in welcome breakthroughs; and a revolution in Gillette's approach to managing for quality.

My tour of the facilities for making razors supported Gambrill's comment. A shocking percentage of the production of razor components was defective and had to be scrapped or reworked. The processes clearly needed an evaluation of process capability. To do so would require much data collection and analysis. I proposed to Gambrill that he assign two engineers to the project—one for razors and one for blades. He was willing, but he didn't have the engineers. We ended up recruiting two engineers from the outside. One of them, Leonard Seder, was assigned to razors; the other, Douglas Benedict, was assigned to blades.

Gillette: Cost Reductions on Razors

Seder was a competent analyst. We met with the accountants and secured information on the extent of costs traceable to poor quality and where these costs were concentrated. We also met with the factory managers and identified the components that were the worst offenders. One of these—the inner tube—was the first to be selected for in-depth analysis. It turned out that the measuring tools were not adequate to control the process. When this was corrected, it became possible to discover the causes of the defects and provide remedies. The defect level on the inner tube then fell from about 10 percent to about 2 percent.

Another high-loss component was the cap; it was produced in a complex pressing operation. Seder collected data on the suspect variables: within a single cap, from cap to cap, from one hour to another, and so on. He ended up with an ingenious set of diagrams that enabled the press operators to discover from their gage measurements how to align the tools to produce good-quality caps (Seder 1950).

Hamilton Watch Company

Hamilton Watch Company, a Clark client, was a leading American maker of fine watches. My mission was to improve quality and reduce costs.

In those days (1946) a watch was an assembly of many tiny mechanical bits and pieces. There were numerous shafts and gearwheels, along with springs to supply energy, and mechanisms to regulate the measurement of time. After being shown the processes used to produce a watch, I decided to start by studying the process for making the tiny shafts. The shafts were turned out by precise lathes, after which each shaft was gaged for all dimensions. This detailed gaging was necessary because many of the shafts, typically about ten percent, were out of tolerance on one or more dimensions. Those defects resulted in a loss to the company consisting of the cost of scrapping the defective shafts plus the time inspectors spent in gaging those myriads of dimensions.

In dealing with such problems, I already knew that a fundamental question to be answered related to *process capability:* is the production process inherently capable of meeting the design tolerances? It is tempting in such cases to assume that the answer can be gotten from people at the work level—the product designer, the process engineer, the production supervisor, the production worker, the inspector. They should be asked; their opinions are useful, and they welcome being consulted. However the authoritative answer must come from the process itself—*we must ask the process.* That was the lesson I had learned twenty years earlier during my study of the "heat coil" in the Western Electric Company.

What we did was to station an engineer all day at one of the lathes, with instructions to capture each piece as it was made, and to preserve the order of manufacture. In addition the engineer was to keep a log of all the events that took place at that lathe. On subsequent days he was to measure each of the five dimensions of each piece—about 2500 measurements in all—using a precise gage. The results were then charted to produce Figure 20-1.

The disclosures of Figure 20-1 are numerous:

- The progressive "drift" in dimensions (due to wear of the tools) was very small. During the run of 500 pieces, the average diameter changed about 0.0001 inch—about a third of the narrowest tolerance range. This uniformity exceeded the expectations of most supervisors.
- The changes due to "restocking" were less than expected. (Restocking consists of inserting a fresh rod into the lathe after the preceding rod has been converted into watch shafts). Note the small effect at pieces number 55 and 493. The effect at piece number 271 is negligible.
- The operators' gages were inadequate to "steer" the machines. Note at piece number 140 how both short end diameters dropped suddenly (these diameters are controlled by a single tool holder). The explanation was that the operator had concluded from his gage that the parts were becoming oversized. He therefore made an adjustment and (unwittingly) began to produce defectives. At piece number 197, after a check by the patrol inspector, the operator restored the previous adjustment. At piece number 392 the operator was again misled by his gage.
- Measurement of the pivot-shoulder distance was highly variable during the first 50 parts. This was due to early unfamiliarity with the precise gage.

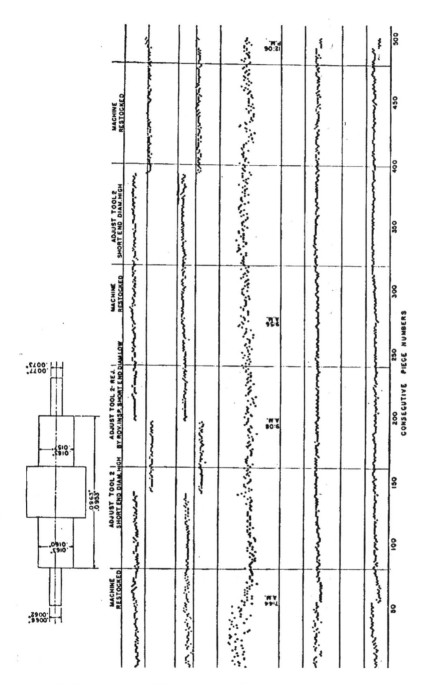

Figure 20-1. Process capability study for a lathe

From these and other disclosures, the supervisors concluded that: (1) the process capability was adequate for the job; (2) the operators' gages were inadequate for the job; (3) it was possible to make more pieces with less frequent checking and less frequent adjustment than before; (4) the costly detail gaging could be replaced by sampling; (5) a number of prior beliefs were unfounded.

By providing better gages and by periodic measurement at the machines, the company greatly reduced defect levels while increasing the volume of production. The associated gaging of every piece was replaced by sampling.

The cost savings made in the lathe department were far greater than the size of the consulting contract. Those same savings served to convince company skeptics that it was possible to simultaneously improve quality and reduce costs through use of modern ways of managing for quality. It then became easier to carry out additional studies and to secure additional improvements.

In addition, it was possible to train a few company engineers in how to analyze quality problems through such tools as evaluation of process capability. This was in keeping with Clark's way of enabling the client to carry on after the consulting engagement came to an end. Still another result was to broaden the outlook of company managers, and in some cases to influence their careers. Most notably, the young quality manager (A. B. Sinkler) later became president of Hamilton Watch Company.

"In connection with our Tech razor cap, Statistical Quality Control methods were able to cut the variability of the product in half, after *all* other methods had failed." (Marcy 1949).

Mechanics Universal Joint (MUJ)

Mechanics Universal Joint, a division of Borg-Warner, made automotive components. In this brief engagement I tackled and solved several long-standing problems of poor quality and the associated high costs. I also trained one of their engineers in how to conduct diagnosis in order to make them more self-sufficient in terms of quality improvement.

An example of MUJs problems was "dynamic unbalance" on torque tubes—the steel tubes used to transmit power from the engine to the wheels. Torque tubes were made in twenty-three different combinations of diameter and length, so as to respond to the power needs and other design features of the various models of vehicles. However, the ends of the tubes were all made to a single common diameter. (To do so, all the large diameter tubes underwent a "swaging" operation.) This operation enabled the company to standardize the sizes of fittings—universal joints, bearings, and others.

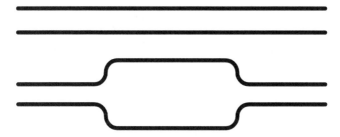

Figure 20-2. Swaged and unswaged torque tubes

Each completed torque tube was placed into a test device and rotated at high speed. A shocking percent of the tubes failed the test; they vibrated excessively. These rejects then went to a repair crew, which tried to beat the tubes into shape with hammers. There were many theories and debates about the cause of this long-standing problem, but no agreement could be reached. So the rejects and hammering continued.

One theory was that the swaging operation caused the dynamic unbalance. I discovered an easy way to test this theory. The inspectors had long kept records showing, for each type of torque tube, the percentage of tubes rejected for dynamic unbalance. I prepared a table listing the types of tubes in their order of percent defective, and showing which ones had undergone the swaging operation.

Figure 20-3 shows that the worst seven types of tubes all had been swaged, while of the best seven types, none had been swaged. That finding produced unanimous agreement that the swaging operation was the major contributor to dynamic unbalance. The managers promptly

Type	% Defective	Swaged (marked X)	Type	% Defective	Swaged (marked X)
A	52.3	X	M	19.2	X
B	36.7	X	N	18.0	X
C	30.8	X	O	17.3	
D	29.9	X	P	16.9	X
E	25.3	X	Q	15.8	
F	23.3	X	R	15.3	
G	23.1	X	S	14.9	
H	22.5		T	14.7	
I	21.8	X	U	14.2	
J	21.7	X	V	13.5	
K	20.7	X	W	12.3	
L	20.3				

Figure 20-3. Effect of swaging on dynamic unbalance

dug deeper into the swaging process and came up with a remedy that greatly reduced the percent rejected for dynamic unbalance.

Mutual Gains from the Alliance

The alliance with Clark was beneficial to both of us. Clark liked my work, based on client feedbacks. He hoped I would join him fulltime, but that did not square with my long-range plans. However at the time neither of us wished to terminate the alliance; it was terminated by Clark's passing.

In my case I learned much about the economics of the consulting business and about the process of securing clients. I also learned that I was naturally sure-footed when serving clients. No client complained about the quality of my work; some, perhaps most, were more than satisfied. In addition, I learned much from the clients' engineers and managers. Each faced gritty realities, forcing me to face those same realities.

On the income side, the future of consulting looked promising indeed. Clark paid me seventy dollars per diem, soon raised to ninety. In his contracts with clients, however, he billed my time at 200 dollars per diem. I could foresee securing such fees directly from clients. In that event I might attain an income well beyond the scales prevailing at Western Electric and far beyond what could be envisioned from government or academia. Of course this optimism was contingent on my ability to generate enough billable days. Based on my experience with Clark, I was optimistic that I could solve that problem in the long run, but I was at risk for the short run—my assets were not sufficient to enable me to survive a few lean years. In that event I could be forced into the job market in my late forties.

References

Juran, J. M., "Inspectors' Errors in Quality Control," *Mechanical Engineering*, October 1935.

Marcy, Herbert, "The Business of Making a Quality Product," *Industrial Quality Control,"* January 1949, pp. 20-22.

Seder, L. A., "The Technique of Experimenting in the Factory," *Industrial Quality Control,* March 1948, also in *Mechanical Engineering,* July 1948. (This paper won the 1950 Brumbaugh Award of the American Society for Quality Control.)

Seder, L. A., "Diagnosis with Diagrams," *Industrial Quality Control,* January 1950.

Spang, J. P. Jr., dinner address at the Third Annual Convention, American Society for Quality Control, published in *Industrial Quality Control,* May 1949.

Q

21
Freelance:
1949-1959

With the end of the Clark alliance, I was on my own in terms of consulting; I had truly become a freelance consultant. Now I had the sole challenge of finding clients, but the resulting fees all belonged to me—there was no longer a middleman.

In 1949 I was still a professor at New York University (NYU), where my salary was not enough to meet my family's needs. I had gambled that my moonlighting income from consulting would help me to bridge the gap; instead it soon exceeded my salary at NYU.

During the decade from 1949 to 1959, I served about forty clients. In the descriptions that follow, I will tell about what took place at only a few of these companies. I have selected this sample to illustrate the results achieved and to show how assignments tended to expand as the original mission generated confidence with clients.

Bigelow-Sanford Carpet Company

My association with Bigelow-Sanford Carpet Company (BSCC) began when its president, James D. Wise, attended an Executive

Round Table I conducted with Peter Drucker at NYU. Soon I was invited to look at BSCC's approach to managing for quality and to participate in the company's upcoming conference on the subject. Following those events, the managers asked me to help them on a variety of projects with the following objectives:

- Improve quality
- Examine the profitability of the Thompsonville Plant
- Improve expense control
- Make comparisons with principal competitors
- Examine the effectiveness of advertising
- Create an executive instrument panel
- Revise the organization structure
- Resolve the conflict between Product Research and Manufacturing Engineering departments

Most of those projects took place during a four-year period; the final entry in my files is dated March 1952. Later I was asked to look at BSCC's Australian subsidiary during my 1957 visit to Australia.

Some of the projects' subject matter was new to me, yet I found that all yielded to a common approach. In collaboration with the managers, I tried to identify the chief problems, theorize as to the causes, test the theories, propose remedies, deal with cultural resistance, apply the remedies, and establish controls to hold the gains.

An interesting application of this approach was used to break the impasse that existed between Reinhardt, head of Product Research (PR), and Catlin, head of Manufacturing Engineering (ME). The plaintiff was Reinhardt, and there were two counts in his indictment:

1. ME takes too long to get the factory ready to manufacture.
2. In doing its work of process engineering, ME makes changes in the process already developed by PR.

ME's response to the first count was "not guilty." Its response to the second count was, "Our changes are necessary." Those responses settled nothing. Reinhardt continued to press his assertions to such an extent that PR's relations with ME deteriorated to a dangerous level.

I began by interviewing all who were affected by the impasse: the top executives, the heads of PR and ME, their subordinates, and the factory chiefs. These interviews confirmed the seriousness of the impasse but shed little light on how to break it.

Next I dug into the case histories of the development of ten products. For each I determined the dates associated with every stage of the progression, from the original concept to the "ready to manufacture" stage.

Each product development followed a well-defined progression of steps, first within PR and then within ME. To protect the secrecy of potential products and inventions, none but PR personnel were admitted into the research laboratory. Once PR had completed its work on a project, however, it made a full disclosure to ME, which then began its work. I found that in the aggregate, the time elapsed from concept to disclosure was about nineteen months, wheras the time elapsed from disclosure to "ready to manufacture" was about four months.

This finding was an eye-opener—of the total of twenty-three months, ME consumed only four months. Clearly, any major reduction in total time would have to come from PR.

As to whether ME's process changes were "necessary," I dug into the technology of the changes and was forced to conclude that PR was simply mistaken in its assertions. The crux of the controversy lay in the fact that PR did its work in a "pilot plant" using small-scale facilities. As part of its work, it developed a production process but it used the small-scale facilities. Thus, the resulting process was not necessarily adequate for use in the large-scale facilities of the factory.

For example, to develop a new type of carpet weave ("Nob Hill"), PR employed the twenty-seven-inch loom available in its pilot plant. In full-scale production, however, Nob Hill would be woven on looms much wider—from twelve to eighteen feet. Large looms exhibited phenomena such as greater thermal expansion, vibration, and so on that might be of little importance in small-scale facilities but had to be dealt with in large-scale facilities.

Despite these differences, the PR engineers exhibited a fierce loyalty to their creations, which they regarded as the proven ways to safeguard meeting the schedules. Their creations were indeed proven, but not on the equipment that would be employed by the factories. (The subsequent engineering for full-scale production faced additional needs that were not faced in the pilot plant: factory economics, production schedules, equipment maintenance, and so on.)

My recommendations included: conduct new product development on a concurrent rather than a consecutive basis; create a New Products Committee to provide oversight and coordination, and to serve as a forum for dealing with jurisdictional and allied disputes; and retain secrecy but give prompt clearance to those ME personnel who have a need to know. Those recommendations were adopted by the senior executives.

During my engagement with BSCC, I also guided the company through a fascinating project for improving the uniformity of carpet yarns. The project included "cutting new windows" in the process in order to measure the effect of key variables. Two of the men associated with the project then published a paper about it (Klock and Carter, 1952).[1] The paper won the Brumbaugh Prize for the best paper of the year.

Koppers Company, Inc.

Koppers was a very large multidivision manufacturer. Managers at the Metal Products Division (MPD) contacted me early in 1951 to help them improve quality in their piston ring factory. The results achieved in that factory led to many additional engagements. It all came to an end in December 1959, more than eight years later.

Piston Ring Quality

The piston ring factory was a marginal operation—there was already talk of shutting it down. The major problem was the high level of scrap and rework during the production processes, plus the cost of inspection to find the defects in the final product.

The MPD top managers accepted my suggestion that they create a multidepartmental team whose mission would be to find the causes of the defects and provide remedies. They also asked me to be a consultant to the team. To carry out its mission, the team conducted many experiments and collected and analyzed much data. It turned out to be a rewarding project. (One of the experiments aroused much interest, nationally and internationally, when I later described it in my videocassette series, "Juran on Quality Improvement.")

Mass-produced piston rings originated in the foundry by casting a hollow metal cylinder in a centrifugal casting machine. Those cylinders, called "pots," then went to the machine shop, where they were cut up into rings and then sent through various machining operations. The finished rings then underwent inspection to separate the good from the bad.

The principal defect was pits or porosity in the finished rings. Because the processing steps abounded with variables and the pits were not visible until all steps had been completed, an elaborate experimental design was required to discover the causes of the pits. Since the factory had no laboratory for conducting such experiments, *we were forced to use the factory processes as an experimental laboratory.* We stationed engineers in the foundry to record, for each of many pots, the state of the prevailing variables: which casting machine made it, who was the "melter," what was the pouring temperature, and so on. The identity of the pot was then preserved throughout the machining operations (no simple feat), so that the presence or absence of pits on the finished rings could be related back to the process variables.

The most notable finding from the experiments was that one of the nine melters—a Mr. Knight—produced pots that yielded rings of distinctly superior quality in terms of freedom from pits. Evidently Knight had some knack not possessed by any other melter. We discovered the nature of this skill and trained all the melters in how to develop it. The resulting improvement was sizeable; it also made it easier to identify the other contributing variables and then to make further reductions in the number of pits. And so it went for other defects. Within the first year of the project, the annual loss in the piston ring factory (about $120,000) had been converted to a profit of about $300,000. In terms of today's dollars that gain of $420,000 would become over $6,000,000.

Additional Projects

Those stunning results stimulated MPD's top executives to apply the team approach to additional areas of their business. Starting in September 1952, they created seven more teams during a six-year period. (I was asked to serve as consultant to each team.) The missions of the teams were as follows:

- Review the organization of MPD's engineering function.
- Improve the overall performance of the piston ring business.
- Review the system of incentives for the wood preserving operation, a part of Koppers' Chemicals Division.
- Improve the overall performance of the couplings business.
- Review the systems of incentives for MPD.
- Review the overall organization of MPD.
- Improve the overall performance of the electrical precipitators business.

As consultant, I urged each of those teams to carry out their mission in the following sequence: identify the specific problem areas needing improvement, arrange these in their order of priority, diagnose the major problems to learn the causes, find remedies for the causes, deal with the cultural resistance, and introduce controls to hold the gains.

Without exception those teams achieved gratifying results. As a result, the participating managers greatly enlarged their understanding of their business as a whole, and they emerged better motivated to optimize *company* results rather than *departmental* results.

Consulting Without Staff

During the MPD projects (as in others), I employed no staff. Instead I employed Koppers' staff people. They collected and analyzed the data, prepared and published the advance agendas, published the minutes, and did the follow-up to assure that the assigned "homework" got done on time. The man in charge of this exacting work was the young head of the Operations Research group, Walter Aring. We all relied on him because he was absolutely reliable.

My method of operation was to visit Koppers every few weeks

and remain for about three days. On the first day, I reviewed with Aring the progress made since my previous visit, after which we prepared and distributed the agenda for the team meeting. The team met on the second day, reviewed progress, and assigned the work to be done by members before the next meeting. On the third day, Aring and I agreed on the staff work to be done before the next meeting and on a draft of the minutes. It was a busy and exciting three days.

When preparing the book *Managerial Breakthrough* (1964), I wanted to include some of the case material from those Koppers' projects, but I was unable to secure clearance from the company. Therefore, I included the material on an anonymous basis. I also wanted very much to give credit to Aring but needed to do so by abbreviating his name to "Mr. Ring." Now, more than fifty years later, I assume that some statute of limitations has kicked in and I am free to use his full name.

Cumulative Failure Analysis

During the project on electrical precipitators (EP), I developed a useful improvement for interpreting field failures. The EP Division's record system collected cost data on field failures, service calls, and claims. These were summarized and reported monthly. All this data collection was useful but of little value for testing theories about the causes of failures. The innovation I introduced has come to be known as "cumulative failure analysis."

An EP is a large, costly piece of equipment installed in the exhaust system of an industrial process. The EP prevents air pollutants from going up the chimney and settling on the neighboring (and distant) towns and farms. The cost of an EP plus its installation can run to a few million (in year 2000's dollars).

When an EP failed, a service engineer went to the site to restore service. His report described the nature of the failure and what was done to restore service—time spent, materials used, and so on. Accounting then computed the costs, which became inputs to the published reports. For the purpose of cumulative failure analysis, the unit of measure became cumulative repair charges as a percentage of the original cost of the EP.

A major obstacle to the EP Division's profitability was the high level of repair charges arising from the EP's field failures. It was known that one of the models of EP had more repair charges than all other types combined, but the cause of these charges was hotly debated. Cumulative failure analysis then helped to shed light on the causes, as shown in Figure 21-1.

Figure 21-1 covers five years of repair charges for one model of EP. During the year 1948, three units were sold. In the first twelve months of operation, they accumulated repair charges to a level of 4 percent of the cost of the EPs, after which the units remained stable.

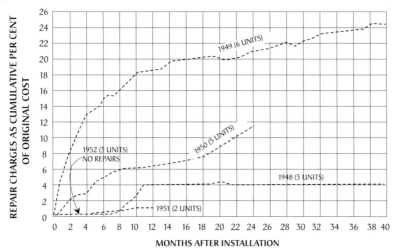

Figure 21-1. Study of design effectiveness of large equipment through analysis of cumulative repair charges

In the year 1949, six units were sold. For these the repair charges soared, exceeding 18 percent within the first twelve months and still climbing after forty months.

The five units sold in 1950 fared better, but still were at an unsatisfactory level; cumulative repair charges were over 11 percent within the first twenty-four months and were destined to climb higher.

The two units sold in 1951 were models of reliability; twelve months after installation, they had required repair charges of only about 1 percent. The three units sold in 1952 were free of repair charges at the time the chart was prepared.

It remained to compare the trend of repair charges with the corresponding chronology of events that had taken place in the EP design department. The files showed that late in 1948, the engineers changed the product design to introduce features that would improve the product's salability. Analysis then showed that those design changes were responsible for the rise in repair charges. Late in 1950, the engineers came up with a remedy that reduced the rate of charges. The design was then further improved, resulting in near immunity from field failures.

International Latex Company

International Latex Company (ILC) made consumer products from latex—gloves, diaper covers, womens' girdles, and so on. I was hired to review their approach to managing for quality. The end result was creation of a corporate Quality Control department with responsibility for preparing manuals, conducting audits, and reporting on performance. All of this was done amid moderate cultural resistance. (Dealing with the cultural resistance was aided by spelling out what the new department would *not* be doing.)

An interesting result of this assignment was an application of the concept of cumulative failure analysis to consumer products. The application involved an article of womens' clothing. The innovation I introduced was to plot monthly the cumulative rate of returns for each product type. The unit of measure became the cumulative percentage of units returned relative to the cumulative number of units sold. The lower curve of Figure 21-2 is an example of such a report for a product that first went to market in December 1951.

The returns were almost exclusively because of the product tearing during use. The continuing rise in the curve suggested that the longer the products were used, the more they became torn. By December 1953, the cumulative percentage of returns as reported had reached 1.95 percent, but matters were actually much worse. For products of low unit price (which was the case here), most customers do not complain. In addition, the company discouraged returns by

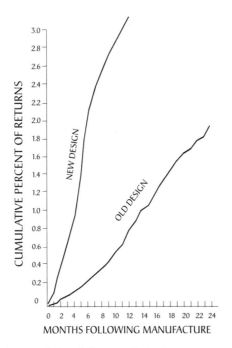

Figure 21-2. Cumulative failure analysis for a consumer product

putting a notice on the containers stating that the product was not returnable. We estimated that actually about 20 percent of the product became torn within a matter of months after going into service. It was a high failure rate that the company reluctantly endured.

Meanwhile, the research department had designed a new model of the product that exhibited new features attractive to consumers. The new product went to market in February 1953. The upper curve of Figure 21-2 shows, month by month, the new product's cumulative rate of return. (The two curves are directly comparable because the horizontal scale is "Months following manufacture.") It is obvious that the new product's failure rate greatly exceeded that of its predecessor. The higher rate of return forced the company to take the new design off the market. Had the company test-marketed the product, a report on cumulative rate of return could have provided early warning that the new design was headed for disaster.

Bausch & Lomb Optical Company

Bausch and Lomb Optical Company (B&L) was a leading maker of optical instruments and ophthalmic lenses and frames. In 1951, I was invited to help improve managing for quality in their Precision Optics Division. The results were so impressive that I was then asked to help other divisions as well. In all, my engagements with B&L continued through 1956, a six-year span.

Precision Optics Division

The Precision Optics Division (POD) made the precise lenses, prisms, and such used in microscopes, binoculars, and other optical products. The cost of poor quality was severe; almost half the factory hours went into making, finding, repairing, or scrapping defective products. We followed the already familiar approach: identify the "vital few" defects, theorize about causes, test the theories, etc. The company put together an excellent team to tackle the project, and we made solid progress that soon became evident in the bottom line.

When the POD project was nearly completed, the team made a presentation to the company's senior executives, explaining the problem they had tackled, the method of attack, and the results achieved. (The presentation used the terms "hidden plant" and "gold in the mine" to dramatize the extent of loss as a result of poor quality; it was an early use of those terms.) The executives were very impressed. The presentation likely was also influential in accelerating the career progress of the team members.

Carl Day, the Works Manager, was soon promoted to vice president of Manufacture. Herb Ashcroft, the Industrial Engineering manager, was soon promoted to Works manager. Ed Close, the Inspection supervisor, later became vice president of Manufacture. Jack Harby, the young supervisor in Industrial Engineering, was put on a fast track for promotion and ultimately became the company's president.

Another outcome of the POD project was a paper presented by Carl Day, then Works manager at B&L, at an AMA Conference. The title was "Quality Control: Tool for the Manufacturing Executive." Day estimated the cost of poor quality in POD to be about

$500,000 per year. (In today's dollars, that would be closer to $8,000,000.) As an example he cited cutting the incidence of chipped lenses from 27 percent to 5 percent. The paper was presented at an AMA Manufacturing Conference and was published in AMA's Manufac-turing Series Number 206 (1953). Day was generous in crediting my participation.

I pondered whether to advertise by sending out reprints of Day's paper. I decided not to; it might be interpreted as engaging in self-aggrandizement. In retrospect, I was just naïve. Ironically, one result of Day's paper was an invitation from B&L's chief competitor (American Optical Company) to provide them with consulting assistance. I turned them down; I thought it unethical to help a client's competitor.

Ophthalmic Lens Division

Following the successes achieved in POD (and the enthusiastic response of the senior executives), Carl Day concluded that the next manufacturing project to be tackled would be to improve quality in the Ophthalmic Lens Division (OLD). The division made numerous kinds of ophthalmic lenses that B&L sold to optometrists, opticians, and others who sold directly to the public.

A new team was created to carry out this project. It soon found that the approach used in POD was applicable to OLD. As in POD, yields were sharply improved, resulting in notable effects on the company's bottom line.

Other Manufacturing Areas

B&L's manufacture extended beyond POD and OLD. The company made microscopes, binoculars, and other instruments, as well as frames for eyeglasses. As in POD and OLD, teams were created to improve quality and to reduce the cost of poor quality. I was not asked to participate actively with those teams, although they occasionally asked for my opinion on specific matters. The manufacturing managers had concluded that their experience in POD and OLD made them self-sufficient for tackling new projects. This view was reinforced by the fact that some team members were being promoted, so that in their higher posts, they became strong advocates for improving quality.

Meanwhile, the top executives, elated with the results achieved in manufacture, raised the question, "Is the approach we used to improve performance in manufacture applicable to nonmanufacture?" I suggested they choose some nonmanufacturing division as a testing ground. They chose the Ophthalmic Sales Division.

Ophthalmic Sales Division (OSD)

OSD was the marketing arm that sold eyeglass lenses and frames to various outside wholesalers, retailers, ophthalmologists, optometrists, and opticians. I began by interviewing the pertinent personnel within B&L as well as a sample of those outside. Their comments yielded nominations for over fifty potential improvement projects. A team was formed to tackle those projects in their order of priority. The team membership consisted of managers within OSD; the chairman was G. H. Phreaner, the head of OSD.

The team turned out to be most effective, and within a year, its work had led to improvements in numerous problem areas, some long-standing. The financial results went well beyond the hopes of the B&L chief executives. Those same results added to my status as "the only consultant who ever paid off."

Instrument Sales Division

Following the stunning improvements made in OSD, I was asked to look at the Instrument Sales Division (ISD). The flagship product line for ISD was microscopes. Other lines included optical measuring instruments, photographic lenses, and binoculars. ISD's profitability in recent years had been high chiefly as a result of the adoption of wide-screen motion pictures. B&L had a near-monopoly on making the lenses needed to modify the projectors and cameras. That business was now past its peak, resulting in a serious decline in ISD profitability.

I followed the customary approach. I interviewed numerous company personnel, both at headquarters and in the field. I also interviewed a sample of outsiders, including dealers and employees from hospital supply houses, school supply houses, and in-house laboratories. I classified the comments into forty-one categories, which then became a list of potential projects to be tackled by a coordinating team.

After a few team meetings, it became evident to me that progress would be minimal as long as the head of ISD remained on the job. It also became evident that the morale problem in the division was largely traceable to the same individual. (Morale was one of the selected projects.) When I conveyed my findings to Carl Hallauer (the president of B&L), his response was, "That confirms my own belief." Hallauer not only replaced the head of ISD, but he also concluded that he would look to the new head to find remedies for ISD's problems.

Advisor to Senior Management

During the final stages of my work with B&L, I was frequently sought out by the top executives to discuss matters of high-level importance. The executives included the president, Carl Hallauer; the vice president and treasurer, William McQuilkin (later president); and the vice president of manufacture, Carl Day. The subject matters included the following:

Enlarging the Product Line. The question was whether B&L should "go beyond the lens" and enter the field of scientific instruments generally. This would require taking some sizeable risks—enlarging the product research and development budget, revising the organization structure, changing the company name, and so on.

Going International. Growing competition from Japan was forcing B&L to consider forming an alliance with some Japanese company, such as Nippon Kogaku (who made Nikon cameras, Nikkor lenses, and so on). As it so happened, I had visited Nippon Kogaku and established an excellent rapport with its president, Masao Nagaoka. I also had an excellent rapport with A. B. Sinkler (now president of Hamilton Watch Co.), who had acquired useful experience in forging alliances abroad.

Changing the Organization from Functional to Product Type. This was an idea whose time had come. Hallauer sensed this, but he preferred that his successor preside over something so messy. (His vice presidents were generally eager to tackle that change.)

Recruitment. I was asked to nominate potential candidates for high-level jobs. An example was the new job of International Manager.

Promotions. I was occasionally asked for my appraisal of managers who were being considered for promotion to higher-level jobs.

The Young Family Hopeful. One young manager (in OSD) was a member of a family that owned a significant bundle of B&L stock. He had become deluded into thinking he would soon become president of the company. It was essential to get him to leave, but how to do so was unclear. Fortunately, I had developed a good rapport with him during the OSD project. That enabled me to contribute usefully to solving the problem.

General Foods Corporation

General Foods Corporation (GF) was—and is—a huge food processor. It produced many products in many factories. Its sources of supply were international, as were its markets. The management approached me in November 1955 to conduct a survey of managing for quality throughout the corporation: at corporate headquarters; in the purchasing department; in the marketing department; and in the factories (based on visits to a sample of them).

We reached an agreement in February 1956 on the scope of the survey and on the method of approach. I enlisted Leonard A. Seder to collaborate with me.

By May 1956 we had published three reports. These dealt with corporate headquarters, the Jell-O division, and the Maxwell House (coffee) division. The remaining reports related to the Post Cereals division, the Walter Baker (chocolate) division, the Birdseye (Frozen Foods) division, and the Gaines (dog food) division.

I was also asked to help out in related matters, such as nominating quality managers for recruitment.

While Seder and I came up with many recommendations, we found that basically, GF was uncommonly competent at managing for quality. The people we dealt with were capable and professional, and they had evolved practices that were at the cutting edge.

Consumer Preference and Share of Market

One of my innovations during the GF assignment was a diagram relating, for many GF products, their "consumer preference" to their share
of market.

In Figure 21-3, the horizontal scale shows consumer preference
over the leading competitor. The vertical scale shows share of market
versus the leading competitor, considering the two as 100 percent.
Each of the (41) dots represents a type of product on supermarket
shelves. It competes with other products for the same shelf space.
Competing products are packaged in similar-sized boxes containing
identical amounts of product and sold (usually) at identical prices.

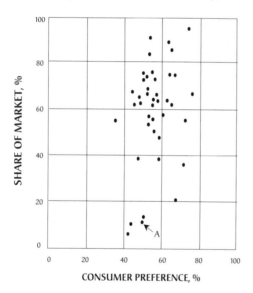

Figure 21-3. Consumer preference versus share of market

In no case does any product exhibit a consumer preference below
25 or above 75 percent. The likely reason is that a product with a preference of over 75 percent drives its competitors out of the market.

In contrast to the vacant areas in the horizontal direction, the vertical scale has dots throughout the entire spectrum. The product
marked A lies squarely on the 50 percent preference line yet has only
a 10 percent of the share of market. The reason is that its principal

competitor (which has a 90 percent share) had pioneered the product and thereby acquired a "prior franchise," which it then maintained through good marketing.

Discussion of Figure 21-3 resulted in the evolution of several theories:

- When quality preferences are clearly evident to users, such differences are also decisive in share of market, all other things being equal.
- When quality differences are slight, marketing skills are the decisive factor in share of market.
- Companies are well advised to undertake quality improvements that will (1) take them from a clearly weak level to an acceptable level of preference, or (2) take them from an acceptable level to a clearly dominant level of preference.
- Companies are not well advised to make quality improvements that will merely move them from one acceptable level to another, since the dominant role in share of market in such cases is played by marketing skills.

I elaborated on this concept in my paper "A Note on Economics of Quality."[2]

The Exhilaration of Discovery

Many client problems yielded to simple methods of analysis; there was little need for innovation. In cases in which I was forced to innovate, I was always exhilarated by the experience. To innovate requires embarking on a voyage of discovery. The fascinations of the voyage then can exceed those of the destination; the road can yield deeper satisfactions than the inn. In addition, and marvelous to relate, *consulting was fun*; small wonder that during my nearly ninety years of gainful employment, I spent about fifty years as a freelance consultant.

What Did I Bring to the Table?

By 1959 I had begun to ask myself, *Why do company managers need to call in outsiders to help get rid of chronic quality waste and other such quali-*

ty problems? Certainly the managers know much about the technology—the materials, processes, machines, tools, and so on. In such matters, they are the experts; I am the amateur. The managers are also intelligent. Each can think logically, and each possesses creativity. The facts needed for diagnosis are often lurking in the house, waiting to be analyzed, as was the case at Gillette and many other companies. (At Gillette, the shave test was inherently flawed, yet knowledge of this critical information lurked for years in company records, waiting to be discovered.) It puzzled me that such situations could go on and on for years.

As I pondered this phenomenon, two theories emerged to explain the impasse.

1. The "alarm signals" had been disconnected. Under this theory, the managers had learned years ago that the processes' yields were well below 100 percent. The resulting wastes made it impossible to meetschedules, budgets, and other departmental goals. The seemingly "obvious" remedy was to reengineer the processes. However, the process engineers claimed that their orders were to give priority to new processes—those needed to produce new products and thus generate more sales. So the managers met their departmental goals by buying more machines, hiring more workers, and perpetually ordering more materials. By creating those wastes, they could meet their goals, but as a result, they had disconnected the alarm signals and thus had enabled the wastes to go on and on.

2. The managers were simply unskilled in the quality improvement process. They were not even aware that such a process existed. In company after company, the managers openly expressed their admiration of the various steps: use of the team concept to bypass functional roadblocks, use of a systematic method for thinking about causes, testing theories through the factual approach, and so on. Of course, that series of steps for making improvements was itself only a part of the overall science of managing for quality, but that science was still in its infancy and, in any case, had never been a part of the curriculum studied by my clients.

What I contributed as a consultant was a collection of concepts, methods, skills, and tools, all related to managing for quality. As of 1959, that collection was not yet a fully matured body of knowledge that had been recognized as a new science. But managing for quality was developing into a thing of elegance as well as a great benefit to society.

Notes

1. Klock, A. G., and C. W. Carter. "Woolen Carding Meets Quality Control." *Industrial Quality Control,* May 1952.

2. Juran, J. M. "A Note on Economics of Quality." *Industrial Quality Control,* February 1959: 20–21.

Q

22

My First Visit to Japan: Teaching Quality to a Country in Ruins

In 1954 I went to Japan to lecture and to consult with companies on matters relating to managing for quality. That visit marked the beginning of a long, productive alliance that contributed usefully to Japan's emergence as a world quality leader and economic superpower. It began with the convergence of two events: (1) the Japanese military defeat in World War II, and (2) publication of the first edition of my *Quality Control Handbook* in 1951.

Japan's Quality Revolution

Japan's surrender in 1945 put an end to its efforts to "find a place in the sun" by military means. Now such efforts would have to be through peaceful means—by trade. For a nation of few natural resources, trade demanded an economy based on the import of materials and export of finished goods. Such an approach had enabled Great Britain, also a small island nation with few natural resources, to become an economic superpower.

The Japanese manufacturers did convert production to civilian goods but promptly ran into a serious marketing problem. Japan's exports, while low in price, had a long-standing reputation for poor quality—so poor that foreign importers were reluctant to buy them. To change that reputation required that Japanese industry improve its quality to a level competitive with that of the West. The Japanese chief executives soon became aware of this, but as of the late 1940s, there was no consensus on how to bring about such a change. The emphasis in Japanese companies (as in Western companies) was on use of inspection to separate good products from bad. The concept of annual quality improvement had yet to be grasped, and the process for such improvement had yet to be evolved.

Despite the seeming impasse, within four decades Japan made enough progress in managing for quality to become the world quality leader, and then it used that leadership to emerge as an economic superpower. In my view, the chief contributions to that progress included the following:

1. The actions of Japanese managers who saw the need to make revolutionary improvements in quality and then did so successfully. Their work became the model for other companies to follow. I have often said that "the unsung heroes of the Japanese quality revolution are the Japanese managers."
2. The work of the Japanese Union of Scientists and Engineers. It became a sort of quality center for Japan.
3. The lectures of two Americans, W. E. Deming and J. M. Juran, which provided the seed training courses in statistical methodology and managing for quality, respectively.

Still other events contributed to Japan's remarkable achievement. (See, for example, Nonaka 1995).[1] I will leave those events to be explained by some future researcher who sets out to prepare a comprehensive history of the Japanese quality revolution.

Although the prewar quality of Japan's exported consumer goods was indeed notoriously poor, the situation was different in other product categories. Some Japanese handicraft products had long been of world-class quality. During the early days of World War II, some Japanese military hardware (such as the Zero fighter airplanes and the naval torpedoes) were superior in quality to their American counterparts.

The Japanese Union of Scientists and Engineers

In 1946 the Japanese Union of Scientists and Engineers (JUSE) was created. It was an independent, nonprofit organization with a vague mission of helping the nation during the postwar period. JUSE's first managing director, Ken-ichi Koyanagi, soon identified the quality problem as critical to Japan's prosperity. He therefore oriented JUSE to give top priority to that problem.

At the outset, JUSE had virtually no source of earned income. To get things done, it recruited volunteers—professors from universities and engineers from companies. One team of such volunteers evolved a training course, "Statistical Quality Control," which was offered to industrial companies during the period September 1949 to August 1950. The course, which emphasized advanced statistical methodology, attracted little interest.

JUSE did receive modest subsidies, principally from industry. It was JUSE's good fortune that its chairman, Ichiro Ishikawa, was probably the most influential industrialist in Japan. In addition he was chairman of Keidanren, the Japanese Federation of Economic Organizations. (Its functions parallel those of the U.S. National Association of Manufacturers and the U.S. Chamber of Commerce.)

The Deming Lectures

W. Edwards Deming was trained as a physicist (Ph.D., Yale 1928). From 1921 until 1927, he was an instructor in engineering and physics at several universities. He then served the U.S. Department of Agriculture as a physicist from 1927 to 1939. Meanwhile he became attracted to the subject of statistics and especially to the work of Dr. Walter A. Shewhart, a mathematician on the staff of Bell Telephone Laboratories (Bell Labs). (This was the same Shewhart I had met in 1926 during the life of the Joint Bell Labs–Western Electric Committee on Inspection Statistics and Economy.)

Deming next moved to the U.S. Bureau of the Census as an advisor on sampling (1939–1946). Finally he became a professor of statistics at New York University and at Columbia University, as well as a consultant in statistical surveys. Deming's association with Shewhart taught him the new methods Bell Labs had evolved, especially the control chart (a Shewhart invention) and new concepts and tools relative to sampling. During World War II, Deming was an active participant in designing the War Production Board's training course in statistical quality control (SQC); he also was one of the lecturers during the early courses.

Deming's name was familiar to the volunteers in JUSE; he was a coauthor of some of the English-language papers that had helped JUSE to prepare its basic course. In 1947, when Deming was in Japan to help the occupation forces plan the 1951 Japan census, he met some of the Japanese associated with JUSE. Those meetings resulted in an invitation for Deming to conduct lectures in Japan on use of statistical methods for quality control.

Deming accepted that invitation and gave the lectures in the summer of 1950, basing them on the courses offered by the War Production Board during World War II. The lectures were spread over eight days, were attended by 330 engineers, and were well received. That reception led Koyanagi (the managing director of JUSE) to believe that it should be feasible for JUSE to adapt the course to the Japanese culture and then offer it over and over again to Japanese companies.

Subsequent events bore out Koyanagi's belief. JUSE did offer the new course, and it was heavily attended year after year. The course then proliferated; there were courses designed for the workforce, for supervisors, for engineers, advanced courses, and so on. Large companies soon became organized to carry out much of the training themselves. JUSE also created journals to publish case examples of quality improvement. Conferences were created, and prizes were offered for superior papers. Courses were even offered over the national radio. The resulting income from attendance at courses, publications, attendance at conferences, and so on soon reached levels that helped to solve JUSE's financial problems.

A further important result of Deming's lectures was JUSE's creation of the Deming Prizes. I will return to Deming and the Deming prizes in a future chapter.

My Invitation from Japan

My invitation to lecture in Japan was a result of the publication of my *Quality Control Handbook*. Koyanagi told me he was interested in the *Handbook* because most of it dealt with matters beyond statistics—matters such as economics of quality, specification, organization, inspection, assurance, and supplier relations. He thought that Japan had reached a state of self-sufficiency in SQC but that to achieve quality required much more than application of statistics. He hoped to make arrangements to translate the book into Japanese.

Koyanagi also hoped it would be possible for me to come to Japan and conduct lectures in the nonstatistical subjects that were treated in the *Handbook*. I told him I was definitely interested.

By December 1952, I had received Koyanagi's formal invitation and accepted it. I was to visit Japan during June and July of 1953 for about six weeks, giving lectures and visiting companies. I was also to prepare a text and send it on to be translated in advance. It was a daunting timetable, but I was rescued by a ghost out of the past.

In June 1926, during my first week at Western Electric, I failed the medical entrance examination when the physician discovered an incipient hernia (a hernia waiting to happen). I was accepted for the job anyway, and the hernia waited for 28 years, happening late in 1952. That required surgery and a convalescence of several weeks. At the time I still had some teaching commitments at New York University, so I was forced to schedule the surgery for the summer of 1953 and to postpone going to Japan until the summer of 1954.

Koyanagi also asked me to help him get permission to translate the *Handbook* into Japanese. I discussed the matter with McGraw-Hill, but they balked and finally turned down the proposal. (The problem was currency controls in Japan.) I then learned that the publisher Richard D. Irwin had given Koyanagi the right to translate Acheson Duncan's book on statistics. That action by a competitor persuaded McGraw-Hill to relent and authorize a Japanese translation of the *Handbook*.

Preparing the Courses

The program envisioned by Koyanagi consisted of four courses for industrial managers. Two of these would be for middle managers and would occupy two weeks each. The other two would be for chief executives and would occupy two days each. During late 1953 and early 1954, I was much occupied with preparing the texts for those courses and getting them to Koyanagi in time for translation and publication.

For the middle managers I divided the subject matter into twenty topics. These included some of the following:

- Economics of Quality
- Specification of Quality
- Planning for Quality
- Producing Quality
- Inspection and Measurement
- Staff Quality Functions, Quality Assurance
- Training for Quality
- Quality-mindedness
- Case Examples of Quality Improvement

I also included a lecture on the role of statistical methods.

At the time, that text material was largely at the cutting edge of good practice; few specialists in managing for quality had acquired my breadth of experience or had written so extensively about the subject. Yet today, on rereading those lectures, I am impressed by the extent to which the subject matter has grown in scope, in depth, and especially in importance to world economies. Keeping up with all those advances would occupy me for decades to come.

Mr. Koyanagi and I had much correspondence. The translators ran into problems because of the multiple meanings of many English words and phrases. I needed information on the state of Japanese industry as well as on the Japanese culture. In addition, I needed an overhead projector for use during the lectures.

I had begun to use such a projector at NYU and found it greatly superior to a blackboard. (It was a Beseler model and, at the time, the only one on the market.) I had also shown one to Koyanagi when he was in the New York area during a stopover on one of his intercontinental trips. He found that there was no such machine in Japan, and he was unable to obtain the dollars to buy and import one. We finally agreed that I would buy one and ship it to Japan, where Koyanagi would reimburse me in yen (so we thought).

The Journey

In those days of piston engines, a trip from New York to Tokyo consumed about forty hours of flying time plus waiting time for changing planes on the west coast. Sadie and I chose to break up the journey by making an overnight stay in Los Angeles.

Koyanagi met us on our arrival and took us to our hotel, a converted office building. It was Saturday evening, so we had Sunday in which to relax from the effects of the trip. On Sunday afternoon, Koyanagi took me to meet many of the JUSE volunteers, as well as Mr. H. Kano, who was to be my interpreter. My activities did not commence until Tuesday, but on Monday afternoon, Koyanagi and I went to Yokohama where the customs office was holding my overhead projector hostage. The customs officer was willing to admit the projector but insisted that after my lectures, the thing must be returned to the United States. Koyanagi assured the officer that it would indeed be returned; I winced—the projector had cost me $345, and I had no need to own one.

Meetings with Companies

During July and August, I visited ten manufacturing companies, a testing lab, and a newspaper plant, as follows:

Showa Denko. It was a chemicals manufacturer and one of the first winners of the Deming Prize. I visited a factory that made ammonium sulphate (a component of fertilizer).

Nippon Kogaku. It made Nikon cameras and other optical products.

Tokyo Shibaura (now Toshiba). It made electrical products. The factory I visited made lamps and vacuum tubes for radio sets.

Nippon Kokan. It was a steel maker, especially of steel tubes.

Noritake China. It was a pottery company, making high-grade chinaware.

Toyo Spinning. It made yarns and fabrics, chiefly from cotton.

Toyo Rayon. It made yarns and fabrics, chiefly from synthetics.

Takeda Pharmaceutical. It made a broad line of pharmaceutical products.

Toyo Bearings. It made anti-friction bearings for the automobile industry and others.

Furukawa Electric Company. I visited its Nikko Copper Works, which used electricity from the company's hydro power plants to produce copper and other nonferrous metals as well as products made from those metals.

Chubu Nippon Shimbun. This was a newspaper.

Japan Spinners Inspecting Association. This was an independent testing laboratory. To manufacturers of cotton yarns and textiles, it offered a service of testing their products and awarding a certificate that could be helpful in selling their products to skeptical foreign importers.

A company visit typically consumed half a day. Each visit followed a common sequence: a tour through the facility; a meeting with senior executives, at which I would offer comments and respond to questions; and a social event that could range anywhere from an informal gift presentation to an evening dinner party. In some cases I was also asked to give a brief lecture.

On some days I conducted a course in the morning and then visited a company in the afternoon. The course attendees were divided into groups to discuss assigned problems and to prepare reports for presentation on the following morning.

The questions raised at the companies I visited exhibited much similarity. The most frequent question was on how to organize—who was to be responsible for what. Such questions were not limited to organization of managing for quality; they included all parts of the management hierarchy, including the top levels. Questions on organizing tended to be phrased in vague terms, such as "Who is responsible for quality?" Most companies had not yet learned that the precise definition of "responsibility" requires that the questions be stated in terms of responsibility for making which decisions and taking which actions.

Another frequent question was "What is the practice in the United States?" Many Japanese had been greatly impressed by the outpouring of U.S. military products during World War II; to some it was an awesome achievement.

The company visits presented me with a continuing procession of fascinating sights. For example, some factories, such as Toyo Spinning, were located in rural areas where the workers were unable to commute from their homes because of inadequate transport facilities. In such cases the companies provided dormitories to enable workers to live on the premises. Additional amenities included schools and shops, as well as facilities for sports, hobbies, social clubs, and more.

The visits were also interesting in the professional sense. I will comment on only two of them.

Nippon Kogaku was a good example. I was quite familiar with the optical industry as a result of my work with Bausch & Lomb, and, luckily, the company chairman, Mr. Nagaoka, spoke excellent English. Nippon Kogaku (it made cameras and lenses) originally learned how to make optical glass from a pamphlet published by the U.S. Bureau of Standards. (No need to buy licenses.) During World War II, the company was busy with military contracts: gun sights for the Army, periscopes for the Navy, bomb sights for the Air Force, and so on.

When I visited Nagaoka, on his desk was a German Leica camera that he was copying. (Again, no need to buy licenses.) He was amused when I told him that in America, the Japanese had the reputation of being good copyists but not innovators. He pointed out that "for a country to have new product development requires schools of technology, engineers, laboratories, literature, and so on. It takes a long time to create all that, and Japan was late to industrialize."

Following the war, Nagaoka converted the company's output to civilian products chiefly by copying the Leica and selling the camera to members of the occupation forces. The word soon got around that the Nikon was an excellent camera at a price well below the Leica's; business was brisk.

Toyo Bearings was also of special interest. This company had measured the quality capability of the production processes and found them to be much better than had been thought. By modest changes in tooling, the machines became able to make bearings an order of magnitude more precise than customers' specifications. Following that breakthrough, the company pondered what to do with the increased precision.

It offered to supply customers with bearings of greater precision but at a premium price. That didn't work; the customers balked on the ground that the less precise bearings met specifications and were also adequate for use. Toyo Bearings then offered to sell the more precise bearings at no increase in price. That strategy was successful because it enabled the company to increase its share of the market.

The Lecture Courses

My chief mission during this visit was to conduct the four lecture courses that Koyanagi had organized. The enrollments had grown to substantial numbers:

- The course for senior managers (two days) at the Fujiya Hotel— 62 enrollments
- The course for middle managers (ten days) at Waseda University—160 enrollments

- The course for middle managers (ten days) at the Osaka Chamber of Commerce—106 enrollments
- The course for senior managers (two days) at Koyasan—62 enrollments

Organization for the courses included recruiting assistants to manage the incidentals, such as recording the questions and my responses, recording the sketches I drew on the projector, setting up and assisting the discussion groups, and more. At the Waseda course there were thirteen such assistants, chiefly university professors and engineers from the companies.

The Lectures at the Fujiya Hotel

The Fujiya Hotel was one of the most elegant in Japan. Located in the Hakone resort area amid spectacular scenery, it offered impeccable service—quite appropriate for a gathering of Japan's industrial leaders.

My lectures to the upper managers centered on their responsibilities for quality, which I listed as follows:

- Establish the quality policy and goals—the company's code of conduct with respect to quality, and the results to be achieved.
- Choose the quality of design—the grade of product appropriate to the market the company has chosen to enter.
- Create an organization appropriate for designing, producing, and marketing the company's products.
- Establish measures of actual quality performance.
- Regularly review quality performance against goals and take action as needed.

I expanded on this list in some detail, bringing in topics such as these:

- The functions relating to achievement of quality
- Whether higher quality costs more or less
- Evaluating the cost of poor quality
- The critical distinction between sporadic and chronic problems; mobilizing to attack chronic problems

- The sequence of steps needed to achieve defect prevention
- Control of quality at the senior managers' level; quality audits

At the time I was not fully aware of the different priorities between senior managers and factory managers. The focus of senior managers was on how to penetrate foreign markets with products bearing their companies' own name. The focus of factory managers was to meet the specification, the schedule, and the budget. I understood manufacturing goals, but it would take more years of consulting before I acquired a complete grasp of senior executives' goals.

A critical need, both during the company visits and the lectures, was to interpret my English into Japanese. (In 1954, few Japanese understood English.) Koyanagi provided for sequential interpretation. I would speak several sentences and then pause while the interpreter translated what I had said. That method doubles the time required to cover the ground, but the quality is superior to that of simultaneous translation. During the entire visit, I had the good fortune to have Hisamichi Kano as my interpreter. He had a mastery of the English language, including the idioms. We became a well-synchronized team.

A highlight of all the lecture courses was the overhead projector— the "lecturing machine." The Japanese had never seen such a device; during each break a few came up to examine it in detail. At the Fujiya Hotel their attendees' interest solved my problem about the projector being sent back to the United States. When I announced that in view of the participants' interest, I was donating the projector to JUSE, a wave of smiles illuminated the room. A few days later, Mr. Nagaoka came to see me and presented me with one of his Nikon cameras. That presentation may well have been related to my disposition of the projector.

The Lectures at Waseda University

The first ten-day course for middle managers was held at Waseda University, located in the Tokyo area. Usually I lectured for half the day, and then the attending managers were divided into project groups of about twenty men each. Each group was asked to analyze an assigned problem and write a report to be presented the following morning.

The first of many training courses in Japan

As part of their project, each group was asked to "take a census"—to go around the room to discover what was the practice prevailing (relative to the assigned problem) in each of the companies represented. Taking the census and discussing the findings turned out to be an exercise of much interest to the managers. Only rarely had they had the opportunity to meet with managers from other companies to discuss common problems so freely.

Those middle managers were much more informed than their superiors about the realities and details of how to manage for quality, so their questions were more pointed. I was familiar with most of the problems they posed and could provide head-on answers. Also, in contrast to the senior managers, virtually all attendees at Waseda were aggressive note takers.

At Waseda, as well as at other courses, the assistants provided by Koyanagi recorded all the goings-on—my oral lectures, the questions and answers, the project reports, and the diagrams I drew on the projector. Those records then became inputs to the book that JUSE would publish in 1956.

The questions raised by the middle managers reflected their close involvement with realities. Their most frequent question, as in other courses, related to organization and responsibility. Because important problems usually involve multiple functions, clear definition of "who is to be responsible for what" becomes essential to solving such problems. Each middle manager (middle in the hierarchy) is, in effect, also on a team with other middle managers.

The Course in Osaka

The second ten-day course for middle managers was held at the Chamber of Commerce in Osaka, Japan's second largest city. Osaka, like most major Japanese cities, had suffered extensive damage during World War II. The New Osaka Hotel, where we stayed, was indeed new.

The course, attended by 106 managers, was essentially a duplicate of the Waseda course—lectures, project assignments, questions, and so on, including the farewell party. Again Kano and the course assistants conspired to make life easy for me.

The Course at Koyasan

The second two-day course for senior managers was conducted at Koyasan (holy plateau mountain). It was a unique experience. At the time, women were not allowed to go there, so I provided Sadie with an account for her diary, which follows:

> To get to Koyasan, we (Koyanagi, Kano, many of the attendees, myself, and the projector) climbed aboard a train at one of Osaka's minor stations. It was a narrow-gauge railroad, and ours was a three-car train. The little train then wove its way along the sides of the mountains, snaking into and out of tunnels, constantly climbing while the valleys receded below us. After we had climbed about 2,500 feet, we left the train and took a cable car that climbed yet another 500 feet, at a steep angle. That brought us to the mountaintop—Koyasan.
>
> Koyasan is a sort of center of Buddhism in Japan. It was founded in the year 774 by Kobo Daiishi, a Buddhist priest. I was told that there were close to one hundred Buddhist temples there and that about five million pilgrims visit annually. Our

destination was Kongobuji temple, the headquarters of one the sects of Buddhism. To get there we left the cable car and rode a bus. The lectures would be held at Kongobuji, and we would stay there overnight.

On arrival we ran into a crisis—where to connect the projector? The temple was not wired for electricity, but Japanese resourcefulness came to the rescue. There was a power line running down the street, so someone climbed a pole, connected a wire, and brought the other end into the temple. A bed sheet served as a screen, and I gave the lectures while sixty-two senior managers sat on the floor and listened. (The temple was virtually devoid of Western furniture.)

The lecture sessions at Koyasan were essentially a repeat of those at the Fujiya Hotel. The questions raised by the attendees were also like those raised at Fujiya.

We had time to visit the cemetery area. It was vast, containing close to 300,000 monuments as well as groves of huge cryptomeria trees, some over 500 years old. Many of those monuments consisted of massive stones stacked one above the other. These were built by piling up a mound of dirt high enough to permit rolling or sliding each stone to the top of the pile, then more dirt, another stone, and so on until the monument was fully stacked up. Then the dirt was removed. The labor to bring those stones up the mountain without roads, animals, or equipment defies the imagination.

Learning about Japan

Beyond the events relating to my mission, Sadie and I had an opportunity to learn about Japan under conditions that would be the envy of any tourist. Sadie's escorts included Koyanagi's teenage daughter Liko, along with Japanese and American ladies whom she had met at social functions. I was usually escorted by company managers or members of JUSE. All our escorts were willing and even eager to explain what we were seeing plus the associated cultural background. There was much to see and ask about.

Except for the few nights we spent in a converted office building in Tokyo, we enjoyed Japanese hotels. The Fujiya was exceptional. We were housed in the "flower palace," where each room bore the name of a flower; ours was "cherry." On the evening of the course banquet, our table setting was a sight to behold. It consisted of a miniature landscape: a garden, rocks, bridges, statuary, many miniature (bonsai) trees—an artistic triumph.

During most of our time in Tokyo, we stayed at the legendary Imperial Hotel. Designed in 1916 by Frank Lloyd Wright to "float on a sea of mud," it survived the 1923 earthquake that claimed 120,000 lives. By 1954 it was showing its age, but we relished the flawless service it provided. In still other cities we also enjoyed luxurious hotel facilities, thanks to Koyanagi's planning.

Quite appropriately, I encountered my first earthquake while sitting in the Imperial Hotel; it was an eerie feeling. At the time I was chatting with a visitor, Mr. Suzuki. He reacted calmly, saying "That was a strong one."

Social Functions

Thanks to the powerful sponsorship of Keidanren and JUSE, the Japanese regarded us as distinguished guests and treated us accordingly. We soon learned that courtesy was deeply ingrained in Japanese culture, and we relished being engulfed by it. (I also learned, years later, that some of the Japanese I met were amazed that an American was willing to travel all that distance to help a former enemy of his country.)

All visits to companies terminated with a gift-giving event. Usually the gift was some decorative piece of handicraft, such as a cloisonné vase. In some cases the gift, such as a bolt of decorative fabric, was directed to Sadie. At the Noritake China Company, I signed a ceramic plate, which they then fired and presented to me.

Each course ended with a ceremonial dinner or farewell party. The Japanese were evidently surprised to learn that I was a total abstainer from alcohol. To some, that fact was enough to give me an image of someone formal and austere. I was not aware that such was their conclusion.

The final reception, on the day before our departure, took place on the estate of Prince Takamatsu, brother of Emperor Hirohito. It was most enjoyable as well as a high honor. The prince spoke excellent English and showed interest in my mission. He expressed concern that making all those intended improvements could add to Japan's unemployment problem. I tried to point out that improving quality and reducing waste would improve the salability of Japanese products and thereby would reduce unemployment. I doubt I convinced him. Nevertheless, within two decades, Japan's high unemployment rate had vanished; there was a labor shortage, and Japan was building factories abroad to create added sources of labor.

My Report to Japanese Industry

About halfway through my mission, Koyanagi told me that Mr. Ishikawa and some other senior executives hoped that at the end of my visit, I would prepare a summary of my observations and conclusions relating to quality in Japan, to serve as a list of recommendations to Japanese industry. What now follows is derived from that report.

"Quality control in Japan has evolved generally along the lines followed in other countries.

1. A strong wave of interest in the statistical tools for quality control.
2. Some overenthusiasm and overextension of the use of statistical tools, with underemphasis on other essential tools.
3. A search for a broader base for the solution of quality problems through use of additional essential tools. (This is the present stage.)
4. Japanese industry appears to have compressed these steps into fewer years than have some Western countries. In this way, though starting later, Japanese industry has reduced the extent to which it was lagging behind Western development. Much of this gain in time has been due to the training activities of JUSE and to the receptivity of Japanese companies to this training.

5. The present trend toward broadening the approach to managing for quality (by setting quality goals, quality planning, organization changes, and economic analysis) is wholly constructive.
6. It is my conviction that notwithstanding the grave obstacles facing the Japanese economy as a whole, the outlook for improved quality and improved quality reputation for Japanese goods is bright."

Aftermath

The 1954 visit to Japan was only the beginning of my alliance with the Japanese. For years thereafter, JUSE organized teams to visit Western countries in order to keep abreast of developments. As part of the planning for such visits, Koyanagi would ask me to recommend which companies to visit and which managers to see. When such teams visited the United States, Koyanagi arranged for them to meet with me. I also heard directly from some Japanese companies wanting introductions to American companies and heard from American companies looking for information about, or introduction to, Japanese companies. All this generated extensive correspondence for Sadie and me, but I was willing to comply.

In 1956, JUSE published (in Japanese) the complete *Planning and Practices in Quality Control*. It ran to over 500 pages and included the written text of my 1954 lectures plus the associated oral elaborations, the diagrams I had drawn, questions and answers, and so on. It was my sixth book.

Note

1. Nonaka, Izumi, in J. M. Juran, ed., *A History of Managing for Quality*. ASQ Quality Press, 1995, pp 523–529.

23

The Bible of Managing for Quality: *Quality Control Handbook*

The urge to write came to me during my teens and intensified as my experience generated topics to write about. At Western Electric my written papers were few; they resulted chiefly from my job duties. Factory managers tended to discourage employees from writing papers for external publication—the prevailing attitude was "anyone who writes papers is likely neglecting his job." In addition, the company clearance procedure was lengthy and distasteful.

Such restrictions were minimal during my years in government and at New York University, and they vanished during my decades as a freelancer. In the absence of restrictions, my pent-up urge to write responded with a fury. While in government and academia, my writings related mainly to improving management in government and in the field of industrial engineering. However, the 1950s found me focusing almost exclusively on managing for quality.

Books Published

During the twentieth century I authored, coauthored, or edited over 30 books. Half of these were first editions; the rest were revisions of the first editions. (Each revision demanded substantial effort.) In what follows, I will discuss only those books that became significant contributions to managing for quality.

Quality Control Handbook

The idea of a handbook on quality control probably originated late in 1944 and was part of my decision to become a freelance consultant after World War II. I had in mind a whole series of books: the *Quality Control Handbook*, which was to be a comprehensive reference book; and separate manuals on quality control for executives, engineers, foremen, and inspectors.

I prepared an extensive outline for the *Handbook* plus a brief description for each of the other books. My publisher was McGraw-Hill, who offered me a contract (a mere one-page document!) in December 1945. Publication was in 1951. It became the flagship of the many books I have written.

The concept of the *Handbook* was to create a compendium of knowledge in the field of managing for quality. The emphasis was to be on universals—"principles that are valid no matter what the product, the process, or the function." I was only dimly aware that I would be contributing to the evolution of a new science—managing for quality. I ended up with fifteen chapters. I wrote six of these; other authors wrote the remaining nine, which I then edited.

The *Handbook* demanded typing work galore: preparing and revising my drafts, revising the drafts of the contributing authors and the associated correspondence. I had not learned touch typing, so I deeply appreciated the competence and dedication with which my wife Sadie responded.

The first edition fully lived up to my economic expectations. It sold about 19,000 copies during its eleven years of life. The original price was $10 per copy; by 1962 (the publication date of the second edition), the price had risen to $16.50. The total royalties during those eleven years came to $27,300. To me that was an ample financial reward; I had devoted the equivalent of about a year's time to the project.

To my surprise, the financial returns from future editions would multiply to a point that could enable me to live affluently solely from the royalties, were I to choose such a life. The second edition, published in 1962, sold 32,000 copies in its twelve years of life. The third edition, published in 1974, sold 94,000 over fourteen years. The fourth edition, published in 1988, sold 85,000 during eleven years. The fifth edition was published in 1999 and ran to 1800 pages. During those forty-eight years, the price soared from $10 to $150 per copy. (All figures exclude translations and student editions.)

From the outset, the *Handbook* became the "bible" of managing for quality and has increasingly served as the international reference book for professionals and managers in the field. It has retained that position; no serious competitor was visible as of the year 2000.

Publication of the *Handbook* was also a milestone on my journey through life. Over the years it attracted many followers, opened many doors, and contributed to my being sought after by institutions in the United States and internationally. It vaulted me into a position of leadership in the field; the decades that followed would solidify and enlarge that status.

With publication of the fifth edition, the name was changed to *Juran's Quality Handbook*; the joint editors-in-chief were Dr. A. Blanton Godfrey and me. For the sixth edition and beyond, Dr. Godfrey will be the editor-in-chief.

Managerial Breakthrough

This book, also published by McGraw-Hill (in 1964) took a long step toward creating a science of managing for quality. It set out in detail two of the major processes for managing anything. They consisted of: (1) breakthrough—creation of beneficial change; and (2) control—prevention of adverse change.

The first edition sold 57,000 copies during its twenty-nine year life. It also generated much fan mail. Many men were "turned on," and some wrote to tell me that the book had changed their lives.

Management of Quality Control

In 1967 I began offering a one-week training course in managing for quality. I called it "Management of Quality Control" (MQC). To that end I prepared a 200-page training manual dealing with numerous aspects of the subject. At the time, courses on quality control already existed—they had begun during World War II, using various universities as venues—but their subject matter was limited to statistical tools. MQC broke with tradition; it broadened the scope to include many managerial subjects.

In 1967 I offered five courses, limiting the number of attendees to forty per course. All courses filled up and became oversubscribed soon after being announced. Meanwhile, I also began to conduct the course for companies who preferred holding it at their own sites.

By 1969 I had concluded that I was spending too much time on the administration of the courses. I solved that problem by licensing American Management Association (AMA) to administer them. That arrangement began in 1971 and continued through 1980, at which time I created Juran Institute. The Institute then took over the administration of the courses.

Under AMA's sponsorship, the number of courses grew to seven each year. To accommodate waiting lists, I raised the limit on attendees from forty to sixty. Also, AMA was aggressive in its pricing. In 1971 it charged $425 per attendee (with a discount for members). By 1980 this figure had risen to $935 per attendee. The resulting income became substantial, especially for AMA but also for me—I received a goodly percentage of the gross income. Meanwhile, I used feedback from the attendees to update and revise my presentations; by 1990 I was using the sixth edition of MQC.

Long before 1990, the course had become a virtual rite of passage for quality managers. The proliferation of this course in numbers and in locations is evident from the announcements for the 1980 courses. They included information somewhat as follows:

Over the last 30 years, this course was conducted over 250 times and has been the basis for training much of a whole generation of managers in management of quality control. Over 75 of these courses have been conducted abroad, in over 30 countries on all continents. They include Argentina, Australia, Czechoslovakia, France, Great Britain, India, Israel, Italy, Japan, Mexico, the Netherlands, South Africa, Spain, Sweden, Yugoslavia, and six of the Eastern European countries, including the Soviet Union.

Quality Planning and Analysis

I teamed up with Professor Frank Gryna to write *Quality Planning and Analysis* (QPA); it was published in 1970 by McGraw-Hill. QPA was a textbook for engineers and other professionals in the field of managing for quality. Beyond its use as a textbook, its mission included helping users prepare for the Certified Quality Engineer (CQE) examination conducted by ASQC.

QPA was welcomed by its intended audience. The first edition sold 25,600 copies during its ten-year life. The second edition soared to 88,000 copies during its twelve years. It also brought many thank-you letters from users who had passed the CQE examination.

When the time came to prepare a third edition, I had become incredibly busy—on top of all the other activities, I was now chairman of Juran Institute. I bowed out by making Gryna a gift of my interest in QPA. He produced the third edition, which was published in 1993. I was persuaded to let my name be used as co-author on the grounds that much of the text still reflected my inputs.

Upper Management and Quality

During my first visit to Japan (1954), I conducted two courses for senior executives. Each ran for two days and each was attended by about sixty very senior executives of Japanese industries. At the time there was no broad demand in the West for such courses. Occasionally a company invited me to spend a day with upper managers, but such invitations were rare. The demand quickened during the 1970s; in response, I prepared a formal set of notes and designed a course which I called Upper Management and Quality (UMQ). The notes became yet another book, which was published in 1978.

The first course offering of UMQ took place in 1978. It was well attended but the feedback from attendees disclosed serious weaknesses, chiefly that the course did not address the problems as seen by upper managers. I promptly revised the notes and continued to revise them—UMQ went through five editions in ten years—while the ratings from attendees kept improving, as did the demand for both public and inhouse seminars.

Translations of Books

Some of my books have been widely translated and published into foreign languages—about twenty translations into twelve languages. Most translations were for countries in southern Europe and the Socialist bloc; others were into Japanese and Chinese. (Amazingly, when the Chinese translated the *Handbook*, their first printing was for 100,000 copies!) Some northern European publishers who researched the market told me that most of their local managers and engineers were multilingual and that they preferred my books in the original English.

Juran on Planning for Quality (JPQ)

JPQ was published in 1988 by the Free Press. It set out in detail the process of planning for quality, thereby becoming the third managerial process in what has become known as the Juran Trilogy; the other two such processes were quality improvement and quality control. They were first described in my book *Managerial Breakthrough* (1964).

Published Papers

During my professional journey, I published more than 200 papers, many of which were also presented to live audiences internationally. Most were published by the American Society for Quality Control (ASQC), the Japanese Union of Scientists and Engineers (JUSE), and American Management Association (AMA). The summaries that follow cover a selection of papers of special interest.

Directions for ASQC (1951). This paper reflected my growing dissatisfaction with the statistics-oriented leadership of ASQC. In contrast, industrial managers were oriented to problems and results, not techniques. I researched the affiliations of members of ASQC as indicated by their job titles. The data showed convincingly that the members' interests covered the broad quality function rather than being limited to the narrow field of statistics. I recommended:

1. Creation of divisions oriented to specific industrial *functions*—vendor relations, product design, inspection, and so on; and

2. Creation of divisions oriented to principal *processes* in industry, such as foundry and machining. I thought that such divisions could become a source of research in quantifying process capability.

The paper was published in *Industrial Quality Control* (IQC), November 1951.

Universals in Management Planning and Control. During 1952 and 1953, I served as leader of one of the four units of AMA's management course—the unit devoted to planning and controlling. During those sessions, there was much interest in universals—principles that were valid in planning and controlling no matter what the company, the function, or the process. This paper discussed some of those universals. Included in the list were the Pareto Principle, the improvement process, responsibility for improvement, use of multiple options, reducing risks in forecasting, the feedback loop for control, and the criteria for accountability. Publication was in AMA's *Management Review*, November 1954, pages 748–761.

Improving the Relationship Between Staff and Line (1956). This paper was born in a flash of illumination that came to me when I was reading Margaret Mead's book *Cultural Patterns and Technical Change*. Mead, a cultural anthropologist, described a number of projects undertaken by the United Nations Educational, Scientific, and Cultural Organization (UNESCO) to improve conditions in developing countries—projects for improving agriculture, public health, transportation, and so on. The improvements were proposed by visiting teams of experts selected by UNESCO. Nevertheless, the intended improvements ran into severe resistance to change and seldom became effective.

Mead contended that the resistance to change was due mainly to a clash between two cultures: the culture of the experts, which was based on their undoubted scientific expertise, and the culture of the developing countries, which was based on their long-established beliefs, habits, practices, and traditions.

In Mead's view, the experts' proposals demanded too great a price in cultural values. Moreover, the experts were not aware that the resistance was of cultural origin; instead they assumed that the resistance was due to superstition, ignorance, stubbornness, and the like. An impasse was inevitable. To her credit, Mead went beyond just describing the case examples; she included a list of "rules of the road" for dealing with resistance to change.

As I read Mead's book, I recalled many instances in which I had recommended changes to clients only to have them rejected for reasons that to me seemed illogical and even irrelevant. Mead's book opened my eyes to the real reasons. I dropped everything I was doing and wrote this paper, in which I used examples drawn from my consulting experience. Its publication was in AMA's *Personnel*, May 1956.

I have never let go of those insights. My paper was only a first response to the new revelation; later I wrote additional papers. Cultural resistance to change became a stand-alone chapter in my book *Managerial Breakthrough* (1964). It also became one of the sixteen videocassettes in *Juran on Quality Improvement* (1980).

Industrial Diagnostics (1957). This paper took a long step toward evolving a unified improvement process, whether for quality or anything else. It began by showing the distinction between two very different management goals: preventing adverse change (control) and creating favorable change (improvement).

The paper then described the repetitive steps taken to achieve control through use of the familiar feedback loop. In addition, it described the steps required by the unfamiliar improvement process:

- Identify and prioritize the specific goals for improvement;

- Diagnose to discover the cause(s) of the conditions needing improvement;
- Design a remedy—a beneficial change that can provide the improvement;
- Apply the remedy by solving the technological problems and the more subtle problems of cultural resistance.

Publication was in AMA's *The Management Review*, June 1957. The paper received favorable attention from industrialists. Later still, it became an essential input to the book *Managerial Breakthrough*.

First Graph Contrasting Control vs. Breakthrough. I have in my files a longhand diagram dated about 1952, showing the distinction between control and improvement. It may have been my first effort to explain that distinction graphically. This is shown in Figure 23-1.

Operator Errors—Time for a New Look. This paper (plus the earlier *Quality Problems, Remedies and Nostrums*) was my response to the "zero defects" fad of the 1960s. Government officials were goading their contractors to stage motivational spectacles; the contractors complied in order to maintain their customer relations. Those two papers became influential by providing company managers with material for resisting their superiors' tendency to be stampeded by the publicity. Publication was in ASQC's journal (now called *Quality Progress*), February 1968.

The QC Circle Phenomenon. I presented this paper at EOQC's annual conference, held in Stockholm in June of 1966. I had studied the concept in Japan in April 1966; this was the first paper to tell the West about it. The conference exhibited great interest. The paper was then published in IQC in January 1967 and attracted a great deal of attention. However, not until more than ten years later did companies in the West try out the QC Circle concept on a significant scale.

In the same paper I published the prediction I had been making orally during 1966:

The Japanese are headed for world quality leadership and will attain it in the next two decades, because no one else is moving there at the same pace.

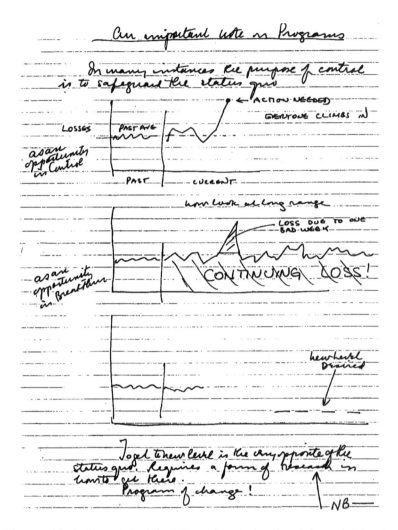

Figure 23-1. The original depiction of control vs. breakthrough (about 1952)

At the time, no one else believed that the Japanese, of all people, could accomplish such a feat.

Mobilizing for the 1970s. This was a sweeping review of quality needs for the 1970s along with suggestions for action. In addition, it presented the then-new concept of "life behind the quality dikes." The paper, published in *Quality Progress,* August 1969, was well received.

Consumerism and Product Quality. This extensive examination of the "consumerism movement" pointed out that the initiative for action on consumer grievances had passed from the industrial companies to consumerists, and that there was a risk of creating a bargaining agent between companies and their customers. It was first published in *Quality Progress*, July 1970.

And One Makes Fifty. This was a mini diary of how I spent the year 1974, my fiftieth year in quality control. I was already seventy years old, but during that year (as in many years), I flew more than 100,000 air miles. I lectured and consulted in fourteen foreign countries, as well as in the United States. I gleefully mentioned that "My journey from breakfast to work is 20 meters long and is made on foot." I had no intention of stopping: "I would be mad to give up so fascinating a way of life." The paper was published in *Quality Progress*, March 1975.

The Non–Pareto Principle; Mea Culpa. This is a brief history of how I invented the principle of "the vital few and trivial many" and then elected to name it the Pareto Principle (published in *Quality Progress*, May 1975).

Khrushchev's Venture into Quality Improvement. This paper was derived from a fascinating account in Nikita Khrushchev's memoirs. He had been assigned by Stalin to solve the problem of the poor quality of automobile tires. He knew nothing about making tires, yet he solved the problem (*Quality Progress*, January 1976).

Japanese and Western Quality—a Contrast. This research examined the approaches used by Japan and the West to manage for quality. The example studied was the color TV set. Through my contacts, I assembled the database needed (much of it company-classified). My research was thorough; use of the TV set as an example provided an aura of reality.

The paper was probably the most widely read of any I have ever written. It was published in *Proceedings of ICQC Tokyo*, October 1978, and also in *Quality Progress*, December 1978, followed by many translations and republications.

Training Courses

Over the years, I have presented more than 400 training courses in the United States and abroad. Most of these were sponsored by AMA, by myself, or by foreign national societies, and they were open to any and all who bought tickets. The sponsoring bodies billed the companies for sending their personnel to such events, and I negotiated with the sponsors to receive a percentage of the gross income. (My arrangements with developing countries and the Socialist Bloc were different; I will discuss these later.) I also accepted numerous invitations from industrial companies to hold similar training courses on site solely for their personnel.

Seminars at American Management Association

I joined the American Management Association (AMA) in 1941 while I was still at Western Electric. At the time its activities consisted of running about a dozen large conferences annually. To run these conferences required only a small staff. However, AMA also formed industry "councils," using unpaid volunteers. Each council consisted of about twenty industry managers who met twice a year to advise AMA's staff about ongoing problems, to propose topics to be addressed in future conferences, and to nominate speakers who might be able to share experiences with attendees. In 1947, the AMA invited me to join the Manufacturing Council. I accepted the invitation and remained on that council for many years.

Alvin Dodd, the president of AMA, retired in 1948. He was succeeded by Lawrence (Larry) Appley, whose background was rich in human relations and training. Appley soon added an innovation—the AMA Executive Seminar. Each such seminar brought together about fifteen managers from various companies to discuss a selected topic over a three-day period, under the guidance of a seminar leader.

I became the regular leader of one category of the executive seminars—the category of managing for quality. Those seminars went well, and I invariably received high marks from the attendees. As a welcome outcome, some attendees invited me to do consulting work for their companies.

The students in the seminars were mature managers. From them I learned about the realities they faced and the strategies they adopted for dealing with those realities. In a sense, each manager was also a researcher engaged in finding innovative solutions to his problems. They shared their experiences with each other in the seminars and thereby added to my database.

The AMA Executive Seminars were most successful. At the time no one else offered comparable opportunities for managers to spend several days with managers from other companies to discuss common problems. AMA had a monopoly and made the most of it.

The AMA Management Course

During the early 1950s, Appley came up with a further innovation—the AMA Management Course. It consisted of four week long "units," each dealing with subject matter as follows:

Unit One—Basic principles, skills, and tools
Unit Two—Planning and controlling
Unit Three—Organization building
Unit Four—Appraising results and taking action

Appley asked me to lead Unit Two. I was willing and even eager to accept. The registrations soon made clear that the Management Course was attracting people from high places in company hierarchies. Many were vice presidents or general managers in their companies or divisions; a substantial minority were presidents. It was a consultant's dream to lead seminars attended by such audiences.

As the course got underway, I discovered that not all was well. I knew quite a bit about controlling; I could explain the universal feedback loop and its application. But, in contrast, I lacked solid experience in "planning" as that word was used by most attendees. To them "planning" meant planning for an entire business—a process in which many of them had more experience than I. That became evident as questions were raised.

I was shocked by the low marks I received from too many attendees during my first week of leadership. Some provided constructive suggestions, which I took seriously. In the months that followed my marks did improve, but they never reached the levels I regularly received in the executive seminars on managing for quality. Although my performance was improving, I was unhappy with it, as was William Kushnick, the director of the AMA Management Course. The end result was my departure from the Management Course. I may have rationalized that my increasing busyness had crowded me out of the course, but deep down I knew I had failed because I lacked adequate experience relative to an important segment of the subject matter.

Videocassettes

During the 1980s I recorded about forty videocassettes. One group of these—the sixteen-tape set called "Juran on Quality Improvement"—became the basis for training huge numbers of managers and facilitators in how to make improvements in quality. I will elaborate on that adventure in the chapter on Juran Institute, Inc.

Lecturing and Writing in Retrospect

The activities of writing and lecturing became an essential part of my life. I found that writing imposes a discipline on the writer. My fears that readers could misinterpret my words resulted in frequent use of the dictionary and thesaurus to choose words and phrases with care. I read and reread the text, looking for ways to improve clarity.

In like manner, I began to evolve expertise as a speaker. When speaking from a prepared text, I learned to avoid the sin of looking only at the pages; instead, most of the time I kept my eyes on the audience. I also began to be comfortable by merely preparing notes that I would then flesh out *ex tempore*.

Dealing with questions from the audience gave me problems at first. In most cases I could provide useful answers immediately. I had a tendency, however, to get carried away by my enthusiasm and wander off on some unrelated topic; whether I ended up answering the question then became a matter of luck. I finally learned to jot down the key words of the question at the outset and to periodically peek down at those words to help me stay on track.

A most important byproduct of my training courses was the feed-back I received from thousands of managers in numerous cultures. The feedback consisted of their experiences, questions, challenges, and sug-gestions for improvement. Within this feedback were many nuggets that contributed to evolution of the new science of managing for quality. Lacking such feedback, my attempts to evolve such a science would have been severely handicapped.

A measure of my selectivity in accepting invitations was my rising consulting fee structure. By the early 1960s, my usual fee was $300 *per diem*. By the mid-1960s it was $500; by the early 1970s it had reached $1,000 *per diem*. In a sense I was using the fee structure to price myself out of the excess of invitations. I felt no shame in accepting those fees. No one but me knew how much time I was devoting to pro bono engagements, reading articles, attending conferences, maintaining my database, writing books and training manuals, preparing lecture notes, keeping up with my correspondence, and so on.

Invitations to lecture also came from nonprofit organizations. These seldom provided an honorarium, but they stirred the urge of service to society. Many of those invitations came from professional societies, especially chapters of ASQC. Others came from units of the U.S. Armed Services. The armed services were especially grateful when I responded, but I would remind them, "It's my Navy, too."

24

Consulting During My Mature Decades

At year-end 1959, I was 55 years old. Despite my late start, I had established a secure status as the leading consultant in managing for quality. During the next three decades I served many clients—far too many to discuss in any detail. In this chapter I will discuss only a few domestic clients of special interest. In a later chapter I will do the same with respect to international clients.

Armour & Company

During the 1960s, I had assignments with several divisions of Armour & Company, the giant meat packer. The company divisions included Foods, Leather, Industrial Chemicals, Agricultural Chemicals, Pharmaceuticals, and Dial (soap).

My most widespread finding at Armour was that the quality control systems focused almost exclusively on meeting quality standards and on putting out sporadic fires; only rarely did the systems provide an organized approach for improvement. My recommendations noted this deficit and outlined the steps to be taken to organize for improvement.

Following my reports, some divisions asked me to periodically return to monitor their progress. This was especially the case with the Foods Division, which had embarked on an ambitious program of upgrading quality in order to increase market share and secure premium prices.

The Foods Division's program failed, and the failure reached scandalous proportions. The plant managers had accepted the goals of volume of production but not the new goals of higher quality. In too many cases, the volume goals had been met by shipping out products that did not conform to the quality goals, resulting in serious negative customer reaction.

When Armour's chairman asked me why the plant managers had failed to meet the quality standards, I was forced to point out that the senior executives were part of the problem, because of the design of the "executive instrument panel." The senior executives were well supplied with information on financial performance and on volume of goods shipped to customers. Their report package, however, lacked summarized information on matters such as the extent of customer satisfaction and the state of the competitors' quality. Lacking such information, the executive reviews of plant performance convinced the plant managers that the senior executives considered the goals for volume to have higher priority than the goals for quality. One of the dramatic consequences of this contrast in views was that the general manager of the Foods Division lost his job.

Dennison Manufacturing Company

Dennison was a mid-sized company engaged in making coated papers, labeling systems, machines for printing images on containers, and more. It had been founded by Henry S. Dennison, a visionary with socialist leanings who gave high priority to human relations. His approach left an enduring imprint on the company.

My activities with Dennison had their origin in 1962, when the Dennison president, Dana C. Huntington (DCH), attended an AMA seminar on the Board of Directors. (I was one of the leaders of that seminar.)   Soon after that, DCH invited me to visit Dennison, meet individually with the senior executives, look over the company, and give him my observations. I completed that assignment in March 1963.

DCH next invited me to sit in on Dennison's board meetings as an observer. I did so and offered periodic comments on my observations. That led to my being elected to the board at the 1963 annual meeting of shareholders. I remained on the board until 1974, when I became victim of an age limit that I had initiated and that the board adopted.

Life at Dennison was quite stable and predictable. The senior executives had spent virtually their entire careers with Dennison and (with one exception) had reached a state of peaceful coexistence. The company was quietly progressive and innovative, and it was mostly at peace with its shareholders and employees. An exception to this was the state of its copier.

By the early 1960s the Xerox company had marketed its first electrostatic copier—the 914. It was a sensation; it outperformed all known ways of copying documents. Xerox leased the machines at high mark-ups and enjoyed a phenomenal growth in sales and profits.

During those same early 1960s, Dennison went to market with a copier of an inferior design—it required the use of specially coated paper. Its cost per copy was substantially below that of Xerox, however. The very fact that the Dennison copier was the first machine to break the Xerox monopoly sent Dennison's shares soaring briefly on the stock market.

Despite that rosy beginning, the Dennison copier was soon in trouble. The machines failed often in service, requiring costly redesigns and retrofits. More ominous was the new competition from Japanese companies, which came out with electrostatic copiers that bypassed the Xerox patents. Now the competition was between plain paper copiers, making Dennison's copier obsolete.

Except for the copier, the time spent with Dennison was one of "calm seas and a prosperous voyage."

Ideal Corporation

Ideal Corporation was a small privately held company making automotive parts for the "aftermarket"—parts sold to the merchant chain that supplies automotive repair shops. In May 1953, I was invited to have a look at their approach to managing for quality. Thus began a long, continuing engagement that terminated in 1971 when Ideal was sold to Parker-Hannifin.

Although I was brought in to deal with managing for quality, I soon developed an excellent rapport with Ideal's president, Philip Rauch (Phil). That rapport led to my becoming Phil's consultant on virtually all matters of managing the company. In addition, Phil used me to work with his managers on specific multifunctional problems. For example, he had not been schooled in technology, so he used me to review projects such as product design and process design. He also drew on my contacts to help recruit managers, as well as to find consultants for specific missions.

Phil was a hands-on manager and a master at using outside consultants. He expanded sales through new product designs and imaginative marketing. He was also an aggressive cost-cutter.

Phil's dedication enabled him (in 1971) to sell his company to Parker-Hannifin (PH) at a handsome price. Through that sale he became a major stockholder in PH and a member of its board of directors, which soon elected him as its chairman.

Merck, Sharp & Dohme

Merck, Sharp & Dohme (MSD) is the manufacturing division of Merck & Company, a giant in the pharmaceutical industry. In November 1964, I was contacted by Charles W. Pike, an MSD vice president. That contact led to an agreement for me to look at MSD's approach to managing for quality and to report my conclusions and recommendations.

I found that MSD was well poised to carry out its mission of producing products that met its customers' needs for efficacy and safety. Moreover, MSD was quite progressive in looking for better ways to conduct its operations. For example, MSD was among the first in its industry to adopt new technology such as automated chemical analysis and electronic data processing.

My principal recommendations related to the following:

- Creation of an executive report package to keep the senior managers informed about the state of quality and associated trends;
- The emerging threat from generic products and the associated pricing problems;
- Improving the coordination of departments on joint problems;
- Reducing the cost of the numerous controls on quality.

MSD responded positively to the report, and this response included the senior managers. They organized several meetings to discuss the report with me. This was followed by a consulting arrangement in which I came in one day each month to meet with various managers to discuss ongoing problems. This arrangement was renewed year after year for a total of nine years, terminating in 1973.

I thoroughly enjoyed meeting with those dedicated men. They took their responsibilities seriously and operated on an exemplary level of ethics and competence. They were good listeners and were open-minded with respect to my comments and proposals. This extended even to the problem of pricing, in which they concluded not to accept my proposals. In turn, I learned much from them while admiring their dedication.

Otis Elevator Company

Otis was a multinational company engaged in providing elevators and escalators for buildings. In the United States, it was organized into three operating divisions. The Production Division made the components from which the final products were assembled. The Construction Division did the assembly at the building sites. The Service Division provided inspection and maintenance service to the building managements.

In April 1962 the Production Division invited me to review their approach to managing for quality at their two plants (in Yonkers, New

York, and Harrison, New Jersey). That review led to the creation of a Quality Improvement Committee and my becoming a regular member. For the next five years, I made numerous visits to the Otis factories to attend the committee meetings and for other purposes.

By February 1967 I had concluded that it would be best to terminate the arrangement—the Production Division managers had been fully exposed to my views. Even more important, I had become convinced that the company's major unsolved quality problems were of a multidivisional nature and that a formal multidivisional approach was needed. Such an approach was resisted by the Construction and Service divisions. I therefore decided to "fire" Otis as a client.

Xerox Corporation

Xerox produced and marketed the first xerographic copier, a machine that outperformed every copying process then in existence. The patents gave the company a monopoly and enabled it to grow in sales and profits at a rate seldom matched in financial history.

Prior to the 1980s, my contacts with Xerox were brief. Some Xerox managers had attended my courses. On at least one occasion (1963), I conducted a five-day training course for managers and engineers at the company offices in Rochester, New York. Then, in the early 1980s I was drawn into a most serious problem— Xerox's sales were hemorrhaging, and the reason was poor quality.

The Xerox machines were seriously failure-prone, and there were other quality problems as well. Xerox's chief response had been to create a field service force to restore service, but the customers were not satisfied; they wanted no service interruptions. The depth of this feeling was not known to the Xerox senior managers. Their "instrument panel" kept them up to date on their dazzling financial results but did not give them information about quality, even though customer dissatisfaction had built to dangerous levels.

In due course, competitors found ways to bypass the Xerox patents and came to market with machines that were less failure-prone. The growing competition increasingly ate into Xerox's share of the market.

The impact of competition on Xerox's financial performance finally reached crisis proportions; in the minds of some analysts, the continued existence of Xerox was under threat. The threat then forced the very senior executives to inform themselves on what was taking place with respect to quality. One result was that in the early 1980s, I was invited to look at the problem and then spend a day to brief the entire body of senior executives, from chairman McColough down.

What I was able to tell those executives was essentially the following:

- The executives had complete information on finances but little on quality. That had enabled quality problems to reach crisis proportions without their knowledge.
- The Xerox machines were seriously failure-prone; they failed frequently, creating mini crises for customers.
- The top few failure types accounted for the bulk of the field failures. Those failure types had their origin in the product designs; in addition, they were identical, model after model. *New models went to market with known failure-prone features.*

Xerox had an army of product designers, most of whom were assigned to create new features to go into new models in order to create added sales. Those added sales were not keeping pace with the loss of market share traceable to the field failures.

In addition, Xerox was enduring large chronic wastes caused by internal quality problems—factory scrap, redoing of prior work, excess inspection and test, delays, and so on. No organized approach to reducing these chronic wastes existed.

I never learned what subsequent actions (if any) were traceable to that meeting. However, Xerox soon underwent a reorganization during which David Kearns emerged as the chief executive. Shortly after that, Kearns invited me to meet with him. We had a lengthy session during which he took extensive notes and asked many questions. He also wanted me to become deeply involved, but I was forced to turn him down—I had too many prior commitments.

Under Kearns' leadership, Xerox regained much of its share of the market; it also won national quality awards in the United States, Great Britain, and Japan. It then published a book relating how the company dealt with the crisis. (*A World of Quality: The Timeless Passport*, ASQ Press, 1993.)

My final meeting with Xerox took place in early February 1994. The occasion was its strategic planning conference for senior executives worldwide. I attended the awards session of that conference. The Xerox chairman was now Paul Allaire, successor to David Kearns. He presented awards to some of the executives for outstanding performance in their areas. He also presented me with an award for my contribution to Xerox quality. The physical award was a handsome piece of Steuben glass depicting an American flag. I was deeply moved by the gracious gesture; it was their first such award to an outsider, ever.

U.S. Navy—The Fleet Ballistic Missile System

The Fleet Ballistic Missile System (FBMS) was created in 1955 to provide the U.S. Navy with a capability of launching long-range nuclear missiles from a submerged nuclear-powered submarine. It was a new and terrifying weapon system.

The Navy's approach to managing the FBMS was also new. It involved creating a Special Projects Office to command the project rather than the traditional approach of giving funding and command to the Navy bureaus, such as the Bureau of Ships, Bureau of Ordnance, and so on. It was an inspired approach; the new organizational design greatly reduced the time required to make the FBMS operational.

I was drawn into this project in 1961 by Admiral Raborn, then head of the Special Projects Office. He secured my name somehow and invited me to visit him. He wanted an independent review of the reliability and quality aspects of the FBMS. I turned him down, pointing out that for so vast a system, the survey was beyond the full-time capability of any one person. However, I made a counterproposal: create a committee with membership from the responsible organizations, and I would be willing to serve on such a committee. He would then get the benefit of my views, while the other committee members would see to it that the essential database would be provided.

Admiral Raborn accepted that proposal. The resulting committee included members from the Special Products Office, its technical representatives at the contractors' premises, the prime contractor (Lockheed Missiles and Space Company), principal subcontractors, and the Navy Bureau of Weapons.

The Navy arranged for me to be designated as a consultant to the Applied Physics Laboratory (APL) at Johns Hopkins University. It was APL who secured my top-secret clearance and paid my expenses. I was surprised to learn that my appointment as a consultant to APL carried an honorarium of $100 per diem. I would have accepted the appointment on a pro bono basis—no honorarium; the U.S. Navy was also *my* navy.

The committee's review focused on the missile (which at the time was the Polaris), the submarine navigation subsystem (it enabled the submarine to travel submerged for weeks at a time), and the missile guidance subsystem.

The committee held seven meetings. Its final reports, issued in 1962, made numerous recommendations especially relative to the missile reliability but extending to such matters as the contractors' organization design.

The committee reports were issued seventeen years after the end of World War II. We were no longer in combat, although the new cold war was in progress. I would never again be called to help our armed forces, but I relished the opportunity to be of help in the FBMS, which in its day was the most important military program under development by the United States.

One-Day Diagnosis

During the 1970s and 1980s, as senior executives began to involve themselves in matters of quality, I was often asked to conduct a "survey" of a company's approach to managing for quality. For such engagements I took the broad approach: identify the company's

strengths and weaknesses, identify the threats faced and opportunities available, and offer recommendations.

After a few such engagements, I evolved an approach that parallels
a physician's annual physical examination of a patient. I discovered that
diagnosing the health of a company with respect to managing for
quality could be done in much the same way.

At a time when my fees were in the range of $5,000 to $10,000
per diem, I would offer to conduct such a survey in a single day. It
could be done, but only by adhering to a demanding schedule.

Before making the visit, I would arrange to acquire some briefing.
In part I would request that the company send me information in
advance: the most recent annual report to shareholders, the corporate
quality manual, any executive reports on quality, a list of the top few
unsolved quality problems, the principal improvement projects under
way, and the like. I would review these while flying to the location. In
addition I asked for a face-to-face briefing from the quality manager
during the evening of arrival or at breakfast on the day of the visit.

I divided the eight-hour day of the visit into eight segments of an
hour each. The first six hours (which included the lunch hour) were
used for interviews with six of the senior executives. The seventh
hour was used to enable me to organize my notes and prepare my
summary. The final hour was used to present my report to the senior
executives collectively.

I preferred to begin the interviews with the marketing head, and
I started with the question, "As viewed by your customers, what is
your ranking in quality compared to your leading competitors?" After
the response I would ask, "How do you know that?" I would also ask
many other questions such as, "What is being done to improve the
company's ranking in the marketplace?" Meanwhile I would be making notes such as "There are no hard data on why customers prefer the
competitors' products; there is an atmosphere of blame between the
marketing and product development departments." And so it would
go for interviews with other senior executives.

In some cases the executives were surprised that in one day, I had
learned so much about the company and could shed so much light on

what needed doing. Occasionally my report led to decisions being made then and there. Yet, in retrospect, I hesitate to recommend the "one-day diagnosis" to other consultants. It is probably better to allow two or several days for the diagnosis.

Q

25
Japan, 1960s Through 1990s

During the period of the1960s through the 1990s, I made numerous visits to Japan. With one exception, each was as an invited guest and for a specific mission. Between visits, there was extensive correspondence and other activity. Koyanagi, the managing director of JUSE, regularly kept me informed about activities taking place in Japan and asked for my views on what was going on in the United States and elsewhere.

The Second Visit to Japan—1960

In September of 1957, Koyanagi invited me to return to Japan and give lectures in three areas: industrial engineering; organization, planning, and controlling; and new product development. The lectures were not to be limited to managing for quality; they were to deal with managing generally.

I accepted the invitation even though the focus was not on managing for quality. In part I would be lecturing on fields in which I was not yet fully expert; I would need to acquire research material to prepare the lectures.

At the Kurake Spinning Company in Japan (1960), one of many such company visits

The visit took place from October 28th to November 20th, 1960. Sadie again accompanied me. I gave two one-day courses to senior executives and two multi-day courses to middle managers, as well as a public lecture sponsored by one of the newspapers. In addition I made several plant visits.

During the courses for senior executives, we went around the table, asking each attendee, "What is your company's present quality ranking compared to your competitors? What will your ranking be ten years from now?"

The answers were revealing. Most companies had evaluated their competitive ranking. Most had made tangible progress during the 1950s. A few had attained quality leadership and now faced the problem of proving this to customers. Most were optimistic about future progress.

I also observed the physical goings-on. Japan was in the midst of a huge construction boom, both in factories and in the national infrastructure. There were unmistakable signs of progress in managing for

A public lecture in Japan (1960). I first used the overhead projector there in 1954; at the time the only such machine in Japan was the one I brought with me.

quality. JUSE was heavily engaged in conducting training courses, chiefly in the use of statistical methods but increasingly in how to manage for quality. (The textbook *QC for Foremen* had already sold 1.2 million copies.)

The Aborted ICQC Tokyo—1965

In the early 1960s, Koyanagi proposed to hold an international conference on quality control (ICQC) to be held in Tokyo in 1965. Such conferences were already being held annually in Europe under the sponsorship of the EOQC, starting in 1957. No such conference had ever been sponsored by Japan, however.

To reduce the inherent risks, Koyanagi corresponded with foreign leaders in the field. He traveled abroad for face-to-face visits. He set up committees within Europe and the United States as well as in Japan. He looked to me to help on several fronts: nominating topics to be addressed at the conference, nominating speakers, evaluating speakers nominated by others, coordinating the supporting activities in the United States, and so on. The resulting correspondence was extensive and time-consuming.

Amid all the planning, Koyanagi ran into an impasse with Deming. It began when Koyanagi proposed to include the topic "Total Quality Control (TQC)" at one of the conference sessions. Koyanagi had read a book of that title published in 1961 by A. V. Feigenbaum. Koyanagi was intrigued by the phrase "total quality control"; it denied the idea of "partial quality control."

Deming vigorously protested the term "total quality control." In his "Notes for Mr. Koyanagi" dated May 2, 1964, he stated:

> The word Total Quality Control (TQC) is wrong for Japan and completely unnecessary anywhere. The statistical control of quality means total, and never meant anything else to Dr. Shewhart, and this is what I taught my Japanese students and executives.

Koyanagi was troubled by Deming's claim. Deming's words carried much weight in Japan; the publicity surrounding the Deming Prizes had made him a celebrity. So Koyanagi asked a few foreigners (including myself) for comments before overruling Deming.

I was disappointed by Deming's reaction. He was contending that statistical tools could solve all quality problems—they were a panacea. I knew from experience that this was simply not so; I concluded that his comment was narrow and self-serving. I urged Koyanagi to add TQC to the program, adding, "I would certainly not worry about Deming's reactions. I do not regard his opinions on the integrated approach as being based on experience. Moreover, while a number of mathematicians who had narrow approaches have broadened their views as they have been exposed to industry, Deming has not. He has remained a narrow specialist, one of the very best in his specialty, but his mind seems to have been closed to all else."[1]

Koyanagi reached much the same conclusion. In his letter of June 22, 1964, he had observed, "Frankly speaking, it seems to me that Dr. Deming has had little experience in industrial production, and that he has never handled 'quality' as a complete entity including product, process, and operation (including men's activities)." It was the beginning of JUSE's disenchantment with Deming.

The ICQC in Tokyo was never held. Koyanagi's health was failing. By 1964, matters had worsened to a point that he could not carry on his work. He was so central to the project that it ground to a halt. He passed away on January 16, 1965, at the age of 61.

The Third Visit—1966

My third visit to Japan was in April 1966—cherry blossom time. My mission was to conduct quality-related courses for top executives and middle managers. I was also to include lectures on the "breakthrough" concept. (My book *Managerial Breakthrough*, published in 1964 in English, had aroused interest in Japan; a Japanese translation was underway, stimulated by Nippon Kayaku Ltd.) In addition I was to visit some Japanese companies, especially Toyota and Matsushita. I was also to address the annual Conference on QC Circles. It all went well. I was no longer a stranger to the Japanese; they welcomed me as a friend. And I was also on familiar ground—the subject matter was entirely related to managing for quality.

I had meanwhile exchanged much correspondence with Mr. T. Takamatsu, Koyanagi's successor. During the 1966 visit, I met him face-to-face and was charmed. In contrast to the intense Koyanagi, Takamatsu was relaxed and tactful. From the very outset, our exchanges were easy-going and effective. I also found that Takamatsu was reactivating the work on the aborted ICQC from 1965; it was now to be held in 1969.

The Japanese QC Circles

The 1966 visit introduced me to a surprising Japanese invention—the QC Circle. By the 1960s the Japanese had decided to offer training in managing for quality to the work force. Following the training, they offered workers the opportunity to join improvement teams—QC Circles—that could then tackle improvements, one after another, without end.

At the 1966 Annual Conference on QC Circles, I heard several case examples of improvements made by workers, some very young. My imagination soared. In my address to the conference I included the following:

> Japan has found a way of utilizing the creativity and energies of the people at the very bottom of the company hierarchy to aid in solving problems that would otherwise require the time of managers and engineers, or would go on and on without solution.

I did much to inform the West about the Japanese QC Circle approach. In my speech to the 1966 EOQC Conference (Stockholm, June 1966), I wove in what I had seen in Japan in April. I also published a paper[2] that was widely translated and republished; it brought requests for hundreds of reprints. Nevertheless, Western business cultures resisted adoption of the QC Circle concept.

The Japan Prize

At the end of my final 1966 course, there was the usual farewell party and the usual round of speeches. In Japan it is the custom that each speaker, on concluding his remarks, designates who is to be the next speaker. When Professor Kondo of Kyoto University spoke, he finished with the comment, "We have a Deming Prize; why don't we have a Juran Prize?" Then, after a bit of elaboration, he designated me to be the next speaker.

I was in a quandary—What did Kondo mean, and how should I respond? I finally mumbled out that such a matter should be decided by the Japanese, or words to that effect. Years later I found out what Kondo had in mind.

Before the farewell party, the Japanese had discussed creating a new quality prize to be awarded to companies that had won the Deming Prize for the second time. The discussion favored calling the new prize the Juran Prize. Kondo was asking me, in a roundabout way, whether I would be willing to lend my name to that new prize. My answer was interpreted as a gracious turn-down, and instead they named the new prize the Japan Prize.

In retrospect, I realize now that Kondo's query was actually in accordance with the Japanese custom of avoiding bluntness. Nevertheless it confused me, and today I regret the outcome. I would have been delighted to lend my name to something so symbolic of excellence in quality.

The Fourth Visit—ICQC Tokyo—1969

Soon after becoming the managing director of JUSE, Takamatsu took steps to reactivate ICQC Tokyo, which he rescheduled for October 1969. He asked me to help with the planning, and I agreed. He also asked me to participate actively throughout the conference, including the closing address, in which I was to summarize the event.

Then came a shock. In June 1969 Takamatsu suffered a fatal heart attack while leading a meeting; he died then and there. This time the conference was not aborted. A new JUSE top management was soon in place. Those appointments, plus Takamatsu's prior planning and delegation of authority, enabled ICQC Tokyo—1969, to go on as scheduled.

As it turned out, 1969 was a good year for holding the conference. Japanese products were increasingly invading Western markets, notably those of the United States. This invasion was stunningly successful in consumer electronics but had also become significant in automobiles, steel, and several other product categories. Buyers welcomed the Japanese imports, which were becoming competitive in quality (in some cases even superior) while lower in price than the domestic products.

The conference attracted over 1,000 attendees; 227 came from 36 foreign countries. There were 231 papers from 37 countries; all were published in the Proceedings book and made available to attendees as they registered. Thanks to the detailed prior planning, the attendees' needs were met without a hitch.

To summarize the entire conference required me to read each of the 231 papers! To do so, I spent most of the conference time in my hotel room reading those papers and preparing my summary.

The closing banquet was a glittering affair. Music came from stringed kotos played by women in colorful traditional Japanese kimonos and obis. The attending Japanese wives and other family members added to this color. Flashbulbs popped endlessly. Ample food was available, along with a generous supply of sake, the Japanese rice wine. It was a most memorable occasion.

Following ICQC Tokyo—1969, I spoke at the QC Circle Conference and the Eighth Conference on QC for Foremen. The latter was held in a Sumo wrestling stadium with 3,800 foremen in attendance! I learned that the number of participants in QC circles had roared ahead: in 1962 there had been 200,000 participants; by 1969, the number was two million!

The Fifth Visit—1970

My fifth trip to Japan took place in May 1970. On that trip I accompanied several executives from Ideal Corporation, a small American maker of automotive parts. This company was trying to establish a source of supply in Japan. (I was their management consultant and a member of their board of directors.) The choice of May 1970 was timed to enable the managers to visit Japan's International Exhibition, known as Expo 70. (Expo 70 was indeed worth visiting.)

I informed JUSE of my plans to come to Japan, and while I did manage to meet with some of the JUSE people, these were mainly courtesy meetings.

The Sixth Visit—1974

During the early 1970s, JUSE proposed that I come to Japan to lecture on managing for quality in service industries. I declined the invitation, pointing out that I lacked enough case examples to support lectures on the subject. As a counterproposal, I suggested that they organize a conference on quality in service industries and invite Japanese service companies to present papers explaining their approaches. I would be willing to attend such a conference, critique the papers, and offer general comments. JUSE accepted that counterproposal. (By this time my correspondence with JUSE was through Mr. Junji Noguchi, whose title was Manager, R & D Department.)

The conference on quality in service industries was (to my knowledge) the first such conference ever. Fifteen papers were presented, each a masterpiece of analysis of problems and design of remedies. My subsequent detailed report was published in *Quality Progress,* April 1975. A major surprise (and disappointment) of the conference was the low attendance—only about fifty tickets were sold. We had much discussion on why the response was so limited.

The All-Japan QC Circle Conference featured the presentation of prize-winning papers previously presented at regional conferences. A panel of judges conferred to select the all-Japan winners; medals were hung around the necks of the winners in the manner of Olympic athletes. At the convivial meeting following the conference, I made it a point to visit with the winners and with others less fortunate. Those were heartwarming discussions.

I also had decided that since I would be making the long trip to Japan, I should accept some invitations of long standing to lecture in Taiwan, Hong Kong, and the Philippines.

The Seventh Visit—ICQC '78 Tokyo

In October 1978, the Japanese held their second International Conference on Quality Control—ICQC '78 Tokyo. As in 1969, they invited me to attend as their honored guest. They also asked me to present several papers at the conference and at the post-conference events, and I agreed.

At ICQC '78 Tokyo, my presentations included a paper titled "Japanese and Western Quality—a Contrast." This paper was based on my research relative to color TV sets. It became the most widely read, translated, and republished paper I have ever written.

During my visit to Toyota Motor Company, I presented the paper "Perspective on Automobile Quality." In the section on automotive safety, I drew heavily on the research I had done for the paper "Automotive Safety Legislation—Ten Years Later," which I had presented at the EOQC conference held in Denmark in 1976.

I also met with an audience of senior executives and presented a paper titled "Japanese QC in the Future and the Role of Top Management." During the discussion period, several of the men put me on the defensive by complaining of the "growing unfairness" of American quotas and tariffs on imports from Japan.

I pointed out that serious resistance to the imports now came from labor unions; millions of jobs had been "exported" to Japan because of the imports. The labor unions represented millions of voters. One remedy was for Japanese companies to manufacture within the United States employing American workers, as was being done by Japanese makers of color TV sets. My audience was unhappy with my comments, but in due course, many Japanese companies, even in the automotive industry, established or bought factory facilities within the United States.

A special treat was seeing the annual "Jidai Matsuri" (Festival of Ages) in Kyoto—a procession of about 3,000 actors who portray historical incidents dating back to the seventh century A.D. The actors play the roles of shoguns, nobles, warriors on the march, and so on, all clad in the original costumes of the respective historical periods.

The Eighth Visit—1981

My eighth visit to Japan (in November 1981) was to receive a high honor—the emperor's award of the Order of the Sacred Treasure, Second Class. (The Second Class is the highest award that may be given to a non-Japanese.)

Actually, I missed receiving the physical award (a certificate plus a handsome medal) from the emperor in person. In the normal course of events, all the emperor's awards are made on one day of the year specifically designated for the purpose. As that day approached, I was receiving requests from JUSE urging me to come to Japan during that week but not telling me why. JUSE was in a quandary. Nominations for so prestigious an award must be cleared by numerous officials before the emperor's final approval, and this clearance process had not yet run its course. JUSE dared not invite me to what might end up as a nonevent.

I also was in a quandary. I had scheduled a five-day course for that week in Atlanta; there were already sixty people registered, along with

Receiving the Japanese Order of the Sacred Treasure (1981). A schedule conflict caused me to miss receiving it directly from the emperor. Instead, the presentation was made by Mr. Ichiro Nakagawa, Minister of Science and Technology, at a special ceremony.

a waiting list. Not knowing what JUSE had in mind, I declined the invitation but offered to come the following week. The end result was that I received the physical evidence of the award from Ichiro Nakagawa, Minister of Science and Technology, with a small group of other notables in attendance. The citation for the award read:

> … for the development of Quality Control in Japan and the facilitation of U.S. and Japanese friendship.

The Ninth Visit—ICQC '87 Tokyo

In October 1987, JUSE hosted its third International Conference on Quality Control. For the third time they invited me to attend as their honored guest. This time my duties were limited to the conference itself; I gave a keynote address and also chaired an international panel discussion. Nevertheless, it was a treat to visit with the attendees. Most of the world leaders in managing for quality were there, and I knew them well.

During the conference, my broker in New York phoned to tell me the sky was falling. The Dow Jones Industrial Average had plunged nearly 23 percent in one day, with a corresponding impact on my investments. It would take nearly two years for them to regain their precrash levels.

The Tenth and Final Visit—1990

By the end of the 1980s, I had begun to advise foreign countries that during the early 1990s I would terminate all foreign travel because of my age and my huge backlog of neglected personal and family matters. Noguchi took notice of my intentions and invited me to come to Japan in 1990 to participate in the upcoming International QC Circle Conference and also to give a public lecture. I accepted that invitation and prepared the paper "The Evolution of Japanese Leadership in Quality" for the conference.

Despite my approaching departure from international affairs, I hoped that the relationship between Juran Institute and JUSE would continue. To this end, I asked Dr. Godfrey (the new chairman of Juran Institute) to join me in preparing the public paper as coauthor and to join me in presenting it as well. We did collaborate and gave the public lecture under the title "Total Quality Management—Status in the U.S.A."

During the final paragraphs of each paper, I began to choke up. I was aware that I was bringing to a close a deeply satisfying phase of my journey through life. I especially choked on the word *sayonara*. A simplistic translation is "farewell" or "good-bye." However, the word *sayonara* is not fully translatable into English; it includes connotations of sadness at departure and emotional hopes of return. I knew I would not return.

My Impact on Japan

I am reluctant to make public my conclusions about my impact on Japanese quality management; I prefer to leave it to others to draw such conclusions. "Others" includes the media, some of whom are notoriously flamboyant. They have touted me as "the man who taught quality to the Japanese ..."; "the architect of the Japanese quality revolution"; and other epithets. Maybe so, but some journalists have said the same things about Deming. In my view, the safest sources of such evaluations are the Japanese themselves—their pronouncements and especially their actions.

Some Japanese (Ishikawa, Imaizumi, Kondo, Noguchi, and others) have written articles and books that include comments on the origins of Japanese quality control. They invariably mention Deming's lectures on statistical quality control and my lectures on managing for quality as providing the seed training courses. Their comments note that the lectures on managing for quality were an essential broadening of the training from the prior overemphasis on statistical methods. See for example, Kondo 1995.[3]

While some of the Japanese comments include biases and embellishments, their actions do not. The following list of those actions provides a useful basis for appraising the Japanese view of my contribution:

- JUSE invited me to make nine visits to Japan and to participate actively in the planned events.
- While my correspondence was chiefly through JUSE, I had many invitations to visit Japanese companies, including Toyota, Matsushita, and Bridgestone.
- JUSE translated several of my books into Japanese, along with many of my papers.
- They published Japanese translations of my lectures.
- They incorporated much of my text material into their array of training courses (for professionals, foremen, middle managers, and senior executives).
- They succeeded in having me decorated with the Order of the Sacred Treasure.

- They planned to name an important prize after me, but because of miscommunication, it ended up as the "Japan Prize."

The Role of Dr. W. Edwards Deming

The story of my activities in Japan is incomplete unless I also discuss the role played by Dr. W. Edwards Deming. His work in Japan was influential, and it intersected extensively with mine.

Trying to discover Deming's role is difficult; the facts lie hidden within an avalanche of media distortion. In consequence, I have relied exclusively on my personal observations and records, plus the accounts of two close observers: Junji Noguchi,[4] for many years a high official in JUSE and, finally, its managing director; and Celcelia Kilian,[5] who was Deming's secretary and who worked for him from 1954 until his passing in 1993.

Deming's doctorate was in physics, but he spent most of his career in the field of mathematical statistics, notably by following the work of Dr. Walter A. Shewhart, a Bell Laboratories statistician, and inventor of the control chart that bears his name. During World War II, Deming helped to launch the War Production Board's courses in statistical quality control (SQC). Those courses devoted much time to Shewhart's control chart.

Noguchi's account includes the following observations:

In the spring of 1949, JUSE organized the Quality Control Research Group (QCRG).

In September 1949, JUSE introduced a basic one-year quality control course (prepared by QCRG) of approximately 200 hours, aimed at training engineers from twenty volunteer companies.

As QCRG became more involved in quality control activities, it recognized an inability to apply statistical methods to more difficult problems in the production area and, consequently, decided to invite an American quality control expert to Japan. (Deming became the invited expert.)

Deming arrived in Japan in June 1950. He conducted two eight-day courses in statistical quality control along with ten lectures.

Prior to Deming's visits in the early 1950s, Japanese quality control had been butting its head against a wall created by adherence to difficult statistics theories. With Deming's help, this wall was torn down.

Deming also spent time in Japan during 1951 and 1952 to give courses in quality control and clinics in market research.

Although Deming visited Japan fifteen more times after 1952, the courses he taught in 1952 were his last in Japan. He did speak at eight celebrations that commemorated the establishment of the Deming Prize, as well as three times (1969, 1978, and 1987) at the International Conference on Quality Control held in Japan.

Deming's courses were best received when he lectured on statistical quality control topics in 1950. When he began to shift his emphasis to sampling methods for market surveys on his trips in 1951 and 1952, his lectures drew less attention.

Later, when he returned to Japan to speak at a conference or Deming Prize celebration, people felt that he did not speak about new ideas or methods.

Deming's great legacy was that he opened the way for quality control by means of statistical methods in Japan.

Deming's 1950 lectures on statistical quality control were well received by the Japanese attendees; the reason (according to Noriaki Kano) was that Deming used simple training tools to explain statistical concepts. Suddenly JUSE had a ready-made course that could save them several years of time in going to market. The group showed their gratitude by attaching Deming's name to the prize they were creating as an award to companies who made exceptional progress in improving their quality. The Deming Prize soon became a major stimulus for quality in Japanese industry. (In my view, the Deming Prize has in

Japan become better known than Deming, just as the Nobel Prize has become better known than Nobel.)

The Deming Prizes soon made Deming a celebrity in Japan, but he remained relatively unknown in the U.S. and in Europe until the 1980 videocast, "If Japan Can, Why Can't We?" That videocast claimed that Japan's rise to economic superpower status was due principally to Deming's 1950 lectures in Japan. The claim had little basis in reality, but it was so cunningly presented that it seemed plausible to a lay audience. In addition it was well timed—Japan's leadership in quality had already become a competitive reality to many American companies. As a media event, the videocast was a stunning success.

It made Deming an overnight celebrity in the United States. He was suddenly in demand as a consultant to chief executives, as a lecturer, as a leader of training courses, and as an author. He received honorary degrees from no less than fifteen colleges and universities. Opportunists looked for ways to attach the name "Deming" to their wares.

Meanwhile the journalists and organized media engaged in a feeding frenzy. Biographies emerged, each with an extravagant title: "The Man Who Discovered Quality," "The American Who Taught the Japanese about Quality," and "Founder of the Third Wave of the Industrial Revolution." Writers dug into Deming's life and came up with gross fabrications.

For example, they learned that Deming had worked at Hawthorne during the summers of 1925 and 1926 and that I was already there, having started full-time in 1924. Their imaginations ran riot: Deming and I had worked together; Deming had improved Hawthorne's quality; Deming had produced other wonders. There is not a shred of truth in any of this. Deming and I never met until the 1940s. At Hawthorne, Deming was not involved with quality at all; he was a physicist working on his doctorate and a sort of intern on summer jobs. In his words, he "did nobody any good, but it was a great experience."

Deming and Juran

We first met in Washington, D. C., during World War II. I was chairman at some meeting and he was in the audience. I was pleased when he came up to introduce himself following the meeting—I knew of him because he had been a member of a committee that had produced a useful publication with which I was familiar. I took a liking to this dignified, even courtly scientist. We were active in different fields: he had moved from physics to statistics, and I had moved from engineering to management. Those fields managed to intersect, and we soon formed a warm friendship that endured until his passing in 1993.

Both of us brought structured training courses to Japan—he in statistical quality control, I in managing for quality. JUSE adapted these to the Japanese culture and then used them to train tens of thousands of industrial personnel. The income from all that training took JUSE out of poverty and into affluence.

Deming and I agreed on most fundamentals. We were both crusaders for good quality. We agreed that the main quality problems had their origins in the system, not the worker. We deplored the efforts to solve problems by means of colorful banners and slogans. We were aware that the leadership in quality must come from top management.

We also had our differences. Deming was convinced that applying statistical methods was the complete remedy for quality problems. I agreed that statistics was an essential element of the remedy, but I knew that much more was needed. As discussed earlier in this chapter, Deming had even opposed holding a conference session on "total quality control" on the grounds that statistical quality control was already "total."

I was dismayed by Deming's attitude toward our Malcolm Baldrige National Quality Award—he dismissed it as "awful" or "horrible" despite its similarity to the Deming Prize. He was seldom asked why he thought it was awful. Then came an occasion when Dr. Godfrey and I participated in a George Washington University telecast via satellite to about 125 locations. There was also a studio audience that included Deming. At lunch, my table included Deming and several other members of the studio audience. One of them asked Deming what he thought of the Baldrige Award. The answer: "Horrible." This time I asked him, "Why do you consider it horrible?" After his answer, I was sorry I had asked; his answer was, "They named it after the wrong man." It was as if he felt entitled to have such awards named after him. There were other indications that he resented being relatively unknown in the United States when he was so well-known in Japan. Of course, the 1980 videocast changed all that.

He came to believe that his 1950 eight-day courses were the dominant reasons for Japan's emergence as the world quality leader. He also believed that the elapsed time for Japan to reach that status was only a matter of a few years or even months. Those beliefs had no factual support—they were wishful thinking. Yet his beliefs were sincere—*he believed his wishful thinking.*

To say that someone believed his wishful thinking is a serious charge, and I am not comfortable with it. Yet there is confirmation in an incident related by Lloyd Dobyns and Clare Crawford-Mason. (They were the creators of the videocast, *If Japan Can, Why Can't We?*, which propelled Deming into celebrity status.) The incident took place during one of their monthly dinner meetings with Deming. When they pressed him to say what had made the difference in Japan, "Deming drew himself up to his full seated height, slapped his hand on the table, and said firmly and finally, 'One lone man with profound knowledge.'"[6] It was an absurd, self-serving claim, but in my view Deming was being sincere when he made it.

In time the officials in JUSE became disenchanted with Deming. As far back as 1964, Koyanagi had concluded that while Deming excelled in statistics, he lacked practical experience and had "never handled 'quality' as a complete entity." One JUSE official complained to me that Deming occasionally had invited himself to come to Japan; JUSE was offended but did not dare to say no to so famous a person.

JUSE also resented Deming's having permitted an ASQ chapter to create a Deming Prize. I learned about this when the Metropolitan (New York area) chapter of ASQ wrote to tell me that I had been chosen to receive their annual award of the Deming Prize. I called them to ask, "Have the Japanese approved such an award?" My contact didn't know but found that Deming had given his approval—he had even participated in the award ceremony. I still was not satisfied; I wrote to JUSE to learn their position. Their reply made clear that they had not been consulted and that they were "strongly offended." I then declined the award. I also wrote to Deming, enclosing copies of the pertinent correspondence. He never answered my letter—the only instance in which he failed to reply to a letter of mine.

Our final face-to-face meeting was in May 1986, during the ASQ annual congress in Anaheim, California. We had agreed beforehand to meet in my room to discuss important matters relating to quality in general. We spent about ninety minutes together.

What troubled me most was his random wandering over many matters he disliked—Crosby's offerings, the gullibility of managers who bought those offerings, the stupidity of chief executives who did not accept training in statistical methods, and so on. He wouldn't stop, and I was finally forced to find an excuse to terminate the meeting. I was aware of his tendency to berate chief executives, even publicly, and had given thought to try to explain to him that the practice was detrimental to his goals. I finally decided against it; Deming would not have changed his habits, and I might have ended up losing a respected friend.

Following his passing, I wrote out an appreciation, which I then sent to ASQ, JUSE, and EOQ. In it I stressed Deming's deep dedication to the cause of quality. The appreciation concluded:

> We have been privileged to witness a dedicated professional, fully absorbed in his mission despite personal tragedies, despite old age, and despite serious illness, yet giving freely of his time even when he had little time left to give. For that privilege we should all be grateful.

Notes

1. Juran to Koyanagi, personal correspondence, July 1, 1964.
2. Juran, J.M., "The QC Circle Phenomenon," *Industrial Quality Control,* January 1967.
3. Kondo, Yoshio, *Company-Wide Quality Control,* 3A Corporation, Tokyo: Japanese edition, 1993; English edition, 1995. The following is an extract from the English edition: "In 1954 Joseph Juran visited Japan at JUSE's invitation to hold QC courses for top and

middle managers. These courses had an immeasurably large impact on Japanese QC in the sense that they extended the QC philosophy (which had previously tended to be restricted to the narrower fields of production and inspection) to almost every area of corporate activities and clearly positioned QC as a management tool. Taking its lead from these courses, JUSE initiated the Middle-Management QC course in 1955 and the Special QC course for Executives in 1957. These are improved and are still held today."

4. Noguchi, Junji, "The Legacy of W. Edwards Deming." *Quality Progress,* December 1995.

5. Kilian, Cecelia S. *The World of W. Edwards Deming,* Second Edition (Knoxville: SPC Press Inc., 1992).

6. Quoted from Dobyns, Lloyd, and Clare Crawford-Mason, *Thinking About Quality: Progress, Wisdom and the Deming Philosophy* (New York: Random House, 1994).

Q

26

Internationalist, 1960s-1990s

My travels abroad began in 1950 with a brief lecture stint in Europe (Sweden, Great Britain, and the Netherlands) and a summer in Japan (1954). I became eager to enlarge this exposure, but I lacked the invitations to go abroad. Also, my finances could not support such luxury. By 1960, however, the outlook was much brighter. My finances had improved considerably, and I discovered that the Europeans had begun holding annual conferences on managing for quality.

The European Organization for Quality Control

In Europe, national societies oriented to quality began to appear early in the twentieth century (Great Britain, 1919; and Russia, 1925). The pace quickened starting in the 1950s (Sweden and Germany, 1952; the Netherlands, 1953; Italy, 1955; and France, 1956). In some countries the name of the society was the National Standards Association or a similar title. A European Organization for Quality Control (EOQC, later EOQ) was formed in 1956, and in 1957 it sponsored the first European congress on quality control. Such congresses then became annual. During the years 1957 through 1960, they were held successively in Paris, Essen, Brussels, and London. They have been held annually ever since.

I knew little about those meetings until 1960. In 1961 I attended the fifth congress, held in Turin, Italy, and discovered that here was a forum from which I could learn much. The leaders welcomed me warmly; they were familiar with my writings. (I learned later that they also welcomed the fact that I had been born in Europe.) I then got into the habit of attending those annual congresses, and I went to twenty-five of them from 1961 through 1991, at which time I terminated all foreign travel. At many of those congresses, I presented papers; at some I was asked to give the keynote address or to make the closing address.

International Courses and Lectures

Attending the European congresses and meeting the leaders then led to extensive activity for me abroad. Some of this took the form of my conducting courses and giving lectures. I have counted 178 visits that I made to 34 foreign countries to conduct courses, to give lectures, or both. More than 20,000 managers and specialists attended those events. At the outset, most courses ran for five days and dealt with managing for quality; the course training manual was titled "Managing for Quality." Most sponsors were local professional societies, although a few were private consultants. During the late 1970s I created a one-day seminar titled "Upper Management and Quality" and another titled "Planning for Quality." To make room for these, I shortened the five-day course to four days. Attendance at these events was high, averaging close to 100 persons per event.

Although Western Europe dominated my foreign visits, other countries were well represented; of the total of 178 foreign visits, 55 were outside of Western Europe:

- North America (Canada and Mexico)
- South America (Argentina and Brazil)
- The Socialist Bloc (Russia, Poland, Yugoslavia, Czechoslovakia, Hungary, Romania)
- The Far East (Japan, the People's Republic of China, Taiwan, Hong Kong, South Korea, Philippines, Singapore)
- Other (Australia, India, South Africa, Israel, Jordan)

In the summaries that follow, I will limit my discussion to countries exhibiting matters of special interest.

Sweden

I made thirty-one visits to Sweden; the sponsor was Dr. Lennart Sandholm, a private consultant who had been corporate quality manager for Electrolux. (He grew to become one of the leading consultants in Europe and the leading world authority on managing for quality in developing countries.) It was a joy to work with him— he was a superb organizer and his integrity was absolute. We usually held the events in the Engineers' house in Stockholm and occasionally elsewhere in Sweden.

Great Britain

Most of the twenty-four courses in Britain were sponsored by the nonprofit Institute of Quality Assurance (IQA). Most events were held in London, with the exceptions being those held in Birmingham, Coventry, Brighton, and Bristol. The IQA had a time getting its act together. At first it was undergoing a change in key personnel. Then it persisted in holding the events at hotels that lacked the facilities for holding courses such as mine. But once IQA solved that problem by finding a meeting hall that was well equipped, we got along famously.

The Netherlands

I made twenty-four visits to the Netherlands, where the courses were sponsored by the Dutch Society for Quality (KDI). The courses began in 1968 and were held in Rotterdam. The executive director of KDI, Dr. J. D. N. de Fremery, announced the courses in his newsletter and also in the EOQC newsletter. The courses were well attended, and in some years it was necessary to schedule two courses.

France

I conducted eighteen courses in Paris sponsored by the French Association for Industrial Quality Control (AFCIQ). The association asked me to shorten the course to three days, which I did. The courses were held in La Defense, across the River Seine from Paris. AFCIQ was cautious—for the first course it expected thirty to thirty-five attendees, but instead there were nearly one hundred, with a waiting list of ninety. The subsequent courses averaged more than eighty attendees.

It was fun to deal with AFCIQ in the person of the executive director, Mrs. Liliane Kressman. She faced the problems of translating my text materials, providing for simultaneous interpretation of my remarks, dealing with questions from the attendees, and so on. She overcame all these problems, for she was a sure-footed organizer. The numerous courses proceeded seamlessly. Our correspondence was a delight, as she had a sparkling sense of humor.

Spain

I first went to Spain in 1962 under the sponsorship of the U.S. Aid Mission to Spain. That occasion involved two assignments:

1. Study the Pegaso Company's approach to managing for quality and report my findings and recommendations. (Pegaso made trucks.)
2. Conduct two courses on managing for quality, one in Madrid and the other in Barcelona. Those courses, sponsored by the School of Industrial Organization, were open to all companies.

Both assignments went well. My report on Pegaso was well received by the managers and the school, and the courses were well received by the attendees and the school.

During my stay in Barcelona (with Sadie), the Cuban missile crisis unfolded. Sadie and I became extremely anxious; we held our breath as the climax came and went. It was a close call.

I made nine more visits to conduct courses in Spain under the sponsorship of the Bedaux consulting company, which was now controlled by Enrique Maso, an important industrialist who had once been a graduate student of mine at New York University. We had a superlative rapport.

Israel

My first trip to Israel was in August 1964. I was to attend the EOQC Conference in Baden Baden, Germany, but I indulged in a touristic round-about way to get in and out—Egypt, Jordan, Israel, Greece, and finally Baden Baden. (I managed to see some fascinating archaeological sights and museums.) From Jordan I entered Israel warily—through the tense Mandelbaum Gate.

I made a total of four visits to Israel, chiefly under the sponsorship of Standards Institution of Israel (SII). During those visits I conducted courses, lectured, made visits to factories, met with government officials, and prepared reports of my observations and recommendations. There was a shortage of manufactured goods, so quality was poor. (It usually is during a seller's market.) The poor quality was a handicap to exporters, yet exports were needed if manufacture was to thrive because Israel's domestic market was small.

I also visited with cousins I had known in Gura Humora nearly sixty years before. My cousin Isadore and his family had survived a terrifying ordeal during the Holocaust. Moreover, life in Israel was threatened from without and within. At the time, the little nation was surrounded by sworn enemies who greatly outnumbered the Israelis.

The Israelis treated me as one of their own, which in a sense I was. I felt that relationship most strongly in 1967 during a flight to London, when an announcement came over the intercom: Egypt, Syria, and Jordan had declared war on Israel. I feared the worst—there might be a savage slaughter of Jews. Instead, the war ended in *six days*, with a stunning victory for the Israelis. Never before or since have I been so proud of being a Jew.

Romania

I made two trips to Romania (1970 and 1972), each at the invitation of the Romanian government. Each involved the usual mixture of teaching and lecturing activities. My host was Ing. Dumitru Niculescu. As state inspector general, his duties were similar to those of a corporate quality manager in a large multidivision corporation—independent quality auditing, quality reports to general management, advising on quality policies and objectives, and training.

During the second visit I allotted several extra days to visit the places where I had spent my earliest years, and the Romanians were most helpful. In Braila (on the Danube), I saw the tiny house in which I was born and spent my first three years. I also met some cousins, who took me to the cemetery where my aunt Chaye was buried—she was my dad's favorite sister. I was deeply moved when I laid a rose on her grave.

The Romanians also took me to Gura Humora, the town in which I lived until the age of eight, when my family immigrated to Minneapolis. The house in which I lived had burned down, but I was told that its replacement was probably much like the original.

South Korea

In 1978 I conducted my five-day course in South Korea; sponsorship was by the Korean Standards Organization. The course was held in a country hotel in Dogo, about fifty miles south of Seoul. All attendees were in residence; they exhibited an enthusiastic interest in the subject, well beyond anything I had ever encountered excepting among the Japanese. The hours were long—our discussions began during the early breakfasts and continued on late into the evenings. The attendees' questions were penetrating and insistent. It was easy for me to conclude, "These guys are going to be fierce competitors, even for the Japanese."

Financing the Courses

Foreign demand for my courses began in the mid-1960s. Companies paid the attendance fees but the number of attendees was unpredictable, so the income might fail to recover the costs and effort. I reduced the sponsors' risks by agreeing to modest honoraria. In addition I minimized travel expenses by flying coach.

Once it became clear that the courses would surely fill up (resulting in handsome surpluses), I insisted on a more respectable share. Generally I ended up with about a third of the gross income, and the sponsors kept the rest. I elected not to press for more. I was the rainmaker; my status as the then leading world expert was what brought in the registrations. Yet I needed local sponsors with whom the companies were familiar. Moreover the one-third share resulted in a handsome *per diem* return. The demand for a higher share came from only some of the sponsors.

For developing countries and for the Socialist bloc, I gave the courses on a *pro bono* basis. I knew that these countries were under strict currency controls and had no way to pay me in dollars. This extended even to my international air travel. (They did take care of my local travel and living expenses.) By this *pro bono* approach, I avoided the image of an "ugly American"; instead I was treated as a welcome and trusted guest.

International Consulting

All those foreign contacts soon generated invitations for me to visit companies, examine their approach to managing for quality, and offer critiques. During the 1960s through the 1990s, I received over eighty such invitations. Of these, twenty-three were to companies in six Socialist countries; the rest were in fifteen non-Socialist countries. Many of the engagements were of short duration—a day or even a few hours. Even so, I had little difficulty providing a useful critique. From experience I had learned what to look for and what questions to ask.

Consulting—Socialist Countries

I did consulting in six Eastern European Socialist countries— Hungary, Romania, Czechoslovakia, Russia, Poland, and Yugoslavia. I learned that Socialist economies operated in ways quite different from their non-Socialist counterparts.

The central government owned the means of production and distribution. The key business goals—capital investment, how much to produce, pricing, and so on—were set by central government planning ministries.

At a "discussion club" in Moscow (1969), with Lenin watching

Industry was organized into producing ministries, each of which was granted a monopoly over its sector of the economy.

Much investment was made to meet ideological and political goals.

There were central control ministries over key elements of the economy. Some had the after-the-fact mission of assuring that the national goals were met. Others exercised before-the-fact control on such matters as hard currency.

Quality was generally poor in the Socialist countries. In Russia I identified five levels of quality. Goods for the military and space programs were of high quality. Goods for export were less so—generally adequate but not competitive with the best in the world market. Domestic consumer products were often poor, and domestic consumer services were frequently dreadful—involving waiting in long lines, discourteous and indifferent clerks, and other indignities.

I concluded that the Socialist countries had some common reasons for poor quality:

- There were widespread shortages of goods.
- Quantity of production had a higher priority than quality.
- Their technology was old.
- They lacked internal competition.
- Their focus was on meeting standards and specifications rather than on customer satisfaction.
- They lacked an organized approach to quality improvement.
- They had a mindset relative to "controllability"—they believed that achievement of quality rested chiefly with the workers rather than with the system.

(Some of these same reasons could be found within some companies in non-Socialist countries.)

My discussions with government officials and industry managers led me to conclude that the Socialist countries were doomed to live in poor economies. The division of power among all those central ministries greatly hindered decision making and coordination. The inability to solve problems such as the shortages created an atmosphere of blame, mistrust, and secrecy. (Shortages led consumers to practice hoarding and barter.)

I also became skeptical about the emphasis on ideology and exhortation to retain the loyalty of the workers. I thought the regimes were failing to make adequate use of powerful human instincts such as acquisitiveness, greed, and competitiveness. (I consider these matters to be instinctive because I have seen them exhibited by most of my descendants—children, grandchildren, and great-grandchildren—certainly during infancy and, often enough, extending into adulthood.)

In the United States, we set few limits on the exercise of those instincts; in the case of greed, those limits are not enough to prevent the emergence of outcomes that are widely regarded as unfair. I have often told managers in the Socialist countries, "In America we make too much use of human greed; in your country, you don't make enough use of it." They seldom contested that assertion, even though their ideology frowned on encouraging the use of human greed.

Consulting—Non-Socialist Countries

During the 1960s through the 1990s, I had sixty consulting engagements in non-Socialist countries, most of which were with giant companies. Here again, space constraints require that I limit the details to a few of the more notable cases.

Rolls-Royce, Ltd. In the spring of 1967, I visited Rolls-Royce (R-R) in Great Britain. My mission was to visit several R-R plants, study their approach to managing for quality, and offer a critique. While at each plant, I also conducted a lecture for local personnel and conducted a week-long course for R-R managers, engineers, and others.

It might have been a routine engagement, but it became notable because it brought me two memorable flashes of illumination.

The name Rolls-Royce is well-known to consumers—the Rolls-Royce automobile has a dazzling reputation for quality and a stratospheric price. R-R's chief business, however, was (and is) aircraft engines. Such engines are based on a demanding technology, but R-R was up to it. Their technological capability was awesome, resulting in aircraft engines that were reliable and competitive.

My host and companion was Frank Nixon, the R-R corporate quality and reliability engineer. Nixon was a competent, voluble guide with an encyclopedic grasp of the history of technology in Derbyshire. He also complained regularly that at R-R, the senior executives "exhibit no interest in quality." Together we rode in a chauffeured car (R-R, of course) to visit plants in England and Scotland. On the return journey, we drove along the mountains and lochs immortalized by Sir Walter Scott in his "The Lady of the Lake." We also visited Bannockburn and Hadrian's Wall.

During my factory visits I noted that there were huge amounts of waste as a result of products scrapped, rework, inspection (separating good product from bad), and so on. I secured estimates of the costs and found that they were shockingly high. When I discussed these wastes with the plant managers, I found that no organized approach for reducing them existed.

The final phase of my mission was to conduct the week-long course. Early in the week I was handed a note from Sir Denning Pearson, the R-R managing director, asking if I could stop in and give him my impressions. I did stop in on Tuesday afternoon. After praising R-R's capabilities, I told him of that shocking waste. I had summarized the estimates into a total for all factories; it was a huge sum. I then told him that R-R had the capability to cut the total in half within five years but that no one was working on the problem; also I informed him that *the resulting return on investment would be much higher than the return from selling aircraft engines.*

Sir Denning was impressed. It was his first awareness of the dimensions of such an opportunity. The key to securing his awareness was translating that waste into terms with which he was familiar—money and return on investment. The idea that quality improvement was a form of investment that could provide a return higher than other forms of investment had never been explained to him. His reaction was immediate: "If I am able to convene my directors this week, would you be willing to meet with them and tell them the same story you have just told me?"

We did hold that meeting, and I repeated my story. I then sat back and listened as they discussed why no organized effort to reduce those wastes existed. Then one director came up with what was, to me, a blinding flash of illumination. In his view, the surest way for men in R-R to rise to senior posts was through increasing sales, whether by designing or marketing aircraft engines. In contrast, reducing factory costs was low-caste work. This social hierarchy influenced the company priorities.

As I listened to that director, my mind raced through my experience with other clients. Many companies harbored a caste system; the highest castes dictated company priorities. The castes at the top of those companies might differ from those in R-R, but a caste system was nevertheless in place. I became indelibly imprinted by that brilliant insight. In future consulting engagements, I made it a point to identify and understand clients' caste systems.

The second flash of illumination was quite familiar to me, but at R-R it was more intense than I had previously encountered. It hearkened back to Nixon's complaints that "at R-R, the senior executives exhibit no interest in quality." My experience at R-R was the precise opposite. When I told Sir Denning that for the next few years the return on investment from reducing waste could exceed that from selling aircraft engines, he was promptly energized. The key was to present the information on quality in the proper language; for senior industrial executives, the most persuasive language is money. Had Nixon been "bilingual" and made his presentations using the language of money, he would have found that his managing director had a great deal of interest in quality.

Koninklijke Philips Electronics N. V. Philips is the giant Dutch electronics company based in Eindhoven. I first visited it in 1950 and lectured there briefly. In later decades, the company sent many managers and engineers to my courses in Rotterdam. I came to know and hold informal meetings with some of the Philips quality managers.

By the late 1970s some Philips' products, such as color TV sets, were losing share of the market to Japanese competitors, in large part because of the superior quality and reliability of Japanese products. Each Philips division had a quality manager who reported to the general manager of the division. In addition, one member of the board of management (I will call him Mr. K) was responsible for oversight of the quality function—a sort of corporate quality manager. When Philips' quality problems reached a state of crisis, Mr. K's approach was to scold the quality managers while resorting to exhortation as a remedy. The quality managers resented his approach and staged a palace revolt; they made their dissent known through the grapevine while holding unofficial meetings with me.

The end result was that the entire Philips board of management cleared a day to meet with me. During that day I concentrated on the quality improvement process—how to mobilize the company's resources to identify the most troublesome areas and then to use multifunctional teams to diagnose the problems and provide remedies.

That meeting took place in August 1982 and may well have had an enduring impact. I did not receive periodic feedback about the board's actions, but I do know that the most enthusiastic division general manager later became chairman of the Philips board of management.

Volkswagen (VW). The board of management of this giant German automaker cleared a day to meet with me in June 1982. I had received a modicum of briefing beforehand, but it did not prepare me for what actually came up. At the meeting, the board members' primary interest turned out to be creating a new model that would reproduce the stunning success of the "beetle," a small, fuel-efficient car that VW had produced and sold by the millions soon after World War II.

At the meeting it took some time to sort out the two major meanings of the word "quality." (To this day that dual meaning is a source of confusion in many companies.) One of those major meanings is sales oriented—it relates to those features of the product that provide customer satisfaction. Under this definition of "quality," higher quality usually costs more; more and better product features usually require investment in market research, product research and development, and so on. The other major meaning of "quality" is freedom from failure—freedom from factory scrap and rework, field failures, complaints, lawsuits, and so on. This meaning is cost-oriented; under it, higher quality costs less, often a lot less.

I was in no position to help with respect to product features; to be of help, I would have needed extensive briefing on VW's approach to market research, product research, and more. I made my limitations clear and then went on to deal with how to reduce defect rates and field failure rates. The managers listened and then discussed those matters, but their top priority was creating sales through greater customer satisfaction. I suspect that at the end of the day, they were disappointed.

Royal Dutch Shell. Shell is a huge international company in the energy industry. In December 1986, I lectured at a meeting of their managers in the corporate headquarters at The Hague. The company videotaped the lecture, edited it, and made it a part of the training materials to be used by their numerous locations around the world. Those videotapes generated many requests for consulting service from Juran Institute. For a substantial span of time, Shell was Juran Institute's chief client.

Toyota Motor Company. I visited Toyota Motor Company during several of my trips to Japan. I was much impressed by this company's refreshing approach to managing for quality and by the innovations they brought to their industry. Even the housekeeping in their factories was immaculate in comparison to their counterparts in the United States.

We had some lively discussions in their headquarters in Nagoya. On one occasion I was asked about the need for a corporate quality office:

Question: "What do Ford and General Motors do?"
Answer: "Ford has such an office; General Motors does not."
Question: "Which one is right?"
Answer: "Ford's method is right for Ford; General Motors' method is right for General Motors" (and I explained why).

On another occasion, I asked why Toyota's advertising made no mention of the known differences in failure rates between Toyota's models and those of its competitors. As well as I could gather, the reticence was traceable to Japanese reluctance to be strongly assertive or conspicuous.

I developed a good rapport with Mr. Soichiro Toyoda, a senior executive and later president of the company. (The company name is Toyo<u>t</u>a but the family name is Toyo<u>da</u>.) He was gracious enough to prepare a chapter on quality in the automotive industry for my *Quality Control Handbook*, third edition. It was a masterpiece.

Air Travel

Foreign travel had its romantic moments, but it was often burdened with many restrictions. Travel to (or landings in) some countries required inoculation for such perils as cholera, smallpox, malaria, and yellow fever. Entry to each country demanded passports and visas, and there was baggage clearance as well.

I once avoided passport and baggage clearance. I flew in the Volkswagen plane from the Netherlands to Germany to spend a day with the chief executives of Volkswagen. Their plane then flew me to London's Heathrow airport to take the Concorde home. During all that time, I did not have to deal with passport or baggage clearance. The Volkswagen crew knew how to skirt those offices.

When flying, both domestically and internationally, I logged much distance—over 100,000 air miles per year for many years. My lifetime total was close to three million miles (nearly five million kilometers). I also flew many types of planes, from early DC3s to jets and jumbo jets. At first all air travel was coach class. Affluence later allowed me to upgrade to first class and then to the fully adequate business class. Going home from London or Paris, I ended up using the Concorde. It was luxurious to be home in my apartment within five hours after takeoff.

Some flights (to Brazil, Argentina, South Africa, and Australia) took me across the equator and back. I never quite became used to seeing the sun go from east to west by arcing to the north instead of to the south. Crossing the International Date Line was also confusing. I could lose a Tuesday flying west and end up with two Fridays on the return trip. I also made several round-the-world journeys; they required a precise count of days. (One such journey fooled Phineas Fogg in *Around the World in Eighty Days*.)

The Sights

A welcome bonus of visiting all those countries was visiting their cultural monuments. I often had the enthusiastic support of my hosts in this. My scrapbooks are crammed with photos and literature—mementos of memorable visits.

I have long been interested in ancient ruins. I was awed to set foot in the Roman Forum, the Colosseum, and other structures built by Roman engineers. I was equally awed by Egypt's Pyramids, the Sphinx, and the temples at Luxor and Karnak. It was the same with the Greek temples and the Great Wall of China.

At Delphi I was intrigued to see the many stone plaques contributed by the Greek city-states; their periodic gatherings were in the nature of an ancient United Nations assembly. I asked my guide, a young archaeologist, "Why is it that once the Greeks fought off the Persian invasion, they began to fight with each other?" Answer: "That's the Greek system."

I spent much of my free time in museums; they were all over. Some—such as the British museum, the Louvre, and those in Cairo and Mexico City—were huge, whereas others were small yet were little gems. I enjoyed gaping at the elaborate structures built by autocratic rulers: the Kremlin in Moscow, Schönbrunn palace in Vienna, Versailles in France, the Doge's palace in Venice, and the Tokugawa tomb in Nikko, Japan.

In yet more trips, I took in other "sights": the cathedrals, the Taj Mahal, Teotihuacan, and cities such as Toledo and Florence, where the entire city is a museum. There were also somber and gruesome sights—the once beautiful city of Dresden, with many of its buildings still in ruins following the firestorms of World War II; or the grisly remains of Auschwitz, site of gas chambers that exterminated countless Jews and Poles.

Of course I haven't lacked for sights in the United States (including our national parks), but I found it refreshing to feast also on the sights in foreign lands.

I viewed many famous sites during my visits to about forty countries.

The Media

Over the centuries, "quality" has seldom been in the news, although a disaster traceable to a quality failure might make it. Managing for quality was not newsworthy—the concept that it was an important branch of knowledge had to await the Industrial Revolution and, especially, the twentieth century.

The media took notice once the quality revolution enabled the Japanese to invade U.S. markets. Journalists like Jeremy Main of *Fortune* and Otis Port of *Business Week* dug in, informed themselves, and wrote enlightening articles. I started to be sought out by journalists; to them I was (along with Deming) a "guru." The media seem to love identifying gurus (especially gurus who might be glaring at each other).

By the 1970s I was being interviewed by journalists with increasing frequency. (The sponsors of my lectures routinely sent copies of their announcements to the media.) Some of the journalists were at a disadvantage—they were ignorant of the subject matter and didn't know what questions to ask. It troubled me to see them struggle. In contrast, the more worldly journalists readily explored the impact of quality on the economy and on human affairs in general.

A memorable example of such a journalist was Mr. Richard Spiegelberg, management editor of the *Times* of London. In an article dated October 1, 1971, he showed that during our interview, he had acquired a firm grasp of the fundamental concepts of quality.

During that same visit to Britain in October 1971, other journalists dug into my views on the environment and on consumerism. I asserted that cigarettes were killing many people but that there was no chance in the United States of enacting legislation to ban cigarettes. I thought that the cigarette companies would in time face severe economic damage through "people getting compensation for death from lung cancer ..." I added that I wouldn't be surprised if I lived long enough to see that take place.

At the time (1971) I was 67 years old. It did take place, about twenty-five years later, and I lived to witness it. One of the British journalists had dismissed my prediction as "piffle." I don't remember his name, but I hope he is still living and has occasion to read this account.

Q

27

The Juran Institute

s the 1970s were coming to a close, I was still happily engaged in consulting, training, writing, and the rest, along with increasingly devoting time to *pro bono* opportunities. As I had said in my 1975 paper titled "And One Makes Fifty"—"I would be mad to give up so fascinating a way of life."

Meanwhile, siren voices had been trying to lure me into dangerous waters. The most frequent were those that sang out, "You have an enviable status in industry. You could create a consulting company and earn a fabulous income." But I wanted none of it. I had seen Wallace Clark run his little consulting business. He owned it, yet it was his master more than his servant. Like me, Clark had a solid reputation in industry, yet he was on a perpetual treadmill of finding new clients, dealing with employee turnover, and all the other time-consuming duties. I considered myself free; I had no master and wanted none.

Emptying Out My Head

Late in the 1970s, a new species of siren emerged. Occasionally a course attendee would point out, "You have an endless supply of know-how in your specialty. Some of that know-how is in the course text and some you provide orally. But most of your know-how remains in your head. You ought to empty out that head." I thought those were pertinent observations, and the suggestion seemed to pose no threat to my freedom. So I succumbed and looked into creating a series of audiocassettes. Peter Drucker had already done some of that and (he told me) it had not been painful. I contracted with AMA to produce some audiocassettes, but I never fulfilled that contract. Audiocassettes had become passé and videocassettes (VCs) were coming into vogue.

When I looked into the world of video production, I was shocked. To produce color VCs required skills that I lacked. I spoke to publishers but their proposals required me to invest a great deal of time, after which the resulting division of proceeds would be heavily weighted in their favor.

About that time, I met G. Howland Blackiston, a young man who was dating my granddaughter Joy. Howland was employed by an advertising agency, and his experience included producing color VCs suitable for television advertising. We soon discovered a common interest beyond Joy—producing VCs on managing for quality. I needed a source of expertise in producing color VCs, and he was looking for an opportunity to get into an exciting and rewarding project.

We quickly got into serious planning for the project. As the subject of the VCs, I chose "quality improvement"—it had been a rewarding topic for my clients, and I had an ample supply of case examples to offer. I estimated that it would take about sixteen cassettes of thirty minutes each to tell my story. Based on Howland's estimates, it would cost close to a million dollars to produce the lot. I had the million and was willing to risk it.

Producing Videocassettes

I brought in lawyers to create a corporation—Juran Enterprises Inc. (We soon changed it to Juran Institute Inc.—JII.) It was a Subchapter

S corporation, a form that treats the corporation's income as the owner's income without the intervention of taxable dividends. The date of incorporation was April 19, 1979. We rented office space in my building at United Nations Plaza in New York City. (The lowest four floors contained offices; the two towers housed cooperative apartments.) I now lived above the store. Howland became the first employee, with the title of vice president.

Once we were past the details of setting up the new business, Howland and I evolved a brisk routine. Bit by bit I wrote out the script; Howland then converted those bits into "storyboards"—mini-scenes to enter the VCs. We both became incredibly busy. For me, the work of writing the script was superimposed on my busy schedule of consulting and training, whereas Howland was forced into overtime. In the meantime, I acquired a grandson-in-law.

The Text

I organized the subject matter for the VCs in accordance with the sequence I had used during numerous consulting engagements in which the mission was to reduce defect and failure rates. I included a great many case examples but they were chiefly from manufacturing. Beyond writing the script I prepared the 340 page workbook for the users and an even larger leader's manual for the trainers-to-be.

Despite our planning, we ran into budget overruns. Our first shooting was a failure—the studio camera was not up to our needs, because the aperture was so small that I was unable to read the script out of the camera lens. The result was a dismal flop.

Howland needed a musical introduction to the VCs. I selected an extract from Beethoven's opera *Fidelio*—a delightful, catchy military march. We then were unable to find someone who could license us to copy the forty-five-second extract from some existing recording. We ended up hiring an orchestra to record that extract. The tab: $8,000.

Both Howland and I were aware that the VCs should do more than deliver my text. They also needed to be of an artistic quality comparable to that which the viewers saw daily on television. To this end, Howland provided the needed capability and ingenuity. Some customers went out of their way to compliment the VCs' artistic content; in addition, the VCs received an award from one of the professional media societies.

Marketing

Even before embarking on the project, I sounded out managers attending my courses on questions such as these: What should such VCs contain? What other materials should accompany them? Would your company buy such VCs? Who in the decision-making process has the final word on whether or not to buy?

Howland prepared attractive brochures describing our product and its merits. We mailed brochures to lists of attendees at my courses, as well as lists acquired from ASQ. We placed advertisements in ASQ's journal, *Quality Progress.* We also exhibited the VCs at the May 1981 Annual ASQ Congress and at Hitchcock Publication's Quality Expo. Those exhibits attracted large crowds around our booths and suggested that our product was headed for a good reception.

We called our product "Juran on Quality Improvement" (JQI). It consisted of a set of sixteen VCs, fifty workbooks, two leader's manuals, and a library of the latest editions of *Quality Control Handbook, Managerial Breakthrough,* and *Quality Planning and Analysis.* We set a price of $15,000 for the "package" but offered discounts to companies who made multiple purchases. We priced additional workbooks at $150 each but offered discounts for bulk purchases.

We sold numerous sets of JQI to giant companies such as Texas Instruments, General Motors, and Bethlehem Steel. Each of these large companies had multiple divisions or plants scattered over diverse areas, and such divisions were usually large enough to need their own set of JQI. (Motorola, which had founded an internal school on managing for quality, paid us half a million dollars for a license to reproduce VCs and workbooks without limit.)

During the six-year period from 1982 to 1989, we sold 927 sets and 71,000 workbooks for a total gross income of about $16 million. Other cassette-related activity, notably foreign royalties, brought this up to $19 million. Many intermediate-sized companies bought one or a few sets of JQI. Small companies usually did not buy JQI; instead they sent their quality managers to our courses on managing for quality.

Soon we were faced with demands for translating the VCs into various languages. Some of these requests came from multinational companies (such as Texas Instruments) that operated facilities in many countries. (The upper-level managers were often fluent in English, but most of the engineers and lower-level managers were not.) In addition, we had demands for translations from foreign companies who planned to use the VCs to supplement their own training programs.

A Surge in Affluence

My annual income from JQI—the VCs, workbooks, leader's manuals, and royalties—greatly exceeded my earlier annual income. The first full year of JQI sales was 1982. During the preceding four years (1978–1981), my federal taxable income averaged about $233,000 per year. Over the four years 1982–1985, that average soared to $2,055,000 per year—a nine-fold rise. During those same four-year spans, my income after federal taxes rose from an average of $122,000 to $1,054,000 per year, again a nine-fold rise.

All that new-found wealth was welcome, but Sadie and I had no intention of changing our lifestyle. Nevertheless, we faced disposing of a large (to us) and growing surplus. An obvious partial solution was to fatten up the college funds we had begun for our grandchildren; we soon had those fully funded. We also started such funds for each of our growing list of great-grandchildren. Another partial solution was to assist our less affluent family members to acquire homes of their own. In addition I had plans to create a *pro bono* foundation to advance the new science of managing for quality. The residue was to be disposed of by our wills.

This still didn't solve the problem of what to do with the shares of Juran Institute. The success of JQI had converted the shares into a valuable asset. By the mid-1980s I was receiving veiled inquiries—was JII for sale? Based on its track record it likely would have fetched a price in the range of $10 million to $20 million. I brushed aside all such inquiries; I had no interest in losing control of the Institute.

I considered various alternatives, each with a strong *pro bono* orientation. In the end I came up with the following approach: I kept 20 percent of the shares; I gave 20 percent to a nonprofit foundation I created; and the remaining shares were to be transferred gradually to the Institute employees in lieu of a pension plan for them. The employees were to end up in control of the company.

Expansion

The success of JQI required that we expand Juran Institute's staff. We needed people to fill orders and handle the associated correspondence. We also needed more storage space to house the inventories of VCs, books, and other materials. Despite the expansion and crowding, the Institute was a friendly place to work. We tried to recruit people who would contribute to a high level of morale. We paid salaries above the market level. We could and did pay generous year-end bonuses; they ran to 50 percent in some years.

I also decided to terminate AMA's license (AMA had for years carried out the details of running my training courses). JII took over that chore, requiring still more staff and storage space. We leased some storage space on our floor, but the staff's quarters became even more crowded.

The conduct of training courses requires lecturers who are experts in the subject matter and who, in addition, are inspiring teachers. During the AMA era, we tested out a few consultants and professors to share the lecturing load with me. At the end of each course, we asked the attendees to rate each lecturer in terms of the adequacy of his contribution. Those ratings were influential in deciding which lecturers to retain. (In those days our lecturers were not full-time employees; they were employed on a course-by-course basis.)

Providing a Consulting Service

As clients began to use the VCs and workbooks, they ran into a serious obstacle. The VCs were indeed helpful in explaining how to carry out an improvement project, but they did not explain how to mobilize the company's resources to *institutionalize quality improvement*—in other words, to carry out quality improvement year after year at a revolutionary pace. Many clients brought this problem to our attention and asked us to help them solve it. Those requests led to a major conversion of the Institute, from a training company to a consulting company.

A consulting service requires professionals—people who have expertise in the subject matter as well as experience in applying that expertise to help clients improve their operations. At the time I was the only such professional in the Institute. I concluded that we had an obligation to help the clients, so we began recruiting professionals in the field of managing for quality,

As we got into the recruiting process, we learned that the full-time professionals we needed were generally unwilling to live in New York City or to commute there. In those days, most areas of the city were noisy, dirty, and even dangerous. This extended to many of the public schools as well. The general feeling was that New York was no place to raise a family. The city did, of course, have some attractive places in which to live and some excellent private schools for children, but only the well-to-do could afford them. Our solution was to move the Institute to Connecticut.

The Move to Connecticut

We rented half an office building in the town of Wilton, about sixty miles from New York City. The move simplified our job of recruiting the needed professionals, but we had to make loans to some to help them relocate. Much of the New York staff was unwilling or unable to move with us, but we readily recruited replacements. At the time, housing in the Wilton area was affordable, but it didn't stay that way. To find affordable housing, our employees increasingly were forced to locate still farther away from New York City, thereby incurring longer commutes to Wilton.

The Impact of JQI

The companies who bought the VCs used them to train their employees in how to make quality improvements. I estimate that more than a million managers, supervisors, and engineers viewed those videocassettes during organized training courses. (The precise numbers have never been researched.)

At the Institute's annual "IMPRO" conferences, I listened to many reports of spectacular results achieved by companies with the aid of JQI. Those anecdotal reports are a biased sample, however; when companies publish their results, they put their best foot forward. I never conducted research to estimate JQI's overall financial effect on the economy.

JQI also was a major force in disseminating the new science of managing for quality. Companies using JQI were a sizeable part of the national economy. For most, JQI was their first exposure to a structured process for improving quality. When these firms wrote their company manuals on quality improvement, they borrowed heavily from the JQI videocassettes. The end result was that one of the most fundamental processes in managing for quality—quality improvement—owes much of its dissemination to JQI.

The Second VC Series

The Institute's highest profitability was achieved from 1982 to 1984, with 1983 being the peak year. Unit sales then declined annually, signaling JQI's obsolescence. In 1985 the Institute actually operated at a small net loss.

I was aware of the trend and set about to create a successor to JQI. Through feedback from course attendees, I learned what their companies' strengths were with respect to the three principal processes of managing for quality: planning, control, and improvement. The attendees' responses were uniform from course to course; they rated their companies as being strong on control and weak on planning and improvement. That gave me three options:

1. Create a second edition of "Juran on Quality Improvement," focusing on how to institutionalize quality improvement year after year at a revolutionary pace.
2. Create a series of VCs focusing on control of quality. I had already

analyzed this subject in the book *Managerial Breakthrough*. That analysis could provide a head start toward preparing the text.

3. Create a series of VCs focusing on planning for quality. This subject had not been analyzed in *Managerial Breakthrough*, so the analysis for "Juran on Planning for Quality" would have to start with a clean slate.

I opted to create "Juran on Planning for Quality" (JPQ) and did so under the worst possible conditions: I was busy conducting courses in the United States and abroad; I was in the middle of writing and editing the massive fourth edition of *Juran's Quality Control Handbook*; and I was still the active head of the Institute, which had meanwhile grown substantially in number of personnel. To make matters worse, I lacked an adequate base of experience in the subject of planning for quality; not enough of my consulting engagements had dealt specifically with this area.

JQP failed miserably. It did not even recover its costs. I was shocked but not surprised.

Passing the Torch

About this time, it was dawning on me that I had lost my freedom—the Institute had become my master! So I set out to regain my freedom and to find someone to replace me as chairman and chief executive officer.

Howland Blackiston had the title of president, but he was not a "professional" in managing for quality. I explained to him that in a firm of lawyers, the chairman had to be a member of the bar, and in the case of the Institute, the chairman would need to be a quality manager. We ended up recruiting Dr. A. Blanton (Blan) Godfrey to become chairman and CEO of Juran Institute. Blan was a brilliant professional; at the time he was Supervisor of Quality Theory and Systems for AT&T. The change became effective on August 1, 1987.

In passing the torch, I took myself out of the chain of command—I did not want to remain harnessed to the Institute's operations. I became "chairman emeritus" but remained on the board of directors. Blan often asked me to attend meetings, such as those with important potential customers. He also asked me to participate in events such as the Institute's annual IMPRO conferences on quality improvement. On such occasions Blan and I found time to talk of Institute affairs. I might raise questions and offer comments, but I left the decisions to him.

As chairman emeritus I attended all board meetings and participated actively. I also arranged to add my son Charles (Chuck) to the board, to serve as a backup for my estate should some disaster overtake me. Chuck was a coexecutor of my estate (and still is). He soon earned the respect of other board members.

Juran Institute: 1987–2002

During the years 1982-1987, the Institute's sales (excluding JQI) came chiefly from its training courses. Then, as the Institute got into consulting work, sales rose year after year, reaching a peak in 1994. The trend in profit was something else. Every year produced a respectable surplus, but virtually all those surpluses were distributed as bonuses to the staff. That left little to be added to the Institute's reserves in the event of stormy weather, so it became vulnerable to a prolonged decline in sales.

That stormy weather arrived in 1995 and persisted. From the peak in 1994, sales declined through 1999. During three of those five years the Institute endured worrisome losses to an extent that its very survival was threatened. As an added alarm signal, the appraised value of a share of Institute stock (by an independent appraisal company) declined dramatically. We had to take heroic measures that involved drastic reductions in personnel and office space, as well as a dip in employee morale.

By 1999 the Institute was actively trying to form an "alliance" with some other company. It was an unpleasant, time-consuming search. The Institute was bargaining from a position of weakness— the worst state from which to negotiate. Happily, the years 2000-2002 brought a turnaround in the Institute's fortunes; sales rose, with an accompanying growth in net earnings after taxes. The crisis was averted, and negotiations for an alliance were terminated. As of mid-2003, this trend has continued, and the Institute seems well on the way to reestablishing a fiscal status in keeping with its professional status.

It troubled me deeply to witness the Institute sinking to those dangerous depths. Nevertheless I elected not to dig into the reasons for the decline. I had these memoirs to finish, and much else to do before my time runs out. So I will leave any such digging to be done by those who are interested and who have the time.

The Last Word

During the early 1990s, I ended my professional career. The first phase was to terminate conducting training courses abroad. I took that step after 1991, during which I conducted courses in many foreign countries.

In 1992 I planned a tour of American cities to present a final one-day course titled "The Last Word." I built the course around a total of 152 visual aids, which were then projected on a screen while I provided an oral commentary. The course manual contained miniatures of all visual aids plus space for taking notes. I encouraged submission of (written) questions, and the attendees responded with enthusiasm. It required grim adherence to the timetable to discuss those visual aids, so most of the questions remained unanswered. It was a mistake to limit The Last Word to one day; it should have been three or four days.

The Last Word was presented during 1993 and 1994 in about twenty cities in the United States and Canada. Attendance varied widely, depending on choice of cosponsors and on the adequacy of the marketing effort.

I also terminated my consulting engagements during the early 1990s. I was still receiving numerous overtures to provide consulting service or to hold in-house courses. Increasingly I declined to make the journeys, but the requests persisted. I then resorted to the tactic of pricing myself out of the market—I raised my *per diem* rate to $10,000.

Most of my would-be clients balked at that rate, but some did not. I then gave the wheel another turn—I raised the rate to $25,000. That did it. Only one client needed me that badly—and bought two days of my time. That income was a far cry from what I earned at my early morning job in 1912, when I sold copies of the *Minneapolis Tribune* for one cent each.

Q

28

The Juran Foundation

As decades passed and as I met more of my conventional human goals, I spent more time on service to society—*pro bono publico*. In September 1983, I decided to raise service to society to the status of a major goal. To this end I created Juran Foundation, Inc. (JFI). Its mission statement included the following:

... to identify the quality-related problems of society and develop remedies for their solution.

This ambitious mission would not be carried out fully—JFI's assets and organization structure never reached levels appropriate for tackling so ambitious an undertaking. However, JFI did manage to provide useful service to society during its lifetime.

Funding

During 1987 and 1988, I transferred 400,000 shares of Juran Institute stock to JFI, composing 20 percent of the authorized shares. At the time, an independent appraisal valued the shares at $3.41 each, for a total value of about $1.36 million. I also transferred shares of some listed stocks to JFI; those shares had a cash value of about $230,000. All told, JFI was funded with assets valued at about $1.6 million.

As foundations go, JFI was of modest size. Because it was too small to justify a full-time director, I functioned as unpaid part-time director, along with my unpaid role as chairman of the board of trustees.

The Board of Trustees

The original board of trustees consisted of Dr. James L. Hayes, Dr. J. Stuart Hunter, and me.

Hayes had for years served as president of AMA. He was also familiar with foundations, since AMA had one as an affiliate—the American Foundation for Management Research. Sadly, within a few years Hayes passed away. We were fortunate to replace him with William W. Eggleston, a retired career manager at IBM, where his final job had been corporate vice president for quality.

Hunter was a professor emeritus, having spent years at Princeton as professor of statistics. He had been an innovator in that field and was held in high esteem among his peers. They later elected him president of the American Statistical Association.

In 1997 we recruited another trustee; he was Edward Fuchs, a career manager at AT&T. When he retired from there, he was the corporate quality manager.

Grants Made by the Foundation

Under prevailing regulations, JFI was required to pay out 5 percent of its assets in grants annually, not including its administrative expenses. JFI employed no staff; it secured its staff services from Juran Institute, which then submitted invoices that were paid out of JFI funds.

The Foundation's routine yearly activity turned out to be making grants to nonprofit organizations for quality-related purposes. For example, during the fiscal year 1994, JFI received twenty-five requests for grants; seventeen of these were approved. Most grants went to schools to be used for books and other training materials or for scholarships to conferences and training courses. Occasionally there were grants to support some conference devoted to managing for quality. One major recipient was the Malcolm Baldrige National Quality Award, which was granted $100,000.

A History of Managing for Quality

In the late 1980s, I proposed to the trustees that JFI prepare a book on the history of managing for quality. The book's numerous chapters would be prepared by experts in various countries, who would set out how quality had been managed in their countries. I volunteered to be the editor-in-chief, and I also planned to write a chapter on managing for quality in the United States and another chapter on "summary, trends, and prognosis."

I had long thought that such a book was overdue. In fact, I took the first step toward its creation in 1982, during my lecture engagement in the People's Republic of China. I asked my hosts if they would be willing to prepare a chapter dealing with the history of managing for quality as it had evolved in China. They agreed to do so, and I agreed to fund the project. They set up a team for the purpose and delivered a superb finished manuscript in 1989.

The JFI trustees approved the book project. I then recruited a distinguished group of coeditors and authors. They prepared chapters dealing with managing for quality in a wide variety of geographical regions and industries; chapters covered such topics as ancient Israel; Greek temples and theaters; Scandinavian shipbuilding; ancient Rome; Germany; the Venetian arsenal; Russia; the French arms industry; the United Kingdom; and Japan.

I contracted with ASQ's Quality Press to publish the book. As editor-in-chief, I found it exciting to be involved in a project with so rich a variety of subject matter and with authors from such a wide range of cultures. It was extremely time-consuming work but, as always, it was rewarding to see the finished book, all 688 pages of it. It also features a handsome picture of the Parthenon on the front of the jacket and a formidable array of "blurbs" on the back: from Robert W. Galvin, chairman emeritus of Motorola; Robert E. Allen, chairman and CEO of AT&T; and Paul A. Allaire, chairman and CEO of Xerox Corporation.

The Proposal from the Quality Leadership Center

By the mid-1990s I had become increasingly concerned about the future of JFI. I was still the executive director, but I was already over ninety years old (and counting). Such was the state of affairs in March 1997, when I received an interesting proposal from the Quality Leadership Center at the University of Minnesota.

The commencement of the proposal began in 1993, when the university's Carlson School of Management created the Quality Leadership Center (QLC) with the ambitious vision of becoming "the world leader in research and education in Quality Management." By 1997 QLC had made significant progress toward that vision—it had already reached leadership status in several respects: it had more research projects submitted to the National Science Foundation than any other university; the most faculty and Ph. D. candidates engaged in research; the most projects selected for funding; and the most funding granted.

The heart of the proposal was to set up an endowment fund that would support continuing research in quality by establishing "Juran Fellowships." (The use of my name was stimulated by my status in the field plus the fact that I am an alumnus of the University of Minnesota.) To this end, the proposal asked JFI to contribute $100,000; it would become the first gift to the new endowment fund.

What impressed me most about the proposal was its vision; it was quite similar to the research mission I had set for JFI in 1986: "... to identify the quality-related problems of society and develop remedies for their solution." In addition, I saw that QLC had what JFI lacked— a full-time staff to carry out such a mission. Those impressions gave rise to a new option: transfer JFI and its assets to the University of

Minnesota! I discussed that option with the JFI trustees, and they agreed in principle, subject to meeting with the leaders of QLC. During those meetings we were well impressed with the leaders—Dean David Kidwell of the Carlson School of Management and the codirectors of QLC, James F. Buckman and Roger G. Schroeder.

Action followed. The transfer papers were signed in October 1997. The university then held several ceremonial events on April 22 and 23, 1998. The climax took place when the university president, Mark G. Yudof, announced that henceforth the Quality Leadership Center would be renamed the Juran Center for Leadership in Quality. I was overwhelmed.

That event also included a retroactive light touch—I received a sweater emblazoned with the university letter M. During my undergraduate years at the university, I had never tried out for any athletic team, but now I was at long last a letterman, having earned that lofty status by winning the university chess championship during the years 1922 to 1924.

In addition to transferring JFI to the university, I agreed to transfer my professional memorabilia. They had for years been displayed in Juran Institute's handsome in-house museum designed by Howland Blackiston. Included in the collection were about 100 framed plaques awarded by as many organizations, along with trophies such as medals, ceramics, crystal, pictures, and the like. The university will need to be selective; their display areas are more limited than was the case at Juran Institute.

I also agreed to transfer my professional papers—a formidable collection. I began accumulating such papers starting in the 1940s: records of consulting engagements, writings, correspondence, tax returns, financial records, scrapbooks, articles, extracts, and much more. Collectively the lot occupied over 100 feet of shelf and file space. Much was well organized and labeled, but the rest was largely helter-skelter. I would have relished having the time to go through all of it at leisure, discarding the chaff but saving the nuggets to serve as inputs for new writings. It did not happen.

Aftermath

The University of Minnesota not only welcomed receiving the assets of the Juran Foundation, it also welcomed receiving the right to use my name for furthering the aims of the Juran Center for Leadership in Quality.

Even before acquiring the Juran Foundation, the Center had a strong record of achievement in the quality field. Now it undertook an ambitious initiative—to stimulate formation of a national movement toward leadership in quality. To this end it created an executive advisory board of industrial and other business leaders to guide the movement while serving as role models. The first meeting of the board was chaired by Paul O'Neill, then chairman of Aluminum Company of America and later secretary of the treasury in the Bush administration.

In addition to the board, the Juran Center has recruited leaders who are active in the field of quality to oversee the execution of the Juran Center program portfolio.

Q

29

Looking Back on the Creation of the Quality Movement

The twentieth century witnessed ever-increasing competition in quality. Much of this resulted from the expansion of international trade, which in turn was stimulated by the growth of multinational companies. The increased competition led to a proliferation of new "inventions" in how to manage for quality. Collectively those concepts, methods, and tools accelerated the evolution of a new science—the science of managing for quality.

As a pioneering freelance consultant, I came up with many such inventions while solving client problems. At the beginnng I wasn't aware that I might be contributing to the evolution of a new science. Then, with growing maturity, I realized that I had been contributing to it all along.

Managing for quality is a branch of the broad science of management. As such, it uses knowledge evolved in other disciplines, such as the behavioral sciences. Managing for quality also exhibits a degree of uniqueness that demands its own special concepts, methods, and tools. In what follows, I will discuss three critical areas in which I made substantial contributions: quality improvement, planning for quality, and control of quality.

The Improvement Process

Many of my early consulting engagements involved helping clients to improve their products' quality. Each company at the outset confided to me, "Our business is different." I found that even though these businesses did indeed exhibit differences in technology, markets, products, and culture, their quality problems were quite similar. To diagnose those problems required common diagnostic concepts and tools, which, in turn, required common remedial concepts and tools. To hold the gains required common control concepts and tools. As I moved from one "different" company to another, I saw that I was going through the same series of steps over and over. The concepts, methods, and tools I used turned out to be applicable to any company.

Those commonalities intrigued me, and gradually I identified the elements of that common series of steps. I disseminated my findings in published papers and in my training courses. In 1964 I devoted half of the book *Managerial Breakthrough* to the universal process for improving quality (or anything else). I then continued to refine the process, and what I learned became an integral part of my training manuals on managing for quality. By 1964 I had gained unbounded confidence in the validity of that universal series of steps. I had field-tested them in many client companies; they repeatedly produced stunning results. In a sense, I had witnessed the miracles and had thereby acquired the faith of the true believer.

A condensed version of that universal series of steps is as follows:

- Estimate the costs of poor quality—the costs that would disappear if quality were perfect.

- Use the Pareto Principle to identify the "vital few" sources of the cost of poor quality.
- Each of those vital few sources becomes a potential project for improvement.
- For each selected project, appoint a team whose responsibility is to improve the quality and reduce the cost of poor quality. Each team should include a facilitator—a specialist who is well-trained in use of the tools for improving quality.
- Conduct the diagnosis—analyzing symptoms, theorizing about causes, testing the theories, and establishing the causes.
- Map out the remedial journey—develop remedies, test the remedies under operating conditions, deal with cultural resistance, and establish controls to hold the gains.

For a more detailed description of the universal process for improvement, see *Juran's Quality Handbook.*[1]

The Quality Planning Process

In *Managerial Breakthrough*, I asserted that "all managerial activity is directed at either breakthrough or control. Managers are busy doing both of these things and nothing else." That turned out to be an overstatement; I should have separated out planning and elaborated it into a third managerial process.

In time I made that separation and identified a universal sequence of the steps that constitute planning for quality. The resulting "road map" is shown in Figure 29-1.[2]

In evolving this road map, I drew heavily on what I had learned from those clients who were also studying the planning process.

The Control Process

In the book *Managerial Breakthrough*, I also set out a universal process for control—the process for preventing adverse change. The anatomy of the feedback loop is shown in Figure 29-2.

The feedback loop consists of five basic elements.

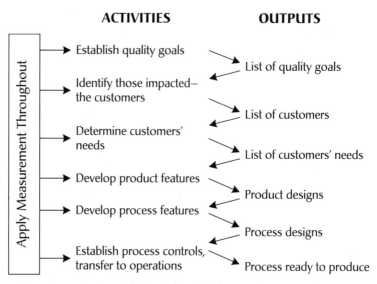

Figure 29-1. The quality planning road map

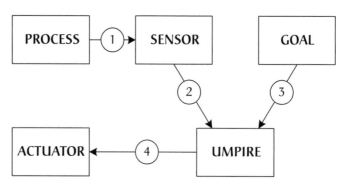

Figure 29-2. The feedback loop

1. A *process*—he, she, or it produces products, such as goods, services, reports, etc..
2. A *goal*—it defines the level of quality that the process should be producing.
3. A *sensor*—he, she, or it evaluates the quality being produced and reports this to an umpire.
4. An *umpire*—he, she, or it compares the actual performance to the goal. If the difference warrants action, the umpire energizes an actuator.

5. An *actuator*—he, she, or it changes the process as needed to bring performance in line with the goal.

A well-known example is the regulation of a building's temperature through use of a thermostat.

I did not invent the feedback loop; that invention took place billions of years ago during the evolution of biological species. In biological organisms, the feedback loop enables the autonomic processes—the digestive system, circulatory system, nervous system, and others—to carry out their work without conscious action by the animal. The feedback loop also regulates critical phenomena— blood pressure, body temperature, and so on—again without the animal's conscious action.

For clients, I examined each station on the feedback loop to identify the decisions and actions involved, as well as to clarify responsibility—who (or what) was to make which decision and take which action. The managers understood the concept of the feedback loop, but most were unaware that to assign responsibility, one must first define the decisions and actions involved.

Interrelationship of Managerial Processes

I also came to realize that those three managerial processes (planning, improvement, and control) were interrelated, so I developed the "Juran Trilogy Diagram," Figure 29-3, to depict the interrelation.

The Trilogy embodies the core processes by which we manage for quality. As a corollary, those same core processes constitute an important sector of the science of managing for quality. To my knowledge there is growing awareness in our economy that mastery of those processes is critical to attaining leadership in quality.

Beyond conducting the three processes of the Trilogy, managers are busy with other essential quality-related activities such as these:

- Training the managerial hierarchy in how to manage for quality.
- Developing the systems for recognizing and rewarding superior performance in quality.

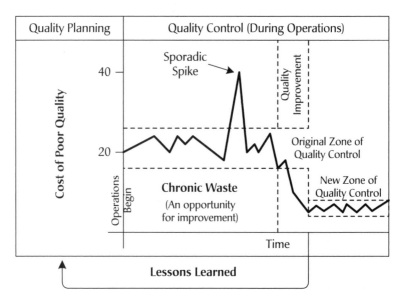

Figure 29-3. Interrelation of planning, improvement, and control (The Juran Trilogy® diagram)

- Developing quality-related expertise in various functions—for example, supplier relations or customer service.
- Securing participation by the workforce.

Nevertheless, to plan, control, and improve each of such activities requires carrying out the invariable steps inherent in the Trilogy.

The Role of Academia

During the twenty-first century, academia will greatly expand its role in the field of managing for quality. I base my belief on economic and social imperatives. Managing for quality already provides career paths for hundreds of thousands of specialists. (The American Society for Quality alone has, as of December 2001, granted more than 100,000 certifications to quality specialists in categories such as Certified Quality Engineer.) Many national and local quality awards have sprung up to stimulate and acknowledge superior performance in managing for quality. Some companies have already approached their academic allies with the warning, "If you wish us to continue recruiting your graduates, it would be best for you to teach them about managing for quality."

During the mid-twentieth century, some U.S. universities and local colleges offered non-degree courses in statistical quality control (SQC). Here and there some business schools and industrial engineering departments offered courses in managing for quality as a part of the school curriculum. However, most of such training was offered by consultants and professional societies such as ASQ. By the 1980s, formal alliances began to spring up between large companies and their favorite business and engineering schools, with a view toward enlarging the schools' roles in offering courses in managing for quality.

To play its enlarged role during the twenty-first century, academia will need to make extensive changes. I believe that these include creation of degree-granting curricular programs in managing for quality. Professors who are knowledgeable in the quality problems of industry, and in the ways of solving those problems, will need to be recruited to teach the courses. The schools will also have to establish close alliances with industry in order to keep up with the changing realities that face the managers. A likely result of these changes will be the growth in research on how to manage for quality, as well as expansion of the content of the science of managing for quality.

The Quality Professional

Until the twentieth century, few "knowledge workers" existed in the field of managing for quality. Such workers (today often called "quality professionals") carry out planning and analysis related to quality policy formation, goal setting, organization, performance measurement, incentives, and the like.

The last century witnessed remarkable growth in the numbers of such quality professionals, beginning during the years of World War II when the War Production Board sponsored numerous (free) courses in statistical quality control (SQC). Companies that wished to apply SQC to their operations then found it necessary to create a new job category of "quality engineer" (or similar title) as a prerequisite for applying the statistical tools.

Eventually the American Society for Quality (ASQ) formalized the professional status of quality engineers by offering certificates to those who successfully passed a written examination. Such certificates then proliferated to other categories of professionals—reliability engineers, quality auditors, and still others.

During the twentieth century there also emerged the concept of "Big Q"—the idea that managing for quality extends beyond the factory; it applies also to offices and warehouses. The Big Q concept also was extended to include such broad matters as customer satisfaction, and the economics of quality. Adopting the Big Q concept broadened the scope of the quality professionals' responsibilities.

The widespread adoption of the ISO series of standards spawned a new category of quality auditors—those who offer a service of reviewing compliance to the standards and issuing certificates of compliance. Such auditors were either self-appointed or sponsored by consulting firms or national societies for quality. In due course, efforts have emerged toward professionalizing these auditors.

An added activity involving professionalism has recently taken place in the "Six Sigma" movement. (Six Sigma is essentially a new name for quality improvement.) An important feature of the Six Sigma movement is the use of facilitators, as has traditionally been done in quality improvement programs. Companies that have preferred to use the Six Sigma banner have also elected to rename the facilitators "Black Belts" (or other colors). These designations are conferred by the companies employing the facilitators, but the extent of prior training and use of examinations has been quite varied.

As of 2002, there are many categories of knowledge workers in the field of managing for quality. Each group strives for recognition as professionals. Yet there is wide variation in the extent of training undergone, experience acquired, and use of pass examinations. There is also competition among the categories over jurisdictional rights.

In my view, the twenty-first century will bring important changes. We will likely witness the emergence of degree-granting college programs devoted to the field of managing for quality, and I believe we will likely witness the creation of a national category of quality professionals paralleling that of certified public accountant (CPA).

Notes

1. Juran, Joseph M., *Jurans's Quality Handbook*, Fifth Edition (New York: McGraw-Hill, 1999), pp. 5.1–5.73.

2. For elaboration, see *Juran on Quality by Design* (New York: The Free Press, 1992).

Q

30

Immigrants and Opportunity

I n this final chapter, I will look back at the lives of those closest to me—my dad, my siblings, and my wife.

The passing of mother in 1920 led to my family's disintegration.
At the time of my graduation from the university, I was still living with Dad. I made periodic visits to the orphanage to see my little
sisters. My other siblings—Betty and my brothers—had already gone
their separate ways; our paths seldom crossed.

Dad

When I left for Chicago, Dad remained alone, living in the rear of
his shop. He was fifty years old. My relationship with him was one
of mutual tolerance. When I left, it was without animosity. The time
came, during the Great Depression, when he was forced to turn to
me for help, and I did not disappoint him.

His final years were sweetened by his many weekend visits with his
younger daughters, Minerva and Charlotte. They looked forward to his
coming to the orphanage to take them for an afternoon in the park.

By 1931, they were young ladies eighteen and seventeen years of age and talked of renting an apartment where he could live with them. It was not to be. He passed away on January 3, 1931. He was 57 years old.

Rudy

Rudy (his given name was Rudolph) was the eldest child—he was born on August 6, 1901. By age sixteen he was six feet tall and was exhibiting the traits of a determined doer. He detested his life of poverty and had no intention of enduring it forever. He wanted respectability, proper clothes, and money to spend. There was no way he could meet these goals while he was dependent on Dad. He also chafed under Dad's discipline. Bad feelings developed, along with a contempt for Dad. Rudy saw how we lived compared with our affluent relatives, and he ridiculed Dad as a failure.

After graduating from high school, Rudy took a clerical job with a manufacturer in Minneapolis. He then studied accounting by correspondence and progressed in the company to accountant and comptroller. Meanwhile he became devoted to the game of golf and soon was playing at championship levels. In 1924 he won the National Southpaw Amateur Tournament at Midlothian. By 1929 he had won that championship four times and retired the cup. He also won the Minnesota State Open Championship. Those feats brought him an invitation to join the prestigious Golden Valley Country Club. (Floyd Olson, governor of Minnesota, was a member.) They also enabled him to meet many affluent, influential men.

Soon he was urged to enter the financial security business, which he did in 1926. Thirteen years later, he and Harold Moody founded the firm of Juran & Moody, specializing in municipal bonds. The company would bid on municipal bond issues and, when successful, would resell the bonds to client investors. During the 1950s Rudy's earnings likely reached $50,000 to $60,000 per year, equal to over $500,000 per year in today's dollars—enough to enable him to reach the status of millionaire.

His family consisted of his wife, Winnifred, and their adopted son, Wynn. In December 1960, he suffered a massive stroke that he did not survive.

Betty

My older sister Rebecca (we called her Betty) had the bad luck to be born a girl early in the twentieth century. Dad restricted her to eight years of grammar school despite her proficiency in art. (She made the posters for the school.) Instead Dad placed her in a secretarial school. Betty's forgiving nature was sorely tested by Dad's conduct. To her, he was a suspicious and frightening person.

By the 1930s Betty was married to Philip Martin and had become the mother of three children, Gloria and the twins, Shirley and Allen. Phil developed emphysema and became incapacitated for work, so Betty was faced with caring for a sick man plus raising her children.

She never gave up. Her life, like her mother's, was devoted to her children. Her artistic capabilities emerged in her superlative needlework. Beyond making crafts for her family, she attracted a clientele. I thought that some of her work was of museum quality. It proved beyond doubt that she deserved to have studied art.

Her children all acquired college degrees. Allen went on to receive an M.D. degree from Stanford University and became a physician. So Betty, who was denied the opportunity to go beyond grammar school, nevertheless attained a form of higher education through witnessing the achievements of her children. It may well be that in her final years (she lived to be ninety), she looked back with satisfaction on what had been her lot. She missed much that life had to offer, but she had many years in which to see how her children made use of the opportunities that had been denied her.

Nat

My younger brother, Nathan, was born in 1907. We usually called him Nat or Nate, and his Hollywood pals called him Jerry.

Unlike me, Nat left the old country without a burden of fears. Also unlike me, he stayed in the real world; he did not withdraw into a world of his own. He was tactful and considerate of the feelings of others. These traits attracted people, and some volunteered to help him. In the years ahead, some of this help became substantial.

Having decided to get a college education, Nat faced the problem of supporting himself and saving the money needed for college. Through hard work and resourcefulness, he did get a degree in architecture. He then got his master's degree at MIT (on a scholarship). He was then ready to practice architecture, but the country was deep in the Great Depression. Building construction had come to a virtual halt, as had employment opportunities for architects. It was hard to find jobs and almost as hard to get paid once the work was completed. Nat finally gave up the struggle and went to California, where he landed a job as a draftsman in the RKO movie studios. From that base he launched a successful career in Hollywood, advancing to art director and movie director.

During World War II he was an officer in the United States Navy, assigned to the Office of Strategic Services. At the end of the war, Nat returned to his wife, Julia, and his career in the Hollywood studios. He worked on many motion pictures and with many of the glamorous people of the industry. Beyond the conventional forms of the art, he mastered the complexities of "special effects." The emergence of television was no problem for him; he adapted easily and presided over numerous productions. In 1941 he won an Oscar for the art direction of *How Green Was My Valley*; in 1946 he was nominated for another Academy Award. Nevertheless he remained a private person—he shunned any celebrity status.

Along the way he directed two movies starring Ronald Reagan, but then he refused to be interviewed about them. Even his mini memoirs were privately published. In 1999 he did accept a "Life Career Award" from a Hollywood academy.

Nat passed away in October 2002 at the age of 95. The *Los Angeles Times* devoted a lengthy obituary (November 1, 2002) to his brilliant career in the motion picture industry.

The Orphans

My youngest siblings, Minerva and Charlotte, both remained in the orphanage until Minerva finished high school in 1931. Charlotte finished a year later. They secured clerical jobs with Prudential Insurance Company, but it was at the depth of the Great Depression when salaries were pitifully low. They roomed with families, sharing the same bed and their mutual poverty until they were married.

Minerva, the "all A's" high-school student, married Hyman Goldberg, a hydraulic engineer employed by the U.S. Army Corps of Engineers. She was a homemaker while rearing her daughter, Judy, but itched to go into higher education. That opportunity arose in the early 1950s and the pent-up urge burst forth with a vengeance. Minerva received a bachelor's degree in 1955 and a master's in 1959, both *summa cum laude*. Her doctorate followed in 1966. She then embarked on a teaching career, attaining the rank of professor of education in 1967. Had our mother lived to witness that achievement, she would have been ecstatic, having a daughter who had reached the exalted status of professor!

Charlotte was the baby in our family. On completing high school, she, like Minerva, went to work for Prudential. A few years later she married Sam Mogilner, a partner in a garment manufacturing company. The Mogilners were an affluent family, and their women were smokers. This induced our young Charlotte to take up cigarette smoking. It would cost her dearly. In her younger years she enjoyed an affluent life and became a good amateur golfer. In later years, her lungs became diseased. She tried to give up the cigarette habit but couldn't—she was inescapably hooked.

Her marriage produced three children, Joseph, Geoffrey, and Karen, who all became college graduates. Once her children were grown, Charlotte devoted much time to community service. She also went into higher education, acquiring bachelor's and master's degrees, including election to the honorary Phi Beta Kappa society. Her illness then precluded further study. She died a premature death at the age of 76. In our family, the nonsmokers have all lived well beyond that age.

Both girls ended up with fond memories of Dad, the only family members to do so. In their view, he had mellowed. Occasionally they visited his shop, but mostly they recalled his Sunday visits to the orphanage to take them to the park.

Thinking back on it, I am sure that had my parents lived longer, they would have been overjoyed to see all their children leading honorable, fruitful lives, all having earned the right to hold their heads high.

The Three Millionaires

As I was sketching out the high points of my brothers' careers, I was struck by their commonalities with my own career, as well as by the differences. All of us shared the same poverty and humble beginnings and were forced to undergo harsh treatment and indignities, yet all were determined to attain positions of respect and affluence, and we all managed to reach those goals. What differed were the roads we traveled to reach our goals. In turn, our choice of roads was strongly influenced by the wide differences in our personalities.

Rudy was the impatient, forceful doer. His courage made him a bold risk taker. He ran off to Hollywood at the age of sixteen, not knowing anyone there and gambling that he could beat the odds by sheer determination. He failed because the odds were simply too great. His emergence as a golf champion gave him access to influential people and enabled him to launch a business enterprise. His integrity and dedication to customer needs then propelled him into the affluence and respect he had sought.

Nat was preordained to reach a state of respectability and affluence. His instinctive friendliness and tact enabled him to make friends and form alliances. People wanted to help him, and they did. His friendliness also made him comfortable in a hierarchy, even in the fiercely competitive environment of the movie industry. He had the bad luck to graduate from MIT when the country was in the throes of the Great Depression. Had he been able to become established in architecture from the beginning, he would (in my view) have become one of the great creative architects of the twentieth century.

My road was different still. When I was en route to Western Electric, my psychological baggage included elements that were antagonistic to survival in a large hierarchy. I was a loner with a thorny exterior. In contrast to Nat's experience, virtually no one went out of his way to help me out.

At Western Electric I progressed rapidly because of my proficiency in analysis and problem solving, despite my limited skills in human relations. Then, as I advanced into managerial posts, those limitations caught up with me, finally reaching a state that barred me from further vertical progress. I had the same experience during my four years of wartime service with the U.S. government.

I concluded that I was out of place in a large bureaucracy, that I was too individualistic. I opted to become a freelance consultant in the field of management—to philosophize, research, write, teach, the works. Some difficult years elapsed before that option became fully viable, but thereafter I enjoyed decades of creative and rewarding activity.

To some it may seem significant that my brothers and I, despite our humble beginnings, all attained the status of millionaires. In my view, what is more notable is that there were opportunities waiting to be seized—opportunities provided by a land of opportunity. Those opportunities went far beyond affluence in worldly goods; they extended to accomplishments that are extremely precious—self-respect, the respect of others, and being of service to society.

Seizing those opportunities required meeting the demands of our country—learning the language; becoming well-educated; if need be, enduring poverty, long hours, and hard work; and living honorably. Our rewards were the byproducts of meeting those obligations.

Is America still a land of opportunity? I doubt I am qualified to answer that. What I can do is to point to the thousands of immigrants, legal and illegal, who continue to press for entry.

A Family of Outsiders

As I look back at my own family, I now realize that in every town in which we lived, we were outsiders. Social life in those towns was centered in the churches and synagogues. I seem to have assumed that since I was an unbeliever in the theological sense, I had no need to belong to a synagogue. I failed to realize that a church or synagogue provides a ready-made social community into which a member is welcomed. Such religious communities provide organized forms of social contact. In my family we were not members; we were outsiders.

For Sadie, being an outsider was a source of acute discomfort. Even though I was likewise an outsider, I was comfortable. I had been a loner for most of my life and accepted that state as the norm.

Our children were also outsiders. In their early years this was not yet serious, or so it seemed. They were, of course, members of our nuclear family, and they also made friends at school. Yet the time came when the lack of belonging to an established social community posed serious problems for two of them.

Sadie

At age 98, Sadie looks back on a good life. The early married years were burdensome, with three infants so close together in age, but she always had help, whether from her mother or from a hired helper. The four years in the Marshall Field Garden Apartments in Chicago were especially happy years. The complex included a well-equipped playground where she could meet with other young mothers. The Pestalozzi-Froebel school, also a part of the complex, provided our children with a superlative entry to the world of education.

By 1937, with the country emerging from the Depression, we realized the American Dream—a home of our own. It was a modest four-bedroom house in Downers Grove, Illinois. We lived in it for ten weeks before I was transferred to company headquarters in New York.

Our years in Summit, New Jersey, and Eastchester, New York, were also happy years. The children were completing their educations and being launched into the world of jobs and family responsibilities. There were significant exceptions to that state of happiness: Bob's antisocial behavior, and passive anti-Semitism in Summit.

During World War II, we lived in Arlington, Virginia, amid the restrictions of shortages, rationing, and crowded conditions. Equally serious was the effect of inflation. During the four years of the war, despite price controls, the weighted cost-of-living index rose by 17.5 percent whereas my weighted government salary rose by only about 2 percent. The difference ate up our savings except for the equity in our house. I ended up broke, living from one paycheck to the next.

Our co-op at 860 United Nations Plaza (in Manhattan) was most welcome to Sadie. Our windows faced the United Nations Gardens and the East River. Despite my frequent trips, we were able to enjoy the museums, concerts, ballets, operas, musicals, lectures, and other delights that flowed from Manhattan's cornucopia. I estimate that during our twenty-five years of living in Manhattan, we attended more than 300 events in the performing arts.

Sadie also appreciated our house in Ridgefield, Connecticut. It was surrounded by generous acreage, well landscaped and with an inspiring view of faraway hills—a deluxe shack in the woods. (We bought it from the widow of Cornelius Ryan, author of *The Longest Day* and *A Bridge Too Far*.) The main house was most spacious. I took over one large room for my office; I used another to accommodate my assistant, Laura Sutherland, a Juran Institute employee who came in several mornings each week. We could easily accommodate visits from family members. There was also a separate studio house, and we used it to provide housing for the caretakers.

By the late 1990s the effects of old age were taking their toll. In July 2001, we moved into a pleasant retirement home in Rye, New York. There we will live out our remaining time.

My Life in the Year 2003

Writing these memoirs has been most rewarding. The exercise has at last enabled me to view what my journey through life has been: the forces that confronted me, my responses, and my impact on the world around me.

At age 98 I am the patriarch of a substantial family. I now realize that I did a mediocre job of raising my four children. My dad had been a poor role model, and my early poverty and our status as social outsiders contributed to my ignorance of how to raise children. An exception to this mediocre job has been education—my descendants have amassed a formidable record of opting for higher education.

My analytical gifts enabled me to progress in an industrial bureaucracy, but being an aggressive social misfit led me to make some stupid decisions, which brought that progress to a halt.

My joining Lend-Lease disrupted our lives, as did our move from Summit to Arlington. Those deprivations resulted from my decisions. I was not forced to accept that invitation to go to Lend-Lease for six weeks, nor was I forced to remain in a war agency for four years. Yet I haven't regretted those decisions for one moment. I owed a debt to the United States and appreciated the opportunity to serve in its defense. In addition, I was also defending my family, whose very existence I felt was under threat.

My decision to become a freelance consultant in management, although risky, was fortunate in the extreme. It enabled my gifts to blossom fully while minimizing the hindrance of my poor political skills. Indeed, the discipline inherent in being a freelancer contributed to my shedding the baggage that had made me a social misfit. Somewhere during my decades as a freelancer, *I lost my urge for revenge.* To this day I don't fully understand how this came about, but whatever the reasons, my entry into freelance consulting changed my relations with personnel in the companies I served. Any urge for revenge was limited to those proven guilty, and even with the guilty, I became willing to overlook their misdemeanors (but not their felonies).

Life as a freelancer offered rewards far beyond meeting my financial needs. Clients brought a continuing procession of challenging problems for which I was able to provide useful solutions. I earned respect from those clients and thereby enhanced my self-respect. I also relished my new-found freedom from the rigidities of big bureaucracies. I had left the security of an ocean liner for the precarious freedom of a canoe, and it was a relief to learn that piloting so puny a craft could lead to a viable and rewarding way of life.

Meanwhile Sadie and I have passed our ninety-eighth birthdays. Also, in June 2001, our entire family assembled to celebrate our seventy-fifth wedding anniversary. Such an anniversary is a rarity. It requires the convergence of three events: each one of us reaching the age of 96, and our marriage enduring for seventy-five years. The probability of such simultaneous occurrences is extremely low, and we are humbly grateful for having been so lucky.

For Sadie and me it has been a turbulent, eventful life, sweetened by the witnessing of miracles—the birth and growth of our progeny. That sweetness has triumphed over the disappointments and tragedies we have endured. We live now in serene harmony.

During my professional career I have touched the lives of many executives, managers, and specialists in the field of managing for quality. They have read my books (over a million copies have been sold); tens of thousands have taken my training courses and attended my lectures; and over a million have studied my videocassette series on quality improvement. In response, I have received much fan mail from my peers—those whose careers are bound up with managing for quality. To them I am the man who wrote the *Handbook*—their bible.

Most of the time I wasn't aware that the subject of managing for quality would, during my lifetime, expand enormously in importance, become a growth industry, and undergo a wrenching world revolution. Neither did I foresee that I would be drawn into that maelstrom and emerge as a leading architect of the quality revolution. Yet it happened.

All that busyness has brought me many honors—over 100 of them. They comprise medals, honorary memberships, honorary degrees and the like, awarded by governments, professional societies, universities,

Autographing books. I did this thousands of times.

and industrial companies in about twenty countries. Some are quite prestigious:

- **The Order of the Sacred Treasure, Second Class,** awarded in 1981 by Emperor Hirohito of Japan for "… positively contributing for a long time not only to the development of Quality Control in Japan, but also to the facilitation of the U.S. and Japan friendship."
- **Membership in the National (U.S.) Academy of Engineering (1988),** for "pioneering contributions in developing the practice of statistical quality control, and in developing engineering design principles based on statistical concepts."
- **The National (U.S.) Medal of Technology,** awarded in 1992 by President Bush, for "his lifetime work of providing the key principles and methods by which enterprises manage the quality of their products and processes, enhancing their ability to compete in the global marketplace."

Receiving membership in the National Academy of Engineering, 1988. The presenters were "Jack" Welch, chairman of General Electric Company, and Robert M. White, president of the National Academy of Engineering.

Receiving the National Medal of Technology from President George Bush (the elder), 1992.

Receiving the medal of the European Organization for Quality from President Tito Conti, 1993.

- **The European Organization for Quality's medal,** awarded in 1993, "in recognition of his valuable contributions to quality in Europe."

Finally, Two Messages

So I have come to the end. I close this book with two messages. To
those whose careers are in the field of managing for quality: thank
your lucky stars. Your field will grow extensively during your lifetime, especially in three of our giant industries—health, education,
and government. There will be exciting opportunities for innovation
and for service to society.

And to my beloved family: when I am gone, let no one weep for
me. I have lived a wonderful life.

Index